CENSUS OF INDIA 1911

CENSUS OF INDIA, 1911

VOLUME - XXIII

TRAVANCORE

PART II - IMPERIAL TABLES

N. SUBRAMHANYA AIYAR

GYAN

Published by

Gyan Publishing House
5, Ansari Road
Daryaganj, New Delhi-110002
Phone: 011-47034999, 9811692060
E-mail: books@gyanbooks.com

Distribution Network
gyanbooks.com
India, USA, Canada, UK, Australia

ISBN: 978-81-212-7127-1 (Set) 23 Vols. In 41 Bindings

ISBN: 978-81-212-7417-3 (PB) Vol. XXIII, Pt. II

First Published, 1912

2nd Impression 2024

Printed at: Gyan Press, Delhi.

CENSUS OF INDIA 1911

CENSUS OF INDIA, 1911.

VOLUME XXIII.

TRAVANCORE.

PART II.

IMPERIAL TABLES.

BY

N. SUBRAMHANYA AIYAR, M. A., DEWAN PEISHCAR.,
CENSUS COMMISSIONER.

TRIVANDRUM:
PRINTED AT THE 'ANANDA PRESS'.
1912.

CONTENTS.

NOTE.

In the Tables of the Imperial Series which comprise this Volume, figures are given for—

i. the State as a whole:

ii. the five Administrative Divisions: and

iii. the two Natural Divisions into which the State is divided for the examination of Census statistics.

The taluks comprised in the Administrative and Natural Divisions are shown below for easy reference:—

ADMINISTRATIVE DIVISIONS.

I. PADMANABHAPURAM DIVISION.

1. Tovala.
2. Agastisvaram.
3. Eraniel.
4. Kalkulam.
5. Vilavankod.

II. TRIVANDRUM DIVISION.

6. Neyyattinkara.
7. Trivandrum.
8. Nedumangad.
9. Chirayinkil.

III. QUILON DIVISION.

10. Kottarakara.
11. Pattanapuram.
12. Shencottah.
13. Quilon.
14. Kunnattur.
15. Karunagapalli.
16. Kartikapalli.
17. Mavelikara.
18. Chengannur.
19. Tiruvalla.
20. Ambalapuzha.

IV. KOTTAYAM DIVISION.

21. Shertallay.
22. Vaikam.
23. Ettumanur.
24. Kottayam.
25. Changanachery.
26. Minachil.
27. Muvattupuzha.
28. Todupuzha.
29. Kunnatnad.
30. Alangad.
31. Parur.

V. DEVIKULAM DIVISION.

32. Devikulam.
33. Peermade.

NATURAL DIVISIONS.

A. WESTERN NATURAL DIVISION.

1. Agastisvaram.
2. Eraniel.
3. Vilavankod.
4. Neyyattinkara.
5. Trivandrum.
6. Chirayinkil.
7. Quilon.
8. Karunagapalli.
9. Kartikapalli.
10. Ambalapuzha.
11. Shertallay.
12. Parur.
13. Vaikam.
14. Tiruvalla.
15. Mavelikara.

B. EASTERN NATURAL DIVISION.

16. Tovala.
17. Kalkulam.
18. Nedumangad.
19. Kottarakara.
20. Pattanapuram.
21. Shencottah.
22. Kunnattur.
23. Chengannur.
24. Changanachery.
25. Kottayam.
26. Ettumanur.
27. Minachil.
28. Todupuzha.
29. Muvattupuzha.
30. Kunnatnad.
31. Alangad.
32. Devikulam.
33. Peermade.

TABLE II.

Variation in Population since 1875.

NOTE:—The population figures given in this Table for the four previous Censuses represent the adjustments for the areas as they stood on the 10th March, 1911.

TABLE II.

Variation in Population since 1875.

DIVISION.	PERSONS.					MALES.				
	1911.	1901.	1891.	1881.	1875.	1911.	1901.	1891.	1881.	1875.
1	2	3	4	5	6	7	8	9	10	11
STATE ..	***3,428,975***	***2,952,157***	***2,557,736***	***2,401,158***	***2,311,379***	***1,731,363***	***1,490,165***	***1,290,415***	***1,197,134***	***1,149,927***
I. PADMANABHAPURAM	**430,087**	384,575	348,982	350,778	348,508	**215,313**	191,105	175,087	172,592	171,219
II. TRIVANDRUM	**557,865**	456,082	377,338	353,852	343,372	**281,225**	230,015	190,537	176,154	171,631
III. QUILON	**1,233,360**	1,070,283	953,758	866,785	832,511	**620,773**	539,491	478,280	431,399	414,381
IV. KOTTAYAM	**1,139,101**	999,607	846,876	807,673	769,601	**576,060**	506,331	428,760	405,359	383,721
V. DEVIKULAM	**68,562**	41,610	30,832	22,070	17,297	**37,892**	23,223	17,751	11,630	8,975
A. Western Natural Division ..	***1,976,154***	*1,705,264*	*1,499,807*	*1,417,265*	*1,381,470*	***994,326***	*856,389*	*752,764*	*702,780*	*684,726*
B. Eastern Natural Division ..	***1,452,821***	*1,246,893*	*1,057,929*	*983,893*	*929,909*	***737,037***	*633,776*	*537,651*	*494,354*	*465,201*

TABLE II.

Variation in Population since 1875.

DIVISION.	FEMALES.					VARIATION, INCREASE (+) DECREASE (−).				NET VARIATION IN PERIOD 1875–1911, INCREASE (+) DECREASE (−).
	1911.	1901	1891.	1881.	1875.	**1901 to 1911.**	1891 to 1901.	1881 to 1891.	1875 to 1881.	
	12	13	14	15	16	17	18	19	20	21
***STATE* ..**	***1,697,612***	***1,461,992***	***1,267,321***	***1,204,024***	***1,161,452***	+ ***476,818***	+ ***394,421***	+ ***156,578***	+ ***89,779***	+ ***1,117,596***
I. PADMANABHAPURAM	**214,774**	193,470	173,845	178,186	177,289	+ **45,512**	+ 35,643	− 1,846	+ 2,270	+ 81,579
II. TRIVANDRUM	**276,640**	226,067	186,801	177,698	171,741	+ **101,783**	+ 78,744	+ 23,486	+ 10,480	+ 214,493
III. QUILON	**612,587**	530,792	475.478	435,386	418,130	+ **163,077**	+ 116,525	+ 86,973	+ 34,274	+ 400,849
IV. KOTTAYAM	**563,041**	493,276	418,116	402,314	385,970	+ **139,494**	+ 152,731	+ 39,203	+ 37,982	+ 369,410
V. DEVIKULAM	**30,570**	18,387	13,081	10,440	8,322	+ **26,952**	+ 10,778	+ 8,762	+ 4,773	+ 51,265
A. Western Natural Division .	***981,828***	*848,875*	*747,043*	*714,485*	*696,744*	+ ***270,890***	+ *205,457*	+ *82,542*	+ *35,795*	+ *594,684*
B. Eastern Natural Division ..	***715,784***	*613,117*	*520,278*	*489,539*	*464,708*	+ ***205,928***	+ *188,964*	+ *74,036*	+ *53,984*	+ *522,912*

TABLE III.

Towns and Villages Classified by Population.

NOTE :—The figures given in this Table as the population of the Quilon and Kottayam Divisions differ from the corresponding figures in Table I, as for the purposes of Division-war classification for this Table, the population of the Alleppey Town which lies within both the Divisions has been included wholly in the Quilon Division where the bulk of the Town lies.

TABLE III.

Towns and Villages Classified by Population.

Division.	Total number of inhabited Towns and Villages.	Population.	Under 500.		500—1,000.		1,000—2,000.		2,000—5,000.		5,000—10,000.		10,000—20,000.		20,000—50,000.		50,000—100,000.		100,000 and over.	
			Number.	Population.	Number.	Population.	Number.	Population.	Number.	Population.	Number.	Population.	Number.	Population.	Number.	Population.	Number.	Population.	Number.	Population.
1	2	3	4	5	6	7	8	9	10	11	12	13	14	15	16	17	18	19	20	21
STATE ...	*3,966*	*3,428,975*	*1,867*	*394,687*	*951*	*689,894*	*789*	*1,098,952*	*328*	*910,394*	*22*	*130,451*	*6*	*85,488*	*2*	*55,548*	*1*	*63,561*	...	...
I. PADMANABHAPURAM.	1,122	430,087	879	138,017	138	98,146	87	117,576	16	41,406	1	5,059	...	...	1	29,883	...	...	...	...
II. TRIVANDRUM ...	460	557,865	149	29,820	110	80,131	130	181,057	67	187,225	3	16,071	...	...	...	...	1	63,561	...	...
III. QUILON	1,289	1,237,730	429	130,073	418	306,203	337	469,710	98	252,857	4	24,074	2	29,148	1	25,665	...	...	...	...
IV. KOTTAYAM... ...	963	1,134,731	310	79,012	267	192,482	227	317,472	142	414,353	14	85,247	3	46,165	...	...	...	...	...	...
V. DEVIKULAM ..	132	68,562	100	17,765	18	12,932	8	13,137	5	14,553	...	...	1	10,175	...	...	...	...	...	...
A. Western Natural Division ...	*2,100*	*1,976,154*	*970*	*185,006*	*453*	*331,413*	*453*	*642,430*	*201*	*558,956*	*18*	*106,619*	*2*	*32,621*	*2*	*55,548*	*1*	*63,561*	...	...
B. Eastern Natural Division ...	*1,866*	*1,452,821*	*897*	*209,681*	*498*	*358,481*	*336*	*456,522*	*127*	*351,438*	*4*	*23,832*	*4*	*52,867*	..	...	..	..	...	...

TABLE IV.

Towns Classified by Population with Variation since 1875.

NOTE :—In 1875 Towns were not separately censused. No figures are therefore given in columns 8 & 12. The net variation shown in column 13 actually refers to the period 1881—1911 and not to 1875—1911 as shown in the heading.

Towns whose boundaries have been changed since 1901 are indicated by asterisks. For purposes of comparison, the present figures on the basis of the 1901 areas are given in the respective columns in brackets.

Alwaye and Tiruvalla are censused as Towns for the first time at the 1911 Census.

TABLE IV.

Towns classified by population with variation since 1875.

TOWN.	DIVISION.	MUNICIPALITY, SUBURBS, CANTONMENT, &c.	POPULATION 1911.	POPULATION 1901.	POPULATION 1891.	POPULATION 1881.	POPULATION 1875.	VARIATION. INCREASE (+) DECREASE (—). 1901 to 1911.	1891 to 1901.	1881 to 1891.	1875 to 1881.	Variation in Period 1875 to 1911. Increase (+) Decrease (—).	MALES. 1911.	MALES. 1901.	MALES. 1891.	FEMALES. 1911.	FEMALES. 1901.	FEMALES. 1891.
1	2	3	4	5	6	7	8	9	10	11	12	13	14	15	16	17	18	19
TRIVANDRUM ...	Trivandrum.	M & C	**63,561**	57,882	27,88[illegible]	41,173	...	**+5,679**	+29,995	—13,286	...	+22,388	**32,292**	29,992	14,707	**31,269**	27,890	13,180
NAGERCOIL ...	Padmanabhapuram.	M	**29,883**	25,782	11,18[illegible]	16,534	...	**+ 4,101**	+14,595	— 5,347	...	+13,349	**14,553**	12,520	5,335	**15,330**	13,262	5,852
ALLEPPEY*	Quilon.	M	**25,665** [24,939]	24,918	22,[illegible]8	25,754	...	**+ 747**	+ 2,150	— 2,986	...	— 89	**13,370**	12,748	11,286	**12,295**	12,170	11,482
QUILON* ..	Do.	M	**18,833** [18,082]	15,691	1[illegible],37[illegible]	13,588	...	**+3,148**	+ 316	+ 1,787	...	+ 5,251	**9,649**	8,095	7,871	**9,190**	7,596	7,504
CHANGANACHERY ...	Kottayam.		**17,242**	14,264	...	...	...	**+2,978**	...	...	...	...	**8,826**	7,166	...	**8,416**	7,098	...
KOTTAYAM* ...	Do.	M	**15,141** [17,910]	17,552	7,09[illegible]	11,293	...	**—2,411**	+10,462	— 4,203	...	+ 3,848	**7,863**	9,147	3,539	**7,278**	8,405	3,551
PARUR ...	Do.		**13,782**	12,962	...	...	...	**+ 820**	...	...	...	...	**7,067**	6,771	...	**6,715**	6,191	...
SHENCOTTAH ..	Quilon.		**10,309**	9,039	8,7[illegible]	7,882	...	**+1,270**	+ 312	+ 845	...	+ 2,427	**4,905**	4,274	4,202	**5,404**	4,765	4,525
TIRUVALLA ...	Do.		**7,969**	...	...	...	...	...	...	...	...	...	**4,268**	...	...	**3,701**	...	...
KAYANKULAM ...	Do.	M	**5,830**	5,745	...	...	...	**+ 85**	...	...	...	...	**2,772**	2,916	...	**3,058**	2,829	...
ALWAYE ...	Kottayam.	M	**3,869**	...	...	...	...	...	...	...	...	...	**2,103**	...	...	**1,766**	...	...

TABLE V.

Towns arranged territorially with Population by Religion.

TABLE V.

Towns arranged territorially with Population by Religion.

Division.	Town, Municipality, Suburbs, Cantonments, etc.	Population.			Hindu.			Musalman.			Christian.			Jew.			Jain.		
		Persons.	Males.	Females.	Persons.	Males.	Females.	Persons.	Males.	Females.	Persons.	Males.	Females.	Persons.	Males.	Females.	Persons.	Males.	Females.
1	2	3	4	5	6	7	8	9	10	11	12	13	14	15	16	17	18	19	20
STATE.		*212,090*	*107,668*	*104,422*	*143,057*	*72,466*	*0,591*	*23,918*	*12,186*	*11,732*	*45,041*	*22,963*	*22,078*	*63*	*45*	*18*	*11*	*8*	*3*
I. PADMANABHAPURAM.		*29,883*	*14,553*	*15,330*	*22,479*	*10,996*	*11,483*	*2,925*	*1,391*	*1,534*	*4,479*	*2,166*	*2,313*	...	...	...	...	...	...
Nagercoil ...	M	**29,883**	14,553	15,330	**22,479**	10,996	11,483	**2,925**	1,391	1,534	**4,479**	2,166	2,313	...	...	...	...	...	...
II. TRIVANDRUM.		*63,561*	*32,292*	*31,269*	*51,346*	*26,180*	*25,166*	*4,648*	*2,475*	*2,173*	*7,552*	*3,626*	*3,926*	*15*	*11*	*4*	...	...	...
Trivandrum ...	M & C	**63,561**	32,292	31,269	**51,346**	26,180	25,166	**4,648**	2,475	2,173	**7,552**	3,626	3,926	**15**	11	4	...	...	...
III. QUILON.		*68,612*	*34,964*	*33,648*	*40,611*	*20,678*	*19,933*	*12,121*	*6,074*	*6,047*	*15,866*	*8,201*	*7,665*	*3*	*3*	...	*11*	*8*	*3*
Shencottah		**10,309**	4,905	5,404	**9,377**	4,447	4,930	**872**	423	449	**60**	35	25	...	...	...	...	...	...
Quilon	M	**18,839**	9,649	9,190	**9,885**	5,149	4,736	**3,358**	1,736	1,622	**5,593**	2,761	2,832	**3**	3	...	...	...	...
Kayankulam	M	**5,830**	2,772	3,058	**3,451**	1,609	1,842	**1,206**	608	598	**1,173**	555	618	...	...	...	...	...	...
Tiruvalla		**7,969**	4,268	3,701	**5,266**	2,797	2,469	**16**	8	8	**2,687**	1,463	1,224	...	...	...	...	...	...
Alleppey	M	**25,665**	13,370	12,295	**12,632**	6,676	5,956	**6,669**	3,299	3,370	**6,353**	3,387	2,966	...	...	...	**11**	8	3
IV. KOTTAYAM.		*50,034*	*25,859*	*24,175*	*28,621*	*14,612*	*14,009*	*4,224*	*2,246*	*1,978*	*17,144*	*8,970*	*8,174*	*45*	*31*	*14*	...	...	...
Kottayam	M	**15,141**	7,863	7,278	**7,547**	3,935	3,612	**577**	323	254	**7,017**	3,605	3,412	...	...	...	...	...	...
Changanachery		**17,242**	8,826	8,416	**9,03[illegible]**	4,509	4,527	**1,855**	1,002	853	**6,351**	3,315	3,036	...	...	...	...	...	...
Alwaye	M	**3,869**	2,103	1,766	**1,293**	603	601	**794**	424	370	**1,780**	985	795	**2**	2	...	...	...	...
Parur		**13,782**	7,067	6,715	**10,745**	5,476	5,269	**998**	497	501	**1,996**	1,065	931	**43**	29	14	...	...	...

TABLE VI.

Religion.

TABLE VI.

Religion.

DIVISION.	Population.			Hindu.			Musalman.			Christian.			Animistic.			Jew.			Jain.			Buddhist.		
	Persons.	Males.	Females.	Persons.	Males.	Females.	Persons.	Males.	Females.	Persons.	Males.	Females.	Persons.	Males.	Females.	Persons.	Males.	Females.	Persons.	Males.	Females.	Persons.	Males.	Females.
1	2	3	4	5	6	7	8	9	10	11	12	13	14	15	16	17	18	19	20	21	22	23	24	25
STATE ...	*3,428,975*	*1,731,363*	*1,697,612*	*2,282,617*	*1,145,511*	*1,137,106*	*226,617*	*116,488*	*110,129*	*903,868*	*461,165*	*442,703*	*15,773*	*8,123*	*7,650*	*73*	*53*	*20*	*11*	*8*	*3*	*16*	*15*	*1*
I. PADMANABHAPURAM ..	**430,087**	215,313	214,774	**296,420**	148,134	148,286	**14,851**	7,419	7,432	**116,778**	58,670	58,108	**2,038**	1,090	948	..	..	..	..	..	..	...	...	..
II. TRIVANDRUM ...	**557,865**	281,225	276,640	**423,909**	213,315	210,594	**51,197**	25,733	25,464	**77,305**	39,371	37,934	**5,438**	2,794	2,644	**15**	11	4	...	...	.	**1**	1	..
III. QUILON ..	**1,233,360**	620,773	612,587	**877,605**	438,137	439,468	**89,750**	46,209	43,541	**262,446**	134,621	127,825	**3,543**	1,793	1,750	**5**	5	...	**11**	8	3	..	...	.
IV. KOTTAYAM ...	**1,139,101**	576,060	563,041	**640,983**	322,027	318,956	**67,061**	34,935	32,126	**428,706**	217,874	210,832	**2,298**	1,187	1,111	**53**	37	16	...	.	..	...	...	.
V. DEVIKULAM ..	**68,562**	37,992	30,570	**43,700**	23,898	19,802	**3,758**	2,192	1,566	**18,633**	10,629	8,004	**2,456**	1,259	1,197	..	...	...	...	...	..	**15**	14	1
A. *Western Natural Division*...	*1,976,154*	*994,326*	*981,828*	*1,417,412*	*709,447*	*707,965*	*135,210*	*68,978*	*66,232*	*419,818*	*213,955*	*205,863*	*3,631*	*1,886*	*1,745*	*71*	*51*	*20*	*11*	*8*	*3*	*1*	*1*	..
B. *Eastern Natural Division*..	*1,452,821*	*737,037*	*715,784*	*865,205*	*436,064*	*429,141*	*91,407*	*47,510*	*43,897*	*484,050*	*247,210*	*236,840*	*12,142*	*6,237*	*5,905*	*2*	*2*	..	.	.	..	*15*	*14*	*1*

TABLE VII.

Age, Sex and Civil Condition.

Part I.—State and Divisions.

TABLE VII.

Age, Sex and Civil Condition.—STATE.

A.—ALL RELIGIONS.

AGE.	POPULATION.			UNMARRIED.			MARRIED.			WIDOWED.		
	Persons.	Males.	Females.	Persons.	Males.	Females.	Persons.	Males.	Females.	Persons.	Males.	Females.
1	2	3	4	5	6	7	8	9	10	11	12	13
0—1 ...	**89,861**	42,659	47,202	**89,861**	42,659	47,202	...	...	...	...	...	...
1—2 ...	**77,462**	37,713	39,749	**77,462**	37,713	39,749	...	...	...	...	...	...
2—3 ..	**104,568**	51,374	53,194	**104,568**	51,374	53,194	...	...	...	...	...	...
3—4 ..	**105,676**	52,166	53,510	**105,676**	52,166	53,510	...	...	...	...	...	...
4—5 ...	**88,244**	43,959	44,285	**88,244**	43,959	44,285	...	...	...	...	...	...
Total 0—5 ..	*465,811*	*227,871*	*237,940*	*465,811*	*227,871*	*237,940*	...	...	...	...	...	...
5—10 ..	**459,383**	230,525	228,858	**457,519**	229,919	227,600	**1,444**	462	982	**420**	144	276
10—15 ...	**417,368**	216,495	200,873	**397,636**	214,266	183,370	**18,838**	1,973	16,865	**894**	256	638
15—20 ...	**326,915**	159,935	166,980	**205,953**	137,973	67,980	**116,444**	21,055	95,389	**4,518**	907	3,611
20—25 ...	**301,853**	144,716	157,137	**94,232**	76,057	18,175	**196,399**	65,697	130,702	**11,222**	2,962	8,260
25—30 ...	**311,234**	153,881	157,353	**41,588**	33,539	8,049	**250,245**	114,653	135,592	**19,401**	5,689	13,712
30—35 ...	**242,440**	122,978	119,462	**13,659**	9,719	3,940	**205,567**	107,015	98,552	**23,214**	6,244	16,970
35—40 ..	**232,867**	127,158	105,709	**7,249**	4,622	2,627	**198,011**	115,833	82,178	**27,607**	6,703	20,904
40—45 ..	**178,998**	94,397	84,601	**3,799**	2,136	1,663	**140,819**	85,090	55,729	**34,380**	7,171	27,209
45—50 .	**146,966**	80,376	66,590	**2,690**	1,406	1,284	**109,971**	71,604	38,367	**34,305**	7,366	26,939
50—55 ...	**115,519**	58,694	56,825	**1,689**	806	883	**73,780**	49,701	24,079	**40,050**	8,187	31,863
55—60 ..	**80,149**	42,659	37,490	**1,024**	451	573	**48,177**	35,143	13,034	**30,948**	7,065	23,883
60—65 .	**70,387**	33,856	36,531	**877**	342	535	**32,540**	25,259	7,281	**36,970**	8,255	28,715
65—70 ...	**34,232**	17,342	16,890	**422**	183	239	**14,999**	12,371	2,628	**18,811**	4,788	14,023
70 and over ..	**44,853**	20,480	24,373	**672**	281	391	**14,256**	12,207	2,049	**29,925**	7,992	21,933
Total ...	*3,428,975*	*1,731,363*	*1,697,612*	*1,694,820*	*939,571*	*755,249*	*1,421,490*	*718,063*	*703,427*	*312,665*	*73,729*	*238,936*

TABLE VII.

Age, Sex and Civil Condition.—STATE.

B.—HINDU.

AGE.	POPULATION.			UNMARRIED.			MARRIED.			WIDOWED.		
	Persons.	Males.	Females.	Persons.	Males.	Females.	Persons.	Males.	Females.	Persons.	Males.	Females.
1	2	3	4	5	6	7	8	9	10	11	12	13
0—1	**59,686**	28,372	31,314	**59,686**	28,372	31,314	...	...	...	...	...	...
1—2	**49,474**	24,103	25,371	**49,474**	24,103	25,371	...	...	...	...	...	...
2—3	**67,332**	33,214	34,118	**67,332**	33,214	34,118	...	...	...	...	...	...
3—4	**68,970**	34,078	34,892	**68,970**	34,078	34,892	...	...	...	...	...	...
4—5	**57,331**	28,700	28,631	**57,331**	28,700	28,631	...	...	...	...	...	...
Total 0—5	*302,793*	*148,467*	*154,326*	*302,793*	*148,467*	*154,326*	...	...	...	...	...	...
5—10	**294,860**	148,188	146,672	**293,614**	147,781	145,833	**935**	303	632	**311**	104	207
10—15	**270,032**	140,123	129,909	**259,603**	139,191	120,412	**9,774**	767	9,007	**655**	165	490
15—20	**216,620**	104,693	111,927	**146,947**	95,821	51,126	**66,098**	8,222	57,876	**3,575**	650	2,925
20—25	**200,952**	95,802	105,150	**71,795**	57,328	14,467	**120,027**	36,186	83,841	**9,130**	2,288	6,842
25—30	**210,099**	103,001	107,098	**32,534**	26,364	6,170	**162,137**	72,296	89,841	**15,428**	4,341	11,087
30—35	**164,186**	82,548	81,638	**11,069**	7,886	3,183	**135,115**	69,842	65,273	**18,002**	4,820	13,182
35—40	**158,252**	85,622	72,630	**5,842**	3,754	2,088	**131,627**	76,910	54,717	**20,783**	4,958	15,825
40—45	**123,999**	64,617	59,382	**2,993**	1,717	1,276	**95,422**	57,730	37,692	**25,584**	5,170	20,414
45—50	**100,573**	54,462	46,111	**2,128**	1,100	1,028	**73,526**	48,237	25,289	**24,919**	5,125	19,794
50—55	**80,095**	40,138	39,957	**1,299**	614	685	**49,663**	33,868	15,795	**29,133**	5,656	23,477
55—60	**55,262**	29,049	26,213	**747**	327	420	**31,958**	23,879	8,079	**22,557**	4,843	17,714
60—65	**49,402**	23,196	26,206	**640**	244	396	**21,368**	17,253	4,615	**26,894**	5,699	21,195
65—70	**23,734**	11,648	12,086	**298**	120	178	**9,868**	8,275	1,593	**13,568**	3,253	10,315
70 and over	**31,758**	13,957	17,801	**467**	178	289	**9,652**	8,371	1,281	**21,639**	5,408	16,231
Total	***2,282,617***	***1,145,511***	***1,137,106***	***1,132,769***	***630,892***	***501,877***	***917,670***	***462,139***	***455,531***	***232,178***	***52,480***	***179,698***

TABLE VII.

Age, Sex and Civil Condition.—STATE.

C.—MUSALMAN.

AGE.	POPULATION.			UNMARRIED.			MARRIED.			WIDOWED.		
	Persons.	Males.	Females.	Persons.	Males.	Females.	Persons.	Males.	Females.	Persons.	Males.	Females.
1	2	3	4	5	6	7	8	9	10	11	12	13
0—1 ...	**5,826**	2,804	3,022	**5,826**	2,804	3,022	...	...	...	...	...	...
1—2 ...	**5,173**	2,497	2,676	**5,173**	2,497	2,676	...	...	...	...	...	...
2—3 ...	**7,391**	3,644	3,747	**7,391**	3,644	3,747	...	...	...	...	..	...
3—4 ...	**7,581**	3,839	3,742	**7,581**	3,839	3,742	...	...	...	..	...	...
4—5 ...	**6,591**	3,211	3,380	**6,591**	3,211	3,380	...	...	...	...	...	...
Total 0—5 ...	*32,562*	*15,995*	*16,567*	*32,562*	*15,995*	*16,567*	...	...	...	.	...	..
5—10 ...	**32,379**	16,280	16,099	**32,288**	16,258	16,030	**68**	13	55	**23**	9	14
10—15 ...	**28,682**	15,029	13,653	**27,670**	14,965	12,705	**966**	54	912	**46**	10	36
15—20 ...	**21,253**	10,711	10,542	**13,609**	9,872	3,737	**7,284**	775	6,509	**360**	64	296
20—25 ...	**20,188**	9,689	10,499	**6,480**	5,700	780	**12,972**	3,766	9,206	**736**	223	513
25—30 ...	**20,022**	9,797	10,225	**2,520**	2,265	255	**16,323**	7,118	9,205	**1,179**	414	765
30—35 ...	**15,450**	7,847	7,603	**776**	657	119	**13,280**	6,840	6,440	**1,394**	350	1,044
35—40 ...	**15,225**	8,499	6,726	**274**	171	103	**13,372**	7,985	5,387	**1,579**	343	1,236
40—45 ...	**11,484**	6,289	5,195	**176**	89	87	**9,412**	5,888	3,524	**1,896**	312	1,584
45—50 ...	**9,027**	5,188	3,839	**79**	37	42	**7,108**	4,842	2,266	**1,840**	309	1,531
50—55 ...	**6,978**	3,823	3,155	**58**	23	35	**4,755**	3,384	1,371	**2,165**	416	1,749
55—60 ...	**4,598**	2,692	1,906	**46**	14	32	**2,999**	2,347	652	**1,553**	331	1,222
60—65 ...	**4,309**	2,233	2,076	**47**	15	32	**2,240**	1,827	413	**2,022**	391	1,631
65—70 ...	**1,899**	1,119	780	**28**	21	7	**986**	855	131	**885**	243	642
70 and over ...	**2,561**	1,297	1,264	**31**	15	16	**1,015**	898	117	**1,515**	384	1,131
Total ...	*226,617*	*116,488*	*110,129*	*116,644*	*66,097*	*50,547*	*92,780*	*46,592*	*46,188*	*17,193*	*3,799*	*13,394*

TABLE VII.

Age, Sex and Civil Condition.—STATE.

D.—CHRISTIAN.

AGE.	POPULATION.			UNMARRIED.			MARRIED.			WIDOWED.		
	Persons.	Males.	Females.	Persons.	Males.	Females.	Persons.	Males.	Females.	Persons.	Males.	Females.
1	2	3	4	5	6	7	8	9	10	11	12	13
0—1 ..	**23,955**	11,300	12,655	**23,955**	11,300	12,655	...		..	..	.	.
1—2 ...	**22,586**	11,000	11,586	**22,586**	11,000	11,586	...	..	..	..	.	.
2—3 ...	**29,416**	14,311	15,105	**29,416**	14,311	15,105	...	..	...	.	..	..
3—4 ..	**28,682**	14,031	14,651	**28,682**	14,031	14,651	...		...	..	..	.
4—5 ...	**23,901**	11,821	12,080	**23,901**	11,821	12,080	..	.	..	.	..	...
Total 0—5 ..	*128,540*	*62,463*	*66,077*	*128,540*	*62,463*	66,077	...	..	...	.	..	...
5—10 ..	**129,969**	64,902	65,067	**129,452**	64,728	64,724	**433**	144	289	**84**	30	54
10—15 ...	**116,857**	60,416	56,441	**108,635**	59,192	49,443	**8,032**	1,144	6,888	**190**	80	110
15—20 ...	**87,566**	43,843	43,723	**44,434**	31,673	12,761	**42,574**	11,963	30,591	**558**	187	371
20—25 ..	**79,381**	38,669	40,712	**15,573**	12,748	2,825	**62,499**	25,486	37,013	**1,309**	435	874
25—30 ..	**79,501**	40,318	39,183	**6,371**	4,785	1,586	**70,425**	34,632	35,793	**2,705**	901	1,804
30—35 ..	**61,573**	31,989	29,584	**1,777**	1,153	624	**56,065**	29,795	26,270	**3,731**	1,041	2,690
35—40 ..	**58,133**	32,298	25,835	**1,104**	674	430	**51,885**	30,271	21,614	**5,144**	1,353	3,791
40—45 ..	**42,573**	22,942	19,631	**622**	325	297	**35,188**	20,982	14,206	**6,763**	1,635	5,128
45—50 ..	**36,659**	20,291	16,368	**470**	265	205	**28,741**	18,132	10,609	**7,448**	1,894	5,554
50—55 ..	**27,930**	14,420	13,510	**324**	165	159	**18,974**	12,172	6,802	**8,632**	2,083	6,549
55—60 ..	**19,962**	10,713	9,249	**231**	110	121	**12,987**	8,745	4,242	**6,744**	1,858	4,886
60—65 .	**16,398**	8,273	8,125	**189**	83	106	**8,280**	6,060	2,220	**7,929**	2,130	5,799
65—70 .	**8,491**	4,509	3,982	**96**	42	54	**4,082**	3,193	889	**4,313**	1,274	3,039
70 and over ..	**10,335**	5,119	5,216	**173**	87	86	**3,512**	2,869	643	**6,650**	2,163	4,487
Total ...	*903,868*	*461,165*	*442,703*	*437,991*	*238,493*	*199,498*	*403,677*	*205,608*	*198,069*	*62,200*	*17,064*	*45,136*

TABLE VII.

Age, Sex and Civil Condition.—STATE.

E.—ANIMISTIC.

AGE.	POPULATION.			UNMARRIED.			MARRIED.			WIDOWED.		
	Persons.	Males.	Females.	Persons.	Males.	Females.	Persons.	Males.	Females.	Persons.	Males.	Females.
1	2	3	4	5	6	7	8	9	10	11	12	13
0— 1 ..	**392**	181	211	**392**	181	211	..	..	..	...	...	...
1— 2 ..	**225**	109	116	**225**	109	116	...	...	...	...	...	..
2— 3 ..	**428**	204	224	**428**	204	224	.	.	...	..		..
3— 4 ..	**440**	216	224	**440**	216	224	...	..	..	..	..	...
4— 5 ..	**421**	227	194	**421**	227	194	..	...	..	..	.	.
Total 0—5 .	*1,906*	*937*	*969*	*1,906*	*937*	*969*	..	...	...	..	..	..
5—10 ..	**2,170**	1,152	1,018	**2,160**	1,149	1,011	**8**	2	6	**2**	1	1
10—15 ...	**1,794**	925	860	**1,725**	916	809	**66**	8	58	**3**	1	2
15—20 ..	**1,470**	685	785	**959**	604	355	**486**	75	411	**25**	6	19
20—25 ..	**1,317**	546	771	**375**	272	103	**895**	258	637	**47**	16	31
25—30 ..	**1,597**	753	844	**158**	120	38	**1,350**	600	750	**89**	33	56
30—35 ..	**1,220**	586	634	**37**	23	14	**1,096**	530	566	**87**	33	54
35—40 ..	**1,251**	733	518	**27**	21	6	**1,124**	664	460	**100**	48	52
40—45 .	**933**	541	392	**8**	5	3	**789**	483	306	**136**	53	83
45—50 .	**698**	428	270	**13**	4	9	**583**	386	202	**97**	38	59
50—55	**513**	310	203	**8**	4	4	**385**	274	111	**120**	32	88
55—60 ..	**327**	205	122	.	..	..	**233**	172	61	**94**	33	61
60—65 .	**276**	154	122	**1**	.	1	**152**	119	33	**123**	35	88
65—70 .	**104**	62	42	.	.	..	**60**	45	15	**44**	17	27
70 and over .	**197**	106	91	**1**	1	..	**77**	69	8	**119**	36	83
Total	***15,773***	***8,123***	***7,650***	***7,378***	***4,056***	***3,322***	***7,309***	***3,685***	***3,624***	***1,086***	***382***	***704***

TABLE VII.

Age, Sex and Civil Condition.—STATE.

F.—OTHER RELIGIONISTS.

Religion.	Division.	Civil Condition.	0—5		5—10		10—15		15—20		20—25		25—30		30—35		35—40		40—45		45—50		50—55		55—60		60—65		65—70		70 & over	
			Males	Females	Males	Females	Males	Females	Males	Females	Males	Females	Males	Females	Males	Females	Males	Females	Males	Females	Males	Females	Males	Females	Males	Females	Males	Females	Males	Females	Males	Females
1	2	3	4	5	6	7	8	9	10	11	12	13	14	15	16	17	18	19	20	21	22	23	24	25	26	27	28	29	30	31	32	33
Buddhist	Trivandrum	Married	..	..	..	..	..	..	..	..	..	..	1	..	..	..	..	..	..	..	..	..	..	..	..	..	..	..	..	..	..	..
	Devikulam	Unmarried	2	..	..	..	2	..	..	..	2	..	2	..	..	..	..	..	..	..	..	..	..	..	..	..	..	..	..	..	..	..
		Married	..	..	..	..	..	..	..	..	..	..	1	..	2	1	1	..	1	..	1	..	..	..	..	..	..	..	..	..	..	..
	Western Natural Division	Married	..	..	..	..	..	..	..	..	..	..	1	..	..	..	..	..	..	..	..	..	..	..	..	..	..	..	..	..	..	..
	Eastern Natural Division	Unmarried	2	..	..	..	2	..	..	..	2	..	2	..	..	..	..	..	..	..	..	..	..	..	..	..	..	..	..	..	..	..
		Married	..	..	..	..	..	..	..	..	..	..	1	..	2	1	1	..	1	..	1	..	..	..	..	..	..	..	..	..	..	..
Jew	Trivandrum	Unmarried	3	..	1	1	..	..	..	..	2	..	..	..	..	..	..	..	..	..	..	..	..	..	..	..	..	..	..	..	..	..
		Married	..	..	..	..	..	..	..	..	..	1	1	1	..	..	..	..	1	..	..	..	1	..	..	..	..	..	..	..	..	..
		Widowed	..	..	..	..	..	..	..	..	..	..	..	..	..	..	..	..	..	..	..	1	..	..	..	..	..	..	1	..	1	..
	Quilon	Unmarried	..	..	..	..	..	..	..	..	1	..	1	..	..	..	..	..	..	..	..	..	..	..	..	..	..	..	..	..	..	..
		Married	..	..	..	..	..	..	..	..	1	..	..	..	1	..	..	..	1	..	..	..	..	..	..	..	..	..	..	..	..	..
	Kottayam	Unmarried	3	1	1	1	..	1	2	1	3	..	2	..	..	..	2	..	..	..	..	..	..	..	..	..	..	..	..	..	..	..
		Married	..	..	..	..	..	..	..	2	..	2	4	2	4	1	1	..	2	1	6	1	2	..	..	..	..	..	3	..	..	..
		Widowed	..	..	..	..	..	..	..	..	..	..	..	..	..	..	1	..	1	..	..	..	..	..	..	..	..	2	..	..	..	1
	Western Natural Division	Unmarried	6	1	2	2	..	1	1	1	6	..	3	..	..	..	1	..	..	..	..	..	..	..	..	..	..	..	..	..	..	..
		Married	..	..	..	..	..	..	..	2	1	3	5	3	5	1	1	..	4	1	6	1	3	..	..	..	..	..	3	..	..	..
		Widowed	..	..	..	..	..	..	..	..	..	..	..	..	..	..	1	..	1	..	..	1	..	..	..	..	..	2	1	..	1	1
	Eastern Natural Division	Unmarried	..	..	..	..	..	..	1	..	..	..	..	..	..	..	1	..	..	..	..	..	..	..	..	..	..	..	..	..	..	..
Jain	Quilon	Unmarried	1	..	1	..	..	..	1	..	1	..	..	..	..	..	..	..	..	..	..	..	..	..	..	..	..	..	..	..	..	..
		Married	..	..	..	..	..	..	..	..	..	2	..	..	1	1	1	..	2	..	..	..	..	..	..	..	..	..	..	..	..	..
	Western Natural Division	Unmarried	1	..	1	..	..	..	1	..	1	..	..	..	..	..	..	..	..	..	..	..	..	..	..	..	..	..	..	..	..	..
		Married	..	..	..	..	..	..	..	..	..	2	..	..	1	1	1	..	2	..	..	..	..	..	..	..	..	..	..	..	..	..

TABLE VII.

Age, Sex and Civil Condition.—PADMANABHAPURAM DIVISION.

AGE.	POPULATION.			UNMARRIED		MARRIED.		WIDOWED.	
	Persons.	Males.	Females	Males.	Females	Males	Females.	Males.	Females.
1	2	3	4	5	6	7	8	9	10
ALL RELIGIONS.	*430,087*	*215,313*	*214,774*	*122,007*	*95,761*	*83,447*	*84,791*	*9.859*	*34 222*
0—5	**57,760**	28,090	29,670	28,090	29,670	.		..	
5—10	**56,596**	28 371	28,225	28,323	28,088	34	114	14	28
10—15	**50,277**	25,674	24,603	25,569	23,496	71	1,059	34	48
15—20	**40,807**	20,246	20,561	19,311	10,495	831	9,802	104	264
20—40	**134,817**	66,574	68,243	20,193	3,577	44,165	56,555	2,216	8,111
40—60	**69,728**	36,173	33,555	472	324	31,330	16,165	4,371	17,066
60 and over	**20,102**	10,185	9,917	49	116	7,016	1,096	3,120	8,705
HINDU	*296,420*	*148,134*	*148,286*	*83,328*	*63,926*	*57,654*	*59,309*	*7.152*	*25,051*
0—5	**39,420**	19,239	20,181	19,239	20,181	.	..	.	.
5—10	**38,221**	19,207	19,014	19,171	18,906	26	86	10	20
10—15	**34,286**	17,407	16,879	17,327	15,940	54	899	26	40
15—20	**27,667**	13,688	13,979	13,059	6,548	542	7,228	87	208
20—40	**92,584**	45,695	46,889	14,147	2,041	30,050	38,947	1,498	5,901
40—60	**49,498**	25,455	24,043	349	284	21,899	11,466	3,207	12,348
60 and over	**14,744**	7,443	7,301	36	79	5,083	683	2,324	6,539
MUSALMAN	*14,851*	*7,419*	*7,432*	*4,023*	*3,101*	*3,119*	*3,214*	*277*	*1,117*
0—5	**1,814**	877	937	877	937	..	.		.
5—10	**2,070**	1,021	1,049	1,021	1,046		3	.	
10—15	**1,749**	925	824	921	784	3	40	1	
15—20	**1,368**	635	733	607	260	26	464	2	9
20—40	**4,689**	2,271	2,418	579	67	1,610	2,094	82	257
40—60	**2,451**	1,301	1,150	15	6	1,177	566	109	578
60 and over	**710**	389	321	3	1	303	47	83	273
CHRISTIAN	*116,778*	*58,670*	*58,108*	*34,138*	*28,359*	*22,187*	*21,781*	*2,345*	*7,968*
0—5	**16,339**	7,879	8,460	7,879	8,460	.	.	..	
5—10	**16,091**	8,024	8,067	8,012	8,085	8	24	4	8
10—15	**14,049**	7,289	6,810	7,218	6,685	14	117	7	8
15—20	**11,532**	5,811	5,721	5,589	3,620	257	2,055	15	46
20—40	**36,839**	18,265	18,574	5,376	1,440	12,283	15,204	606	1,980
40—60	**17,385**	9,157	8,228	105	84	8,088	4,081	1,014	4,113
60 and over	**4,543**	2,295	2,248	9	35	1,587	350	699	1,863
ANIMISTIC	*2,038*	*1,090*	*948*	*518*	*375*	*487*	*487*	*85*	*86*
0—5	**187**	95	92	95	92	..	...	...	.
5—10	**214**	119	95	119	94	.	1	..	.
10—15	**193**	103	90	103	87	..	3	..	.
15—20	**240**	112	128	106	72	6	55	.	1
20—40	**705**	343	362	91	29	222	810	30	23
40—60	**394**	260	134	3	..	216	102	41	32
60 and over	**105**	58	47	1	1	43	16	14	30

TABLE VII.

Age, Sex and Civil Condition.—TRIVANDRUM DIVISION.

AGE.	POPULATION.			UNMARRIED.		MARRIED.		WIDOWED.	
	Persons	Males	Females.	Males	Females.	Males.	Females.	Males.	Females.
1	2	3	4	5	6	7	8	9	10
ALL RELIGIONS.	*557,865*	*281,225*	*276,640*	*165,988*	*129,092*	*105,733*	*105,312*	*9,504*	*42,236*
0—5 ...	**78,062**	38,384	39,698	38,384	39,698	...	...	...	..
5—10 ..	**77,543**	38,939	38,604	38,854	38,344	66	214	19	46
10—15 ...	**69,123**	36,006	33,117	35,836	30,811	132	2,159	38	147
15—20 ..	**53,856**	25,794	28 062	24,531	12,888	1,108	14,230	155	949
20—40 ..	**175,028**	87,424	87,604	27,285	6,611	56,822	68,651	3,317	12,342
40—60 ..	**80,111**	43,183	36,928	970	592	38,771	18,494	3,442	17,842
60 and over ..	**24,122**	11,495	12,6.7	128	153	8,834	1,564	2,533	10,910
HINDU ...	*423,909*	*213,315*	*210,594*	*126,330*	*96,615*	*79,526*	*79,018*	*7,459*	*34,961*
0—5 ..	**58,787**	29,000	29,787	29,000	29,787	...	...	...	..
5—10 ..	**57,580**	29,009	28,571	28,945	28,351	53	178	11	42
10—15 ..	**51,872**	27,155	24,717	27,025	22,909	102	1,678	28	130
15—20 ..	**40,945**	19,628	21,317	18,674	9,882	843	10,675	111	760
20—40 ...	**132,640**	66,368	66,272	21,716	5,142	42,010	50,898	2,642	10,232
40—60 ..	**62,763**	33,262	29,501	863	430	29,694	14,396	2,705	14,675
60 and over ..	**19,322**	8,893	10,429	107	114	6,824	1,193	1,962	9,122
MUSALMAN ...	*51,197*	*25,733*	*25,464*	*15,102*	*11,388*	*9,866*	*10,434*	*765*	*3,642*
0—5 ..	**7,259**	3,593	3,666	3,593	3,666	...	.	..	..
5—10	**7,429**	3,732	3,697	3,727	3,675	1	18	4	4
10—15 ..	**6,578**	3,391	3,187	3,379	2,878	10	297	2	12
15—20 ..	**4,752**	2,304	2,448	2,182	778	104	1,551	18	119
20—40 ..	**15,982**	7,757	8,225	2,184	322	5,287	6,821	286	1,082
40—60	**7,103**	3,886	3,217	29	54	3,595	1,620	262	1,548
60 and over ..	**2,094**	1,070	1,024	8	15	869	127	198	882
CHRISTIAN ..	*77,305*	*39,371*	*37,934*	*23,164*	*19,962*	*15,047*	*14,599*	*1,160*	*3,373*
0—5 .	**11,373**	5,460	5,913	5,460	5,913	.	.	..	
5—10 .	**11,811**	5,822	5,989	5,808	5,976	11	13	3	.
10—15 ..	**10,082**	5,152	4,930	5,125	4,753	19	172	8	5
15—20 ..	**7,667**	3,629	4,038	3,466	2,106	140	1,871	23	61
20—40	**24.504**	12,408	12,096	3,219	1,091	8,843	10,070	346	935
40—60 .	**9,351**	5,475	3,876	73	99	4,969	2,252	483	1,525
60 and over ..	**2,517**	1,425	1,092	13	24	1,065	221	347	847
ANIMISTIC .	*5,438*	*2,794*	*2,644*	*1,386*	*1,126*	*1,290*	*1,259*	*118*	*259*
0—5 ..	**660**	328	332	328	332	...	...	...	.
5—10 ..	**721**	375	346	373	341	1	5	1	
10—15 ..	**591**	308	288	307	271	1	12	...	.
15—20 ..	**492**	233	259	209	117	21	133	3	9
20—40 .	**1,896**	887	1,009	164	56	680	860	43	93
40—60	**891**	558	333	5	9	511	226	42	98
60 and over .	**187**	105	82	...	...	76	23	29	59

TABLE VII.

Age, Sex and Civil Condition.—QUILON DIVISION.

AGE.	POPULATION.			UNMARRIED.		MARRIED.		WIDOWED.	
	Persons.	Males.	Females.	Males.	Females.	Males.	Females.	Males.	Females.
1	2	3	4	5	6	7	8	9	10
ALL RELIGIONS.	*1,233,360*	*620,773*	*612,587*	*333,683*	*273,852*	*260,749*	*252,019*	*26,341*	*86,716*
0— 5 ..	**163,411**	80,021	83,390	80,021	83,390	..	.	.	..
5—10 ..	**164,158**	81,989	82,169	81,720	81,672	205	375	64	122
10—15 ..	**150,472**	77,802	72,670	76,910	66,508	794	5,918	92	244
15—20 ...	**117,236**	56,388	60,848	48,650	26,423	7,437	33,167	301	1,258
20—40 ...	**391,325**	196,725	194,600	44,084	13,661	144,717	158,977	7,924	21,962
40—60 ..	**190,884**	101,253	89,631	1,957	1,633	88,987	49,013	10,309	33,985
60 and over ..	**55,874**	26,595	29,279	335	565	18,009	4,569	7,651	24,145
HINDU ..	*877,605*	*438,137*	*439,468*	*239,460*	*196,297*	*178,426*	*173,576*	*20,251*	*69,595*
0— 5 ..	**112,259**	55,125	57,134	55,125	57,134	..	..	..	.
5—10 ..	**112,396**	56,193	56,203	56,007	55,878	138	231	48	94
10—15 ..	**104,334**	53,918	50,416	53,534	47,394	321	2,831	63	190
15—20 ..	**83,046**	39,297	43,749	36,024	22,294	3,053	20,409	220	1,046
20—40 ...	**283,049**	140,761	142,288	36,844	11,854	97,420	112,127	6,497	18,307
40—60	**140,589**	73,547	67,042	1,683	1,290	64,065	84,811	7,799	30,939
60 and over .	**41,932**	19,296	22,636	243	453	13,429	3,163	5,634	19,020
MUSALMAN ..	*89,750*	*46,209*	*43,541*	*26,171*	*20,097*	*18,593*	*18,271*	*1,445*	*5,173*
0— 5 .	**12,849**	6,290	6,559	6,290	6,559	..	..	...	..
5—10 .	**12,752**	6,873	6,379	6,862	6,351	7	21	4	7
10—15 ..	**11,355**	5,911	5,444	5,886	5,072	22	355	3	17
15—20 ..	**8,593**	4,304	4,289	3,986	1,486	297	2,706	21	97
20—40 ..	**28,025**	14,269	13,756	3,544	506	10,200	11,839	525	1,411
40—60 .	**12,817**	7,273	5,514	84	94	6,675	3,085	514	2,365
60 and over .	**3,359**	1,789	1,570	19	29	1,392	265	378	1,276
CHRISTIAN ..	*262,446*	*134,621*	*127,825*	*67,098*	*56,636*	*62,946*	*59,385*	*4,577*	*11,804*
0— 5 ..	**37,823**	18,383	19,443	18,383	19,443	.	.	.	.
5—10 ..	**38,457**	19,128	19,329	19,056	19,185	60	123	12	21
10—15 ..	**34,371**	17,755	16,616	17,279	13,860	451	2,720	25	36
15—20 .	**25,283**	12,647	12,639	8,509	2,561	4,078	9,967	60	111
20—40 ...	**79,045**	41,114	37,931	3,609	1,258	36,630	34,468	885	2,205
40—60	**36,979**	20,144	16,835	189	246	17,099	10,971	1,966	5,618
60 and over	**10,482**	5,450	5,032	73	83	3,748	1,136	1,629	3,813
ANIMISTIC .	*3,543*	*1,793*	*1,750*	*948*	*822*	*777*	*784*	*68*	*144*
0— 5 .	**476**	222	254	222	254	.	..	..	..
5—10 .	**552**	294	258	294	258	.	.		.
10—15 .	**412**	218	194	217	182	.	11	1	1
15—20 .	**310**	139	171	130	82	9	85	..	4
20—40 .	**1,196**	574	622	84	43	473	540	17	39
40—60 ..	**498**	286	210	1	3	255	143	80	64
60 and over .	**101**	60	41	..		40	5	20	36

TABLE VII.

Age, Sex and Civil Condition.—KOTTAYAM DIVISION.

AGE.	POPULATION.			UNMARRIED.		MARRIED.		WIDOWED.	
	Persons.	Males.	Females.	Males.	Females.	Males.	Females.	Males.	Females.
1	2	3	4	5	6	7.	8	9	10
ALL RELIGIONS.	*1,139,101*	*576,060.*	*563,041*	*298,144*	*241,995*	*251,260*	*247,661*	*26,656*	*73,385*
0— 5	**158,976**	77,679	81,297	77,679	81,297	...	...	...	..
5—10	**153,756**	77,644	76,112	77,465	75,797	137	239	42	76
10—15	**137,871**	72,286	65,585	71,312	58,037	886	7,353	88	195
15—20	**106,897**	53,111	53,786	41,769	16,626	11,028	36,071	314	1,089
20—40	**361,153**	182,419	178,734	28,360	8,129	146,386	153,842	7 673	16,763
40—60	**172,700**	90,450	82,250	1,278	1,789	78,048	45,595	11,124	34,863
60 and over	**47,748**	22,471	25,277	281	320	14,775	4,561	7,415	20,396
HINDU	*640,983*	*322,027*	*318,956*	*168,991*	*135,369*	*136,200*	*135,103*	*16,836*	*48,484*
0— 5	**87,897**	42,918	44,979	42,918	44,979	...	...	.	..
5—10	**82,330**	41,672	40,658	41,570	40,498	70	·110	32	50
10—15	**72,859**	38,460	34,399	38,181	30,901	235	3,371	44	127
15—20	**59,479**	29,155	30,324	25,461	11,180	3,477	18,274	217	870
20—40	**208,470**	104,279	104,191	19,940	6,193	78,854	86,005	5,485	11,993
40—60	**101,979**	52,875	49,104	776	1,408	45,324	25,002	6,775	22,694
60 and over	**27,989**	12,638	15,301	145	210	8,240	2,341	4,283	12,750
MUSALMAN	*67,061*	*34,935*	*32,126*	*19,798*	*15,333*	*13,904*	*13,488*	*1,233*	*3,305*
0— 5	**10,191**	5,021	5,170	5,021	5,170	...	..	..	..
5—10	**9,709**	4,934	4,775	4,928	4,759	5	13	1	3
10—15	**8,610**	4,574	4,036	4,556	3,830	14	200	4	6
15—20	**6,106**	3,223	2,883	2,915	1,175	290	1,641	18	67
20—40	**20,783**	10,669	10,114	2,322	347	7,946	8,908	401	774
40—60	**9,192**	5,193	3,994	35	42	4,701	2,432	462	1,520
60 and over	**2,470**	1,316	1,154	21	10	948	200	347	935
CHRISTIAN	*428,706*	*217,874*	*210,832*	*108,757*	*90,822*	*100,604*	*98,539*	*8,513*	*21,471*
0— 5	**60,618**	29,609	31,009	29,609	31,009	.	.		..
5—10	**61,394**	30,859	30,535	30,788	30,396	62	116	9	23
10—15	**56,101**	29,101	27,000	28,425	23,173	636	3,766	40	61
15—20	**41 103**	20,636	20,467	13,316	4,233	7,242	16,087	78	147
20—40	**131,110**	67,059	64,051	6,041	1,572	59,263	58,504	1,755	8,975
40—60	**61,161**	32,169	28,992	463	339	27,847	18 060	3,859	10.593
60 and over	**17,219**	8,441	8,778	115	100	5,554	2,006	2,772	6,672
ANIMISTIC	*2,298*	*1,187*	*1,111*	*585*	*467*	*530*	*522*	*72*	*122*
0— 5	**266**	128	138	128	138	...	..	.	
5—10	**321**	178	143	178	143	.	...		.
10—15	**300**	151	149	150	132	1	16	.	1
15—20	**204**	95	109	75	37	19	67	1	5
20—40	**768**	395	373	50	17	314	335	31	21
40—60	**355**	197	158	4	..	166	99	27	59
60 and over	**84**	43	41	...	..	30	5	13	36

TABLE VII.

Age, Sex and Civil Condition.—DEVIKULAM DIVISION.

AGE.	POPULATION.			UNMARRIED.		MARRIED.		WIDOWED.	
	Persons.	Males.	Females.	Males.	Females.	Males.	Females.	Males.	Females
1	2	3	4	5	6	7	8	9	10
ALL RELIGIONS.	*68,562*	*37,992*	*30,570*	*19,749*	*14,549*	*16,874*	*13,644*	*1,369*	*2,377*
0— 5 ..	**7,582**	3,697	3,885	3,697	3,885	.	...	..	
5—10 .	**7,330**	3,582	3,748	3 557	3,704	20	40	5	4
10—15 .	**9,625**	4,727	4,898	4.633	4,518	90	376	4	4
15—20 ..	**8,119**	4,396	3,723	3,712	1,553	651	2,119	33	51
20—40 ..	**26,071**	15,591	10,480	4,015	813	11,108	8,999	468	668
40—60 .	**8,209**	5,067	3,142	122	65	4,402	1,942	543	1,135
60 and over .	**1,626**	932	694	13	11	603	1 68	316	515
HINDU ..	*43,700*	*23,898*	*19,802*	*12,783*	*9,670*	*10,333*	*8,525*	*782*	*1,607*
0— 5 ..	**4,430**	2,185	2,245	2,185	2,245	...	...	..	...
5—10 ..	**4,333**	2.107	2,226	2,088	2,198	16	27	3	1
10—15 ..	**6,681**	3,183	3,498	3,124	3,268	55	227	4	3
15—20 ..	**5,483**	2,925	2,558	2,603	1,227	307	1,290	15	41
20—40 .	**16,746**	9,870	6,876	2,685	678	6,900	5,695	285	508
40—60 .	**5,100**	3,127	1,973	87	47	2,732	1,177	308	749
60 and over .	**927**	501	426	11	7	323	109	167	310
MUSALMAN ..	*3,758*	*2,192*	*1,566*	*1,003*	*628*	*1,110*	*781*	*79*	*157*
0— 5 .	**449**	214	235	214	235	...	.	..	..
5—10 ..	**419**	220	199	220	199	...	..	..	..
10—15 ..	**390**	228	162	223	141	5	20	..	1
15—20 ..	**434**	245	189	182	38	58	147	5	4
20—40 .	**1,406**	866	540	164	15	666	491	36	34
40—60 .	**524**	334	190	.	..	313	110	21	80
60 and over .	**136**	85	51	..	.	68	13	17	38
CHRISTIAN	*18,633*	*10,629*	*8,004*	*5,336*	*3,719*	*4,824*	*3,765*	*469*	*520*
0— 5 ..	**2,384**	1,132	1,252	1,132	1,252	..	.	..	..
5—10 .	**2,216**	1,069	1,147	1,064	1,132	3	13	2	2
10—15 .	**2,254**	1,169	1,085	1,145	972	24	113	..	.
15—20 .	**1,978**	1,120	858	848	241	266	611	11	6
20—40 ..	**7,090**	4.428	2,662	1,115	104	3,175	2.444	138	114
40—60 .	**2,248**	1,421	827	35	14	1,188	545	198	268
60 and over .	**463**	290	173	2	4	168	39	120	130
ANIMISTIC .	*2,456*	*1,259*	*1,197*	*619*	*532*	*601*	*572*	*39*	*93*
0— 5 .	**317**	164	153	164	153	..	.	..	.
5—10 .	**362**	186	176	185	175	1	.	.	1
10—15	**298**	145	153	139	137	6	16		.
15—20 .	**224**	106	118	84	47	20	71	2	.
20—40 .	**820**	419	401	47	16	363	368	9	17
40—60 ...	**335**	183	152	...	4	167	110	16	38
60 and over .	**100**	56	44	...	..	44	7	12	37

TABLE VII.

Age, Sex and Civil Condition.—WESTERN NATURAL DIVISION.

Age.	Population.			Unmarried.		Married.		Widowed.	
	Persons.	Males.	Females.	Males.	Females.	Males.	Females.	Males.	Females.
1	2	3	4	5	6	7	8	9	10
All Religions.	***1,976,154***	***994,326***	***981,828***	***553,809***	***439,203***	***398,856***	***395,970***	***41.661***	***146,655***
0—5 ..	**237,942**	131,956	135,986	131,956	135,986	.			.
5—10 ..	**233,443**	132,354	131,089	132,027	130,359	244	580	83	150
10—15 .	**237,377**	123,024	114,353	122,056	106,142	823	7,829	145	334
15—20 .	**188,763**	91,410	97,353	82,718	42,916	8,228	52,157	464	2,290
20—40 .	**629,375**	313,946	315,429	81,303	20,621	220,274	256,247	12,367	33,561
40—60	**302,461**	159,962	142,499	3,206	2,494	139,912	73,039	16,841	66,926
60 and over	**86,793**	41,674	45,119	543	695	29,875	6,038	11,756	33,356
Hindu ..	***1,417,412***	***709,447***	***707,965***	***397,685***	***311,050***	***280,183***	***280,215***	***31,579***	***116,700***
0—5 ..	**188,107**	93,060	95,047	93,060	95,047	.	.		..
5—10 .	**183,694**	92,620	91,074	92,380	90,548	174	412	63	119
10—15 .	**166,315**	86,370	79,945	85,847	74,647	414	4,938	109	310
15—20	**134,560**	64,663	69,892	60,054	32,456	4,264	35,520	350	1,916
20—40 .	**455,768**	225,978	229,790	63,288	15,965	152,884	182,406	9,806	31,419
40—60	**223,467**	116,815	107,152	2,065	1,884	101,053	52,689	12,597	53,579
60 and over .	**65,501**	30,483	35,035	301	508	21,304	4,200	8,651	30,357
Musalman .	***135,210***	***68,978***	***66,232***	***39,224***	***30,169***	***27,565***	***27,829***	***2.189***	***8,234***
0—5 .	**18,958**	9,353	9,605	9,353	9,605	..	.		.
5—10 .	**19,033**	9,540	9,548	9,527	9,501	8	88	5	9
10—15 .	**17,143**	8,892	8,251	8,857	7,637	29	561	6	23
15—20 .	**12,894**	6,297	6,597	5,891	2,410	377	3,908	29	189
20—40 ..	**42,589**	21,180	21,409	5,178	805	14,962	18,320	790	2,284
40—60 ..	**19,301**	10,925	8,876	125	142	10 003	4,553	794	3,631
60 and over .	**5,237**	2,791	2,446	43	39	2,183	359	565	2,018
Christian .	***419,818***	***213,955***	***205,863***	***116.025***	***97,263***	***90,150***	***87.031***	***7,789***	***21,569***
0—5 .	**60,502**	29,360	31,142	29,360	31,142	.			
5—10	**60,222**	29,966	30,256	29,893	30,105	61	139	12	22
10—15	**53,519**	27,555	25,963	27,146	23,630	379	2,275	30	49
15—20 ..	**40,957**	20,391	20,616	16,635	7,968	3,571	12,527	85	171
20—40 .	**129,637**	66,123	63,514	12,471	3,800	51 927	54,895	1,725	4,810
40—60	**59,051**	32,282	26,769	411	453	23,464	15,710	3,407	10,603
60 and over .	**15,931**	8,378	7,553	[illegible]	147	5,748	1,405	2,521	5,911
Animistic .	***3,531***	***1,886***	***1,745***	***852***	***716***	***925***	***881***	***109***	***148***
0—5	**357**	176	191	176	191	.			
5—10 .	**434**	225	209	224	208	1	1		
10—15	**400**	207	193	206	188	1	5		
15—20 .	**347**	152	195	136	81	16	110		4
20—40 ..	**1,344**	638	706	105	43	486	616	47	48
40—60 .	**623**	424	199	5	5	374	135	45	59
60 and over .	**116**	64	52	.	1	47	14	17	37

TABLE VII.

Age, Sex and Civil Condition.—EASTERN NATURAL DIVISION.

AGE.	POPULATION.			UNMARRIED.		MARRIED.		WIDOWED.	
	Persons.	Males.	Females.	Males.	Females.	Males.	Females.	Males.	Females.
1	2	3	4	5	6	7	8	9	10
ALL RELIGIONS.	*1,452,821*	*737,037*	*715,784*	*385,762*	*316,046*	*319,207*	*307,457*	*32,068*	*92,281*
0— 5	**197,869**	95,915	101,954	95,915	101,954	.	...	..	..
5—10	**195,940**	98,171	97,769	97,892	97,241	218	402	61	126
10—15	**179,931**	93,471	86,520	92,210	77,228	1,150	9,036	111	256
15—20	**138,152**	68,525	69,627	55,255	25,064	12,827	48,282	448	1,331
20—40	**459,019**	234,787	224,232	42,634	12,170	182,924	190,777	9,229	21,285
40—60	**219,171**	116,164	103,007	1,593	1,919	101,626	58,120	12,945	42,968
60 and over	**62,679**	30,004	32,675	263	470	20,462	5,890	9,279	26,315
HINDU	*865,205*	*436,064*	*429,141*	*233,207*	*190,827*	*181,956*	*175,316*	*20,901*	*62,998*
0— 5	**114,686**	55,407	59,279	55,407	59,279	...	..	..	..
5—10	**111,166**	55,568	55,598	55,401	55,290	129	220	38	88
10—15	**103,717**	53,753	49,964	53,344	45,765	353	4,019	56	180
15—20	**82,060**	40,025	42,035	35,767	18,670	3,958	22,356	800	1,009
20—40	**277,721**	140,995	136,726	32,014	9,948	102,350	111,266	6,601	15,517
40—60	**136,462**	71,951	64,511	1,093	1,525	62,661	34,163	8,197	28,820
60 and over	**39,393**	18,365	21,028	151	355	12,505	3,289	5,709	17,334
MUSALMAN	*91,407*	*47,510*	*43,897*	*26,873*	*20,378*	*19,027*	*18,359*	*1,610*	*5,160*
0— 5	**13,604**	6,642	6,962	6,642	6,962	...	...	..	...
5—10	**13,291**	6,740	6,551	6,731	6,529	5	17	4	5
10—15	**11,539**	6,137	5,402	6,103	5,038	25	351	4	13
15—20	**8,359**	4,414	3,945	3,981	1,327	398	2,511	35	107
20—40	**28,293**	14,652	13,644	3,365	452	10,747	11,918	540	1,274
40—60	**12,736**	7,037	5,719	38	54	6,455	3,260	574	2,405
60 and over	**3,532**	1,858	1,674	8	16	1,397	302	453	1,356
CHRISTIAN	*484,050*	*247,210*	*236,840*	*122,468*	*102,235*	*115,458*	*111,038*	*9,284*	*23,567*
0— 5	**68,038**	33,103	34,935	33,103	34,935	...		..	.
5—10	**69,747**	34,936	34,811	34,835	34,619	88	160	18	32
10—15	**63,339**	32,861	30,478	32,046	25,801	765	4,613	50	61
15—20	**46,609**	23,552	23,057	15,038	4,793	8,412	18,064	102	200
20—40	**148,951**	77,151	71,800	6,889	1,656	68,257	65,795	2,005	4,349
40—60	**68,073**	36,084	31,989	454	329	31,567	20,149	4,063	11,511
60 and over	**19,293**	9,523	9,770	103	99	6,374	2,257	3,046	7,414
ANIMISTIC	*12,142*	*6,237*	*5,905*	*3,204*	*2,606*	*2,760*	*2,743*	*273*	*556*
0— 5	**1,539**	761	778	761	778	..	..	...	..
5—10	**1,736**	927	809	925	808	1	5	1	1
10—15	**1,394**	718	676	710	621	7	58	1	2
15—20	**1,123**	533	590	468	274	59	301	6	15
20—40	**4,041**	1,980	2,061	331	119	1,566	1,797	83	145
40—60	**1,848**	1,060	788	8	11	941	545	111	232
60 and over	**461**	258	203	1	...	186	42	71	161

TABLE VII.

Age, Sex and Civil Condition.

Part II.—Towns.

NOTE.—In regard to Buddhists, Jains and Jews, only age-periods for which there are returns have been printed.

TABLE VII.

Age, Sex and Civil Condition.—TOWNS.

TOWNS.	AGE.	POPULATION.			UNMARRIED.		MARRIED.		WIDOWED.	
		Persons.	Males.	Females.	Males.	Females	Males.	Females	Males.	Females.
1	2	3	4	5	6	7	8	9	10	11
NAGERCOIL.	ALL RELIGIONS...	*29,883*	*14,553*	*15,330*	*7,743*	*6,059*	*6,236*	*6,424*	*574*	*2,847*
	0— 5 ...	**3,480**	1,676	1,804	1,676	1,804	...	...	.	.
	5—10 ..	**3,811**	1,931	1,880	1,929	1,861	1	16	1	3
	10—15 ..	**3,599**	1,777	1,822	1,764	1,642	8	172	5	8
	15—20 ..	**3,002**	1,463	1,539	1,343	621	108	894	12	24
	20—40 ..	**9,236**	4,442	4,796	986	103	3,327	4,040	129	658
	40—60 .	**5,229**	2,565	2,664	39	23	2,290	1,191	286	1,450
	60 and over ..	**1,524**	699	825	6	5	502	111	191	709
	HINDU ..	*22,479*	*10,996*	*11,483*	*5,725*	*4,216*	*4,808*	*4,940*	*463*	*2,327*
	0— 5 ..	**2,546**	1,283	1,315	1,283	1,315	...	...	..	.
	5—10 ..	**2,847**	1,471	1,376	1,470	1,363	..	11	1	2
	10—15 ...	**2,624**	1,333	1,291	1,323	1,128	5	156	5	7
	15—20 ...	**2,150**	1,060	1,090	949	350	99	720	12	20
	20—40 ..	**7,074**	3,401	3,673	717	43	2,578	3,086	106	544
	40—60 ..	**4,044**	1,976	2,068	28	14	1,753	903	195	1,151
	60 and over ..	**1,192**	522	670	5	3	373	64	144	608
	MUSALMAN ..	*2,925*	*1,391*	*1,534*	*699*	*589*	*653*	*714*	*39*	*231*
	0— 5 ...	**337**	147	190	147	190	...	...	.	.
	5—10 ...	**389**	181	208	181	205	...	3	..	
	10—15 ...	**336**	180	156	173	146	2	10	..	..
	15—20 ...	**267**	109	158	108	42	1	115	...	1
	20—40 ...	**884**	400	484	78	5	315	432	7	47
	40—60 ...	**545**	279	266	6	1	261	141	12	124
	60 and over .	**167**	95	72	1	..	74	13	20	59
	CHRISTIAN ...	*4,479*	*2,166*	*2,313*	*1,319*	*1,254*	*775*	*770*	*72*	*289*
	0— 5 ..	**595**	296	299	296	299	..	..	..	
	5—10 ...	**575**	279	296	278	293	1	2	..	1
	10—15 ..	**639**	264	375	263	368	1	6	..	1
	15—20 ..	**585**	294	291	286	229	8	59	.	3
	20—40 ..	**1,280**	641	639	191	55	434	522	16	62
	40—60 ...	**640**	310	330	5	8	276	147	29	175
	60 and over ...	**165**	82	83	..	2	55	34	27	47
TRIVANDRUM.	ALL RELIGIONS..	*63,561*	*32,292*	*31,269*	*18,091*	*13,127*	*12,801*	*12,319*	*1,400*	*5,823*
	0— 5 ..	**7,514**	3,578	3,936	3,578	3,936	..	..	..	.
	5—10 ..	**7,308**	3,617	3,691	3,615	3,669	2	18	. .	4
	10—15 .	**7,539**	3,849	3,690	3,821	3,277	21	395	7	18
	15—20 ..	**6,621**	3,383	3,288	3,102	1,440	215	1,764	16	84
	20—40 ..	**21,716**	11,402	10,314	3,878	705	7,078	7,942	446	1,667
	40—60	**10.246**	5,434	4,812	93	83	4,717	2,043	624	2,086
	60 and over ...	**2,617**	1,079	1,538	4	17	768	157	307	1,364
	HINDU ..	*51,346*	*26,180*	*25,166*	*14,586*	*10,055*	*10,439*	*10,120*	*1,155*	*4,991*
	0— 5 ..	**6,040**	2,857	3.183	2,857	3,183	..	.	..	.
	5—10 ..	**5,756**	2,892	2,864	2,890	2,842	2	18		4
	10—15 .	**6,013**	3.112	2,901	3,084	2,513	21	371	7	17
	15—20 ..	**5,324**	2,736	2,588	2,525	1,018	199	1,497	12	73
	20—40 ..	**17,579**	9,250	8,329	3,144	444	5,739	6,450	367	1,435
	40—60 ..	**8,492**	4,462	4,030	82	46	3,858	1,662	522	2,322
	60 and over ..	**2,142**	871	1,271	4	9	620	122	247	1,140
	MUSALMAN ..	*4,648*	*2,475*	*2,173*	*1,349*	*887*	*1,026*	*922*	*100*	*364*
	0— 5 .	**524**	260	264	260	264	.	..	..	.
	5—10 ..	**557**	282	275	282	275	.	.	.	.
	10—15 .	**547**	279	268	279	250	..	18	..	.
	15—20 ..	**445**	243	202	236	60	6	184	1	8
	20—40 ..	**1,695**	912	783	289	32	586	637	37	114
	40—60 .	**698**	417	281	3	4	370	121	41	156
	60 and over .	**182**	82	100	..	2	64	12	18	86

TABLE VII.

Age, Sex and Civil Condition.—TOWNS.

TOWNS.	AGE.	POPULATION.			UNMARRIED.		MARRIED.		WIDOWED.	
		Persons.	Males.	Females.	Males.	Females.	Males.	Females	Males.	Females.
1	2	3	4	5	6	7	8	9	10	11
TRIVANDRUM.—(*Concluded*)	CHRISTIAN .	***7,552***	***3,626***	***3,926***	***2,150***	***2,184***	***1,333***	***1,275***	***143***	***467***
	0— 5 ..	**947**	458	489	458	489	..	.	..	
	5—10 .	**993**	442	551	442	551	..	..		.
	10—15	**979**	458	521	458	514	.	6		1
	15—20	**852**	354	498	341	362	10	133	3	3
	20—40 .	**2,437**	1,237	1,200	443	229	752	853	42	118
	40—60 ..	**1,053**	553	500	8	33	487	260	58	207
	60 and over .	**291**	124	167	..	6	84	23	40	138
	JEW ..	***15***	***11***	***4***	***6***	***1***	***3***	***2***	***2***	***1***
	0— 5 .	**3**	3	..	3	.	.	.	.	.
	5—10 ..	**2**	1	1	1	1	.	.	.	..
	20—40 ..	**5**	3	2	2	..	1	2	.	.
	40—60 .	**3**	2	1	.	..	2	.	..	1
	60 and over ..	**2**	2	..	..	..	.	.	2	..
SHENCOTTAH	ALL RELIGIONS ..	***10,309***	***4,905***	***5,404***	***2,698***	***2,086***	***2,045***	***2,204***	***162***	***1,114***
	0— 5 ..	**1,439**	738	701	738	701	..	..	..	..
	5—10 ..	**1,352**	672	680	672	673	.	7	..	
	10—15 ..	**1,225**	591	634	586	540	5	91	..	3
	15—20 ..	**929**	446	483	390	151	55	325	1	7
	20—40 .	**3,119**	1,477	1,642	300	20	1,142	1,378	35	244
	40—60 ..	**1,698**	775	923	9	.	693	377	73	546
	60 and over .	**547**	206	341	3	1	150	26	53	314
	HINDU .	***9,377***	***4,447***	***4,930***	***2,433***	***1,887***	***1,859***	***2,004***	***155***	***1,039***
	0— 5 .	**1,291**	662	629	662	629	..	.	.	..
	5—10 ..	**1,212**	606	606	606	599	.	7		..
	10—15 ..	**1,114**	526	588	521	501	5	84	..	3
	15—20 .	**849**	404	445	351	140	52	298	1	7
	20—40 .	**2,840**	1,346	1,494	281	17	1,031	1,245	34	232
	40—60 ..	**1,569**	716	853	9	.	638	347	69	506
	60 and over .	**502**	187	315	3	1	133	23	51	291
	MUSALMAN ..	***872***	***423***	***449***	***246***	***188***	***171***	***188***	***6***	***73***
	0— 5 .	**138**	71	67	71	67	.		..	..
	5—10 .	**132**	60	72	60	72	..	..	.	..
	10—15 ..	**106**	63	43	63	36	..	7	.	.
	15—20 .	**75**	39	36	36	10	3	26	.	..
	20—40	**255**	117	138	16	3	100	124	1	11
	40—60	**122**	54	68	..	..	51	28	3	40
	60 and over .	**44**	19	25	..	..	17	3	2	22
	CHRISTIAN ..	***60***	***35***	***25***	***19***	***11***	***15***	***12***	***1***	***2***
	0— 5 ..	**10**	5	5	5	5	..	.	.	..
	5—10 .	**8**	6	2	6	2	.	...	.	..
	10—15 .	**5**	2	3	2	3	..	.	...	.
	15—20 ..	**5**	3	2	3	1	.	1	..	..
	20—40 ..	**24**	14	10	3	...	11	9	..	1
	40—60 ..	**7**	5	2	...	..	4	2	1	.
	60 and over ..	**1**	..	1	..	..	..	..	..	1
QUILON.	ALL RELIGIONS	***18,839***	***9,649***	***9,190***	***5,017***	***4,360***	***4,270***	***3,616***	***362***	***1,214***
	0— 5 .	**2,164**	981	1,183	981	1,183	.	..	..	.
	5—10	**2,338**	1,106	1,232	1,100	1,227	6	4	.	1
	10—15 ..	**2,171**	1,070	1,101	1,062	1,016	8	81	..	4
	15—20 .	**1,938**	965	1,008	884	488	75	497	6	23
	20—40 ..	**6,846**	3,639	3,207	946	382	2,584	2,474	109	351
	40—60 .	**2,686**	1,546	1,140	40	63	1,345	508	161	569
	60 and over .	**666**	342	324	4	6	252	52	86	266

TABLE VII.

Age, Sex and Civil Condition—TOWNS.

TOWNS	AGE.	POPULATION.			UNMARRIED.		MARRIED.		WIDOWED.	
		Persons.	Males.	Females.	Males.	Females	Males.	Females.	Males.	Females.
1	2	3	4	5	6	7	8	9	10	11
QUILON—(Concluded)	HINDU.	***9,885***	***5,149***	***4,736***	***2,683***	***2,080***	***2,254***	***1,906***	***212***	***750***
	0—5	**1,078**	498	580	498	580	..	.	.	.
	5—10	**1,175**	574	601	572	598	2	2	.	1
	10—15	**1,036**	540	546	535	481	5	62	..	3
	15—20	**1,120**	576	544	525	240	47	286	4	18
	20—40	**3,603**	1,962	1,641	522	158	1,379	1,253	61	230
	40—60	**1,443**	818	630	28	18	686	277	101	335
	60 and over	**375**	181	104	3	5	135	26	43	163
	MUSALMAN	***3,358***	***1,736***	***1,622***	***838***	***708***	***856***	***728***	***42***	***186***
	0—5	**383**	175	211	175	211	..	..	.	..
	5—10	**410**	183	227	182	226	1	1	.	.
	10—15	**381**	194	187	193	178	1	9		..
	15—20	**316**	146	170	133	66	13	103	.	1
	20—40	**1,293**	696	597	155	21	526	528	15	48
	40—60	**462**	285	177	.	6	270	79	15	92
	60 and over	**110**	57	53		..	45	8	12	45
	CHRISTIAN.	***5,593***	***2,761***	***2,832***	***1,495***	***1,572***	***1,158***	***982***	***108***	***278***
	0—5	**700**	308	392	308	392	.	.	..	..
	5—10	**753**	319	401	316	403	3	1	..	..
	10—15	**704**	336	368	334	357	2	10	.	1
	15—20	**532**	243	289	226	177	15	108	2	4
	20—40	**1,947**	978	969	268	203	677	693	33	73
	40—60	**776**	443	333	12	39	389	152	42	142
	60 and over	**181**	104	77	1	1	72	18	31	58
	JEW.	***3***	***3***	..	***1***	...	***2***	.	..	..
	20—10	**3**	3	...	1	...	2	..	..	...
KAYANKULAM.	ALL RELIGIONS	***5,830***	***2,772***	***3,058***	***1,395***	***1,345***	***1,271***	***1,288***	***106***	***425***
	0—5	**700**	295	405	295	405	.	..	..	..
	5—10	**729**	332	397	332	393	.	4	.	..
	10—15	**701**	336	365	328	325	8	38	..	2
	15—20	**580**	258	322	225	147	33	175	..	..
	20—40	**1,958**	944	1,014	203	65	718	851	28	98
	40—60	**935**	505	430	10	8	452	203	43	219
	60 and over	**227**	102	125	2	2	65	17	35	106
	HINDU.	***3,451***	***1,609***	***1,842***	***788***	***795***	***759***	***775***	***62***	***272***
	0—5	**338**	164	224	164	224	.		.	..
	5—10	**435**	188	247	188	241	.	3	.	..
	10—15	**416**	198	218	193	197	5	19	...	2
	15—20	**323**	146	182	131	84	15	98		..
	20—40	**1,185**	553	632	107	41	433	526	13	65
	40—60	**558**	297	261	4	3	267	121	26	137
	60 and over	**141**	63	78	1	2	39	8	23	68
	MUSALMAN.	***1,206***	***608***	***598***	***340***	***263***	***245***	***254***	***23***	***81***
	0—5	**157**	63	94	63	94	..	..	..	..
	5—10	**138**	75	63	75	63	.	.		..
	10—15	**125**	75	58	74	53	1	5		...
	15—20	**121**	56	65	55	34	1	31		..
	20—40	**415**	203	212	70	17	125	173	8	22
	40—60	**199**	115	84	2	2	103	46	10	3[illegible]
	60 and over	**43**	21	12	1	...	15	2	5	20

TABLE VII.

Age, Sex and Civil Condition.—TOWNS.

TOWNS.	AGE.	POPULATION. Persons.	POPULATION. Males.	POPULATION. Females.	UNMARRIED. Males.	UNMARRIED. Females	MARRIED. Males.	MARRIED. Females.	WIDOWED. Males.	WIDOWED. Females.
1	2	3	4	5	6	7	8	9	10	11
KAYANKULAM.—(Concld.)	CHRISTIAN ..	*1,173*	*555*	*618*	*267*	*287*	*267*	*259*	*21*	*72*
	0—5 .	**155**	68	87	68	87	..	..	..	.
	5—10 .	**156**	69	87	69	86	..	1	...	.
	10—15 .	**152**	63	89	61	75	2	14	..	.
	15—20 ..	**131**	56	75	39	29	17	46	..	.
	20—40 .	**358**	188	170	26	7	155	152	7	11
	40—60 .	**178**	93	85	4	3	82	39	7	43
	60 and over ..	**43**	18	25	...	..	11	7	7	18
TIRUVALLA.	ALL RELIGIONS..	*7,969*	*4,268*	*3,701*	*2,196*	*1,332*	*1,897*	*1,837*	*175*	*532*
	0—5 ..	**1,001**	515	486	515	486	.	.	..	..
	5—10 ..	**833**	476	407	472	402	3	5	1	..
	10—15 ..	**910**	518	392	498	315	20	76	..	1
	15—20 ..	**911**	487	424	383	81	103	334	1	9
	20—40 .	**2,668**	1,429	1,239	306	41	1,069	1,060	54	138
	40—60 .	**1,204**	658	546	18	2	574	319	66	225
	60 and over .	**392**	185	207	4	5	128	43	53	159
	HINDU .	*5,266*	*2,797*	*2,469*	*1,503*	*860*	*1,168*	*1,192*	*·126*	*417*
	0—5 ..	**664**	330	334	330	334	.	..	...	...
	5—10 ..	**545**	305	240	303	238	1	2	1	...
	10—15 ..	**559**	329	230	323	184	6	45	..	1
	15—20 ..	**547**	282	265	252	63	29	194	1	8
	20—40 .	**1,854**	984	870	275	37	667	710	42	114
	40—60 ..	**827**	449	378	17	1	384	208	48	169
	60 and over ..	**270**	118	152	3	3	81	24	34	125
	MUSALMAN ..	*16*	*8*	*8*	*3*	*4*	*4*	*3*	*1*	*1*
	0—5 .	**2**	...	2	...	2	..	..	..	...
	5—10 ..	**2**	1	1	1	1	..	...	..	..
	10—15 ..	**3**	2	1	2	1	...	...	..	..
	15—20 ..	...	...	...	...	.	..	..	..	..
	20—40 ..	**4**	1	3	..	.	1	3	..	..
	40—60 ..	**4**	3	1	.	..	3	..	..	1
	60 and over .	**1**	1	...	.	..	..	..	1	..
	CHRISTIAN .	*2,687*	*1,463*	*1,224*	*690*	*468*	*725*	*642*	*48*	*114*
	0—5 .	**335**	185	150	185	150	.	..	..	..
	5—10 ..	**336**	170	166	168	163	2	3	..	..
	10—15	**348**	187	161	173	130	14	31	..	..
	15—20 ..	**364**	205	159	131	18	74	140	.	1
	20—40	**810**	444	366	31	4	401	339	12	24
	40—60	**373**	203	167	1	1	187	111	18	55
	60 and over ..	**121**	66	55	1	2	47	19	18	34
ALLEPPEY.	ALL RELIGIONS .	*25,665*	*13,370*	*12,295*	*6,876*	*4,649*	*5,957*	*5,611*	*537*	*2,035*
	0—5 ..	**3,174**	1,501	1,673	1,501	1,673	...		.	..
	5—10 ..	**2,732**	1,367	1,365	1,365	1,358	1	4	1	3
	10—15 .	**2,414**	1,258	1,156	1,248	1,059	7	91	3	6
	15—20	**2,562**	1,305	1,257	1,162	386	132	836	11	35
	20—40 .	**9,360**	4,923	4,437	1,518	148	3,234	3,728	171	561
	40—60 .	**4,469**	2,571	1,898	56	19	2,281	909	231	970
	60 and over .	**954**	445	509	26	6	302	43	117	460
	HINDU .	*12,632*	*6,676*	*·5,956*	*3,178*	*2,154*	*3,246*	*2,760*	*252*	*1,042*
	0—5 ..	**1,533**	710	823	710	823	.	...	..	...
	5—10 .	**1,323**	684	639	632	636	1	3	1	..
	10—15 .	**1,145**	615	530	606	468	6	61	3	1
	15—20 ..	**1,233**	649	634	562	161	84	454	3	19
	20—40	**4,655**	2,507	2,148	592	52	1,841	1,797	74	299
	40—60	**2,224**	1,297	927	24	10	1,152	435	121	492
	60 and over ..	**463**	214	255	2	4	162	20	50	231

TABLE VII.

Age, Sex and Civil Condition.—TOWNS.

TOWNS.	AGE.	POPULATION.			UNMARRIED.		MARRIED.		WIDOWED.	
		Persons.	Males.	Females.	Males.	Females	Males.	Females	Males.	Females.
1	2	3	4	5	6	7	8	9	10	11
ALLEPPY—(Concluded)	MUSALMAN ..	***6,669***	***3,299***	***3,370***	***1,807***	***1,229***	***1,356***	***1,554***	***136***	***587***
	0—5	**813**	398	415	398	415	..		.	..
	5—10 ..	**686**	312	374	312	372		1	.	1
	10—15 ..	**591**	303	288	303	272	.	15	.	1
	15—20 ...	**645**	305	340	287	121	14	206	4	13
	20—40 ..	**2,423**	1,166	1,257	481	49	633	1,056	52	152
	40—60	**1,229**	693	536	23		613	264	57	272
	60 and over .	**232**	123	160	3	..	96	12	23	148
	CHRISTIAN ..	***6,353***	***3,387***	***2,966***	***1,887***	***1,266***	***1,351***	***1,294***	***149***	***406***
	0—5 ..	**827**	392	435	392	435	...	.	.	
	5—10 .	**722**	370	352	370	350	.	..	..	2
	10—15 ..	**673**	340	333	339	319	1	15	.	4
	15—20 .	**633**	350	283	312	104	31	176	4	3
	20—40 .	**2,276**	1,247	1,029	414	47	758	872	45	110
	40—60 ..	**1,014**	579	435	9	9	514	220	56	206
	60 and over ..	**203**	109	94	21	2	41	11	44	81
	JAIN ..	***11***	***8***	***3***	***4***	..	***4***	***3***	.	..
	0—5 .	**1**	1	.	1	.	.	..		..
	5—10 .	**1**	1	.	1	.	.	..		..
	15—20 ..	**1**	1	.	1	..	.	.	..	..
	20—40 ..	**6**	3	3	1	.	2	3	.	
	40—60 .	**2**	2	.		.	2	..	.	.
KOTTAYAM	ALL RELIGIONS .	***15,141***	***7,863***	***7,278***	***4,253***	***3,162***	***3,308***	***3,224***	***302***	***892***
	0—5 ..	**2,040**	1,003	1,037	1,003	1,037	..	..		.
	5—10 ..	**2,060**	1,024	1,036	1,023	1,031	.	2	1	.
	10—15 ..	**1,897**	1,017	880	1,008	789	8	90	1	1
	15—20 .	**1,587**	856	731	750	244	102	478	1	9
	20—40 .	**4,731**	2,197	2,234	441	45	1,978	2,029	78	160
	40—60 ..	**2,296**	1,232	1,064	25	8	1,074	596	133	160
	60 and over ...	**530**	234	296	3	5	146	29	85	262
	HINDU. ...	***7,547***	***3,935***	***3,612***	***2,081***	***1,504***	***1,692***	***1,654***	***162***	***454***
	0—5 ..	**952**	469	483	469	483	.	.	..	..
	5—10 ..	**955**	476	479	476	477		2	..	.
	10—15 ..	**893**	489	404	484	358	5	45	.	1
	15—20 .	**784**	392	392	345	154	45	235	2	3
	20—40 .	**2,523**	1,339	1,184	201	23	1,003	1,074	45	87
	40—60	**1,189**	661	528	15	6	569	287	77	235
	60 and over .	**261**	109	142	1	3	70	11	38	128
	MUSALMAN ..	***577***	***323***	***254***	***160***	***113***	***153***	***121***	***10***	***20***
	0—5 .	**81**	43	38	43	38	..	..	..	.
	5—10 ..	**82**	41	41	41	41	..	...	..	..
	10—15	**66**	37	29	37	27	..	2	..	.
	15—20 ..	**56**	30	26	27	6	3	20	.	..
	20—40 .	**182**	109	73	12	1	94	71	3	1
	40—60 ..	**92**	50	42	..	..	46	26	4	14
	60 and over .	**18**	13	5	..	..	10	.	3	5
	CHRISTIAN .	***7,017***	***3,605***	***3,412***	***2,012***	***1,545***	***1,463***	***1,449***	***130***	***418***
	0—5 .	**1,007**	491	516	491	516	..	..	.	..
	5—10	**1,023**	507	516	506	516	.		1	.
	10—15 .	**938**	491	447	487	404	3	43	1	...
	15—20 .	**747**	434	313	378	[illegible]	54	223	2	6
	20—40 ..	**2,026**	1,049	977	138	21	881	684	30	72
	40—60 .	**1,015**	521	494	10	2	459	281	52	211
	60 and over	**261**	112	149	2	2	66	18	41	129

TABLE VII.

Age, Sex and Civil Condition—TOWNS.

Towns.	Age.	Population.			Unmarried.		Married.		Widowed.	
		Persons.	Males.	Females.	Males.	Females.	Males	Females.	Males.	Females.
1	2	3	4	5	6	7	8	9	10	11
Changanachery.										
	All Religions..	***17,242***	***8,826***	***8,416***	***4,711***	***3,601***	***3,303***	***3,797***	***312***	***1,018***
	0—5 .	**2,343**	1,154	1,189	1,154	1,189	..	.	.	
	5—10	**2,347**	1,175	1,172	1,173	1,161	2	8	.	
	10—15 ..	**2,064**	1,083	981	1,065	904	11	74	7	3
	15—20 .	**1,646**	885	761	785	231	98	524	2	6
	20—40 .	**5,417**	2,798	2,619	497	80	2,237	2,363	64	176
	40—60 ...	**2,616**	1,340	1,276	30	24	1,178	762	132	490
	60 and over .	**809**	391	418	7	9	277	66	107	343
	Hindu ..	***9,036***	***4,509***	***4,527***	***2,391***	***1,869***	***1,946***	***2,061***	***172***	***597***
	0—5 .	**1,254**	607	647	607	647		.	.	
	5—10	**1,193**	579	614	578	610	1	4		
	10—15 .	**1,015**	540	475	532	435	6	39	2	1
	15—20 ..	**848**	424	424	386	140	38	279	.	5
	20—40 ..	**2,883**	1,460	1,423	276	26	1,142	1,285	42	112
	40—60 ..	**1,431**	722	709	11	9	636	419	75	281
	60 and over ..	**412**	177	235	1	2	123	35	53	198
	Musalman ..	***1,855***	***1,002***	***853***	***580***	***373***	***399***	***399***	***23***	***81***
	0—5 ..	**238**	131	107	131	107	.			
	5—10 .	**263**	139	124	139	124	.		.	
	10—15 ..	**255**	136	119	136	114	..	5	.	
	15—20 ...	**159**	100	59	96	21	3	38	1	
	20—40 ..	**550**	278	272	75	4	198	255	5	13
	40—60 ...	**295**	161	134	2	1	151	93	8	40
	60 and over ..	**95**	57	38	1	2	47	8	9	28
	Christian ..	***6,351***	***3,315***	***3,036***	***1,740***	***1,359***	***1,458***	***1,337***	***117***	***340***
	0—5 .	**851**	416	435	416	435	.	.	.	
	5—10 .	**891**	457	431	456	430	1	4	.	
	10—15 .	**794**	407	387	397	355	5	30	5	2
	15—20 ..	**639**	361	278	303	70	57	207	1	1
	20—40 ..	**1,984**	1,060	924	146	50	897	823	17	51
	40—60 ..	**890**	457	433	17	14	391	250	49	169
	60 and over .	**302**	157	145	5	5	107	23	45	117
Alwaye.										
	All Religions...	***3,869***	***2,103***	***1,766***	***1,254***	***847***	***763***	***707***	***86***	***212***
	0—5 .	**619**	314	305	314	305	.		.	
	5—10 ..	**477**	248	229	248	229	.			
	10—15 .	**525**	307	218	306	207	1	11		
	15—20 ..	**364**	218	146	199	79	17	66	2	1
	20—40 ..	**1,172**	613	559	168	23	429	404	23	42
	40—60 ..	**584**	382	232	18	3	273	121	41	103
	60 and over ...	**148**	71	77	1	1	50	15	20	61
	Hindu ..	***1,293***	***692***	***601***	***390***	***272***	***263***	***234***	***39***	***95***
	0—5 .	**197**	98	99	98	99	...			
	5—10 .	**161**	89	72	89	72	...	.		
	10—15 ..	**158**	84	74	83	64	1	10		
	15—20 ..	**122**	69	53	61	31	7	21	1	1
	20—40 ..	**403**	209	194	56	6	142	164	11	24
	40—60 ...	**197**	118	79	3	.	98	35	17	44
	60 and over .	**55**	25	30	..		15	4	10	26
	Musalman ..	***794***	***424***	***370***	***243***	***168***	***168***	***163***	***13***	***39***
	0—5 ...	**135**	69	66	69	66	..	.	.	
	5—10 ..	**101**	56	45	56	45	..	.	.	
	10—15 ..	**96**	58	38	58	37	..	1	..	
	15—20 ..	**72**	33	39	28	15	5	24	.	
	20—40 ..	**242**	122	120	29	5	90	108	3	7
	40—60 ..	**114**	69	45	2	..	59	26	8	19
	60 and over ..	**34**	17	17	1	...	14	4	2	13

TABLE VII.

Age, Sex and Civil Condition.—TOWNS.

TOWNS.	AGE.	Population.			Unmarried.		Married.		Widowed.	
		Persons.	Males.	Females.	Males.	Females.	Males.	Females.	Males.	Females.
1	2	3	4	5	6	7	8	9	10	11
Alwaye.—(Concluded.)	Christian ..	*1,780*	*985*	*795*	*619*	*407*	*332*	*310*	*34*	*78*
	0— 5 ..	**287**	147	140	147	140	...	...	...	..
	5—10 ..	**215**	103	112	103	112	...	...	..	..
	10—15 ...	**271**	165	106	165	106	...	..	..	..
	15—20 ..	**169**	115	54	109	33	5	21	1	..
	20—40 ..	**523**	281	245	82	12	190	222	9	11
	40—60 .	**253**	145	108	13	3	116	60	16	45
	60 and over ..	**59**	29	30	..	1	21	7	8	22
	Jew. ..	*2*	*2*	..	*2*	..	..	...	...	...
	15—20 ..	**1**	1	..	1	...	..	...	...	..
	20—40 ...	**1**	1	...	1	..	...	...	...	..
Parur.	All Religions..	*13,782*	*7,067*	*6,715*	*4,130*	*2,906*	*2,648*	*2,737*	*289*	*1,072*
	0— 5 ...	**2,037**	986	1,051	986	1,051	...	...	...	..
	5—10 ...	**1,768**	927	841	927	888	...	2	...	1
	10—15 ..	**1,659**	888	771	885	674	3	96	...	1
	15—20 ..	**1,404**	761	643	721	229	40	398	..	16
	20—40 ..	**4,351**	2,194	2,157	595	95	1,517	1,769	82	293
	40—60 ...	**2,038**	1,050	988	12	16	902	450	136	522
	60 and over ...	**525**	261	264	4	3	186	22	71	239
	Hindu ...	*10,745*	*5,476*	*5,269*	*3,253*	*2,221*	*2,011*	*2,156*	*212*	*892*
	0— 5 ...	**1,572**	755	817	755	817	...	...	...	..
	5—10 ...	**1,368**	726	642	726	641	...	1	..	...
	10—15 ..	**1,271**	686	585	684	499	2	86	..	...
	15—20 ..	**1,124**	607	517	572	181	35	322	..	14
	20—40 ..	**3,397**	1,702	1,695	508	67	1,143	1,380	56	248
	40—60 ..	**1,599**	809	790	11	14	697	350	101	426
	60 and over ...	**414**	191	223	2	2	134	17	55	204
	Musalman ..	*998*	*497*	*501*	*279*	*263*	*199*	*183*	*19*	*55*
	0— 5 ...	**160**	71	89	71	89	..	..	...	..
	5—10 ..	**144**	67	77	67	77	..	..	.	...
	10—15 ..	**127**	54	73	53	70	1	3	...	..
	15—20 ..	**108**	59	49	58	20	1	27	...	2
	20—40 ...	**292**	147	145	30	5	113	126	4	14
	40—60 ...	**141**	84	57	...	1	72	25	12	31
	60 and over ..	**26**	15	11	..	1	12	2	3	8
	Christian ...	*1,996*	*1,065*	*931*	*591*	*419*	*418*	*390*	*56*	*122*
	0— 5 ...	**301**	157	144	157	144	...	...	...	...
	5—10 ...	**254**	133	121	133	119	..	1	...	1
	10—15 :	**260**	148	112	148	104	...	7	...	1
	15—20 ...	**169**	94	75	90	28	4	47	..	...
	20—40 ...	**647**	334	313	60	23	253	259	21	31
	40—60 ...	**286**	147	139	1	1	124	73	22	65
	60 and over ...	**79**	52	27	2	..	37	3	13	24
	Jew ...	*43*	*29*	*14*	*7*	*3*	*20*	*8*	*2*	*3*
	0— 5 ...	**4**	3	1	3	1	...	...	...	...
	5—10 ...	**2**	1	1	1	1	...	...	...	...
	10—15 ..	**1**	...	1	...	1	...	..	...	...
	15—20 ...	**3**	1	2	1	...	...	2	...	..
	20—40 ...	**15**	11	4	2	...	8	4	1	...
	40—60 ...	**12**	10	2	...	...	9	2	1	...
	60 and over ..	**6**	3	3	..	...	3	..	...	3

TABLE VIII.

Education.—Part I. State and Divisions.

NOTE.—[As literate Animists are few in number, they are not shown separately for the Divisions.]

English Education among Christians by Race.

AGE.	LITERATE IN ENGLISH.								
	EUROPEAN.			ANGLO-INDIAN.			NATIVE CHRISTIAN.		
	Persons.	Males.	Females.	Persons.	Males.	Females.	Persons.	Males.	Females.
0—10 ...	**7**	3	4	**33**	19	14	**308**	222	86
10—15 ..	**10**	5	5	**94**	47	47	**1,269**	862	407
15—20 ...	**31**	15	16	**179**	91	88	**2,330**	1,808	522
20 and over...	**311**	211	100	**682**	396	286	**6,222**	5,191	1,031

Education among Native Christians by Sect.

AGE.	NUMBER LITERATE.								
	PROTESTANT.			ROMAN CATHOLIC.			SYRIAN.		
	Persons.	Males.	Females.	Persons.	Males,	Females.	Persons.	Males.	Females.
0—10	**906**	560	346	**895**	644	251	**3,744**	2,442	1,302
10—15	**3,131**	1,858	1,273	**2,499**	1,794	705	**12,558**	8,584	3,984
15—20	**3,882**	2,648	1,23[illegible]	**3,831**	2,742	1,089	**15,660**	11,226	4,434
20 and over	**17,757**	13,980	3,777	**20,025**	16,929	3,096	**80,331**	67,778	12,553

TABLE VIII.

Education.— STATE.

AGE.	POPULATION.									LITERATE IN									LITERATE IN ENGLISH.		
	TOTAL.			LITERATE.			ILLITERATE.			MALAYALAM.			TAMIL.			OTHER LANGUAGES.					
	Persons.	Males.	Females.	Persons.	Males.	Females.	Persons.	Males.	Females.	Persons.	Males.	Females.	Persons.	Males.	Females.	Persons.	Males.	Females.	Persons.	Males.	Females.
1	2	3	4	5	6	7	8	9	10	11	12	13	14	15	16	17	18	19	20	21	22
ALL RELIGIONS.	*3,428,975*	*1,731,363*	*1,697,612*	*513,049*	*428,949*	*84,100*	*2,915,926*	*1,302,414*	*1,613,512*	*453,119*	*378,283*	*74,836*	*108,523*	*95,233*	*13,290*	*8,131*	*7,354*	*777*	*26,250*	*22,924*	*3,326*
0—10 ..	**925,194**	458,396	466,798	**15,415**	10,437	4,978	**909,779**	447,959	461,820	**13,919**	9,488	4,431	**2,524**	1,724	800	**78**	49	29	**612**	457	155
10—15 ...	**417,366**	216,495	200,873	**50,904**	36,565	14,339	**366,464**	179,930	186,534	**46,550**	33,616	12,934	**7,522**	5,487	2,035	**419**	316	103	**2,625**	2,004	621
15—20 ...	**326,915**	159,935	166,980	**67,076**	50,805	16,271	**259,839**	109,130	150,709	**60,954**	46,393	14,561	**10,734**	8,321	2,413	**755**	610	145	**4,828**	4,022	806
20 and over..	**1,759,498**	896,537	862,961	**379,654**	331,142	48,512	**1,379,844**	565,395	814,449	**331,696**	288,786	42,910	**87,743**	79,701	8,042	**6,879**	6,379	500	**18,185**	16,441	1,744
HINDU ...	*2,282,617*	*1,145,511*	*1,137,106*	*324,843*	*276,904*	*47,939*	*1,957,774*	*868,607*	*1,089,167*	*286,992*	*244,059*	*42,933*	*77,404*	*69,256*	*8,148*	*4,198*	*3,931*	*267*	*14,472*	*13,763*	*709*
0—10 ..	**597,653**	296,655	300,998	**9,402**	6,467	2,935	**588,251**	290,188	298,063	**8,810**	5,980	2,630	**1,661**	1,139	522	**27**	20	7	**256**	205	51
10—15 ..	**270,032**	140,123	129,909	**31,169**	23,076	8,093	**238,863**	117,047	121,816	**28,846**	21,485	7,361	**5,008**	3,753	1,255	**122**	96	26	**1,223**	1,061	162
15—20 ..	**216,620**	104,693	111,927	**41,150**	31,977	9,173	**175,470**	72,716	102,754	**37,865**	29,645	8,220	**6,958**	5,453	1,505	**318**	262	56	**2,217**	2,041	176
20 and over .	**1,198,312**	604,040	594,272	**243,122**	215,384	27,738	**955,190**	388,656	566,534	**211,671**	186,949	24,722	**63,777**	58,911	4,866	**3,731**	3,553	178	**10,776**	10,456	320
MUSALMAN ..	*226,617*	*116,488*	*110,129*	*21,342*	*19,911*	*1,431*	*205,275*	*96,577*	*108,698*	*15,744*	*14,852*	*892*	*8,312*	*7,875*	*437*	*3,079*	*2,683*	*396*	*299*	*288*	*11*
0—10 ...	**64,941**	32,275	32,666	**385**	287	98	**64,556**	31,988	32,568	**249**	194	55	**157**	111	46	**51**	29	22	**8**	8	...
10—15 ...	**28,682**	15,029	13,653	**1,402**	1,187	215	**27,280**	13,842	13,438	**1,039**	889	150	**423**	371	52	**261**	196	65	**29**	29	...
15—20 ..	**21,253**	10,711	10,542	**2,312**	2,097	215	**18,941**	8,614	10,327	**1,703**	1,560	143	**745**	687	58	**336**	273	63	**71**	67	4
20 and over .	**111,741**	58,473	53,268	**17,243**	16,340	903	**94,498**	42,133	52,365	**12,753**	12,209	544	**6,987**	6,706	281	**2,431**	2,185	246	**191**	184	7
CHRISTIAN ...	*903,868*	*461,165*	*442,703*	*166,762*	*132,045*	*34,717*	*737,106*	*329,120*	*407,986*	*150,300*	*119,299*	*31,001*	*22,800*	*18,095*	*4,705*	*833*	*722*	*111*	*11,476*	*8,870*	*2,606*
0—10 ..	**258,509**	127,365	131,144	**5,626**	3,683	1,943	**252,883**	123,682	129,201	**5,058**	3,314	1,744	**706**	474	232	.	.	.	**348**	244	104
10—15 ..	**116,857**	60,416	56,441	**18,326**	12,296	6,030	**98,531**	48,120	50,411	**16,658**	11,236	5,422	**2,091**	1,363	728	**36**	24	12	**1,373**	914	459
15—20 .	**87,566**	43,843	43,723	**23,609**	16,727	6,882	**63,957**	27,116	36,841	**21,381**	15,184	6,197	**3,031**	2,181	850	**101**	75	26	**2,540**	1,914	626
20 and over .	**440,936**	229,541	211,395	**119,201**	99,339	19,862	**321,735**	130,202	191,533	**107,203**	89,565	17,638	**16,972**	14,077	2,895	**696**	623	73	**7,215**	5,798	1,417

TABLE VIII.

Education.—STATE. (Concluded.)

AGE.	POPULATION.									LITERATE IN									Literate in English.		
	Total.			Literate.			Illiterate.			Malayalam.			Tamil.			Other Languages.					
	Persons.	Males.	Females.	Persons.	Males.	Females.	Persons.	Males.	Females.	Persons.	Males.	Females.	Persons.	Males.	Females.	Persons.	Males.	Females.	Persons.	Males.	Females.
1	2	3	4	5	6	7	8	9	10	11	12	13	14	15	16	17	18	19	20	21	22
Animistic ..	*15,773*	*8,123*	*7,650*	*62*	*52*	*10*	*15,711*	*8,071*	*7,640*	*60*	*50*	*10*	*5*	*5*	..	..	..	..	..	..	..
0—10 ..	**4,076**	2,089	1,987	**2**	..	2	**4,074**	2,089	1,985	2	..	2	..	..	..	..	..	..	..	..	..
10—15 ..	**1,794**	925	869	**7**	6	1	**1,787**	919	868	7	6	1	..	..	..	..	..	..	..	..	..
15—20 ..	**1,470**	685	785	**5**	4	1	**1,465**	681	784	5	4	1	..	..	..	..	..	..	..	..	..
20 and over..	**8,433**	4,424	4,009	**48**	42	6	**8,385**	4,382	4,003	46	40	6	**5**	5	..	..	..	..	..	..	..
Jew ..	*73*	*53*	*20*	*25*	*25*	..	*48*	*28*	*20*	*23*	*23*	..	*1*	*1*	..	*7*	*7*	..	*3*	*3*	..
0—10 ..	**11**	8	3	..	..	..	**11**	8	3	..	..	..	..	..	..	..	..	..	..	..	..
10—15	**1**	..	1	..	..	..	**1**	..	1	..	..	..	..	..	..	..	..	..	..	..	..
15—20 .	**5**	2	3	..	..	..	**5**	2	3	..	..	..	..	..	..	..	..	..	..	..	..
20 and over .	**56**	43	13	**25**	25	..	**31**	18	13	23	23	..	**1**	1	..	**7**	7	..	**3**	3	..
Jain ..	*11*	*8*	*3*	*5*	*3*	*2*	*6*	*5*	*1*	..	..	..	..	..	..	*5*	*3*	*2*	..	..	..
0—10 .	**2**	2	..	..	..	..	**2**	2	..	..	..	..	..	..	..	..	..	..	..	..	..
10—15 ..	..	..	..	..	..	..	..	..	..	..	..	..	..	..	..	..	..	..	..	..	..
15—20	**1**	1	..	..	..	..	**1**	1	..	..	..	..	..	..	..	..	..	..	..	..	..
20 and over...	**8**	5	3	**5**	3	2	**3**	2	1	..	..	..	..	..	..	**5**	3	2	..	..	..
Buddhist ..	*16*	*15*	*1*	*10*	*9*	*1*	*6*	*6*	..	..	..	..	*1*	*1*	..	*9*	*8*	*1*	..	..	..
0—10 .	**2**	2	..	..	..	..	**2**	2	..	..	..	..	..	..	..	..	..	..	..	..	..
10—15	**2**	2	..	..	..	..	**2**	2	..	..	..	..	..	..	..	..	..	..	..	..	..
15—20	..	..	..	..	..	..	..	..	..	..	..	..	..	..	..	..	..	..	..	..	..
20 and over	**12**	11	1	**10**	9	1	**2**	2	..	..	..	..	**1**	1	..	**9**	8	1	..	..	..

TABLE VIII.

Education.—PADMANABHAPURAM DIVISION.

Age.	Population. Total. Persons.	Total. Males.	Total. Females.	Literate. Persons.	Literate. Males.	Literate. Females.	Illiterate. Persons.	Illiterate. Males.	Illiterate. Females.	Literate in Malayalam. Persons.	Malayalam. Males.	Malayalam. Females.	Literate in Tamil. Persons.	Tamil. Males.	Tamil. Females.	Literate in Other Languages. Persons.	Other Languages. Males.	Other Languages. Females.	Literate in English. Persons.	English. Males.	English. Females.
1	2	3	4	5	6	7	8	9	10	11	12	13	14	15	16	17	18	19	20	21	22
All Religions.	*430,087*	*215,313*	*214,774*	*60,063*	*49,257*	*10,806*	*370,024*	*166,056*	*203,968*	*25,421*	*20,667*	*4,754*	*48,323*	*40,439*	*7,884*	*739*	*633*	*106*	*3,260*	*2,894*	*366*
0—10 ..	114,356	56,461	57,895	2,319	1,511	808	112,037	54,950	57,087	1,372	938	434	1,486	992	494	7	4	3	71	57	14
10—15 ..	50,277	25,674	24,603	6,460	4,254	2,206	43,817	21,420	22,397	3,842	2,532	1,310	4,419	3,101	1,318	46	31	15	298	246	52
15—20 ..	40,807	20,246	20,561	7,282	5,237	2,045	33,525	15,009	18,516	3,833	2,937	896	5,402	3,970	1,432	72	53	19	681	615	66
20 and over ..	224,647	112,932	111,715	44,002	38,255	5,747	180,645	74,677	105,968	16,374	14,260	2,114	37,016	32,376	4,640	614	545	69	2,210	1,976	234
Hindu ..	*296,420*	*148,134*	*148,286*	*42,763*	*35,639*	*7,124*	*253,657*	*112,495*	*141,162*	*22,565*	*18,539*	*4,026*	*32,402*	*27,963*	*4,439*	*314*	*286*	*28*	*1,667*	*1,589*	*78*
0—10 ..	77,641	38,446	39,195	1,600	1,036	564	76,041	37,410	38,631	1,191	806	385	885	599	286	4	4	..	24	23	1
10—15 ..	34,286	17,407	16,879	4,690	3,134	1,556	29,596	14,273	15,323	3,490	2,301	1,189	2,801	2,091	710	10	7	3	156	139	17
15—20 ..	27,667	13,688	13,979	5,008	3,612	1,396	22,659	10,076	12,583	3,414	2,638	776	3,300	2,457	843	34	28	6	329	306	23
20 and over ..	156,826	78,593	78,233	31,465	27,857	3,608	125,361	50,738	74,625	14,470	12,794	1,676	25,416	22,816	2,600	268	247	19	1,158	1,121	37
Musalman ..	*14,851*	*7,419*	*7,432*	*2,391*	*2,213*	*178*	*12,460*	*5,206*	*7,254*	*473*	*442*	*31*	*2,152*	*2,031*	*121*	*340*	*288*	*52*	*55*	*54*	*1*
0—10 ..	3,884	1,898	1,986	75	53	22	3,809	1,845	1,964	13	10	3	67	48	19	3	..	3	1	1	..
10—15 ..	1,749	925	824	159	136	23	1,590	789	801	71	65	6	99	88	11	22	15	7	5	5	..
15—20 ..	1,368	635	733	227	201	26	1,141	434	707	52	47	5	198	181	17	21	14	7	12	11	1
20 and over...	7,850	3,961	3,889	1,930	1,823	107	5,920	2,138	3,782	337	320	17	1,788	1,714	74	294	259	35	37	37	...
Christian ..	*116,778*	*58,670*	*58,108*	*14,909*	*11,405*	*3,504*	*101,869*	*47,265*	*54,604*	*2,383*	*1,686*	*697*	*13,769*	*10,445*	*3,324*	*85*	*59*	*26*	*1,538*	*1,251*	*287*
0—10 ..	32,430	15,903	16,527	644	422	222	31,786	15,481	16,805	168	122	46	534	345	189	..	..	..	46	33	13
10—15 ..	14,049	7,239	6,810	1,611	984	627	12,438	6,255	6,183	281	166	115	1,519	922	597	14	9	5	137	102	35
15—20 ..	11,532	5,811	5,721	2,047	1,424	623	9,485	4,387	5,098	367	252	115	1,904	1,332	572	17	11	6	340	298	42
20 and over ..	58,767	29,717	29,050	10,607	8,575	2,032	48,160	21,142	27,018	1,567	1,146	421	9,812	7,846	1,966	54	39	15	1,015	818	197

TABLE VIII.

Education.—TRIVANDRUM DIVISION.

AGE.	POPULATION.									LITERATE IN									LITERATE IN ENGLISH.		
	TOTAL.			LITERATE.			ILLITERATE.			MALAYALAM.			TAMIL.			OTHER LANGUAGES.					
	Persons.	Males.	Females.	Persons.	Males.	Females.	Persons.	Males.	Females.	Persons.	Males.	Females.	Persons.	Males.	Females.	Persons.	Males.	Females.	Persons.	Males.	Females.
1	2	3	4	5	6	7	8	9	10	11	12	13	14	15	16	17	18	19	20	21	22
ALL RELIGIONS.	557,865	281,225	276,640	80,309	67,214	13,095	477,556	214,011	263,545	69,813	57,972	11,841	25,956	23,859	2,097	3,194	2,952	242	9,932	8,737	1,195
0—10 ...	155,625	77,323	78,302	2,390	1,518	872	153,235	75,805	77,430	2,179	1,396	783	310	204	106	26	13	13	217	139	78
10—15 ...	69,123	36,006	33,117	7,869	5,685	2,184	61,254	30,321	30,933	7,261	5,237	2,024	1,156	914	242	190	153	37	635	485	150
15—20 ...	53,856	25,794	28,062	10,127	7,651	2,476	43,729	18,143	25,586	9,223	6,969	2,257	1,915	1,538	377	229	180	49	1,166	883	283
20 and over...	279,261	142,102	137,159	59,923	52,360	7,563	219,338	89,742	129,596	51,147	44,370	6,777	22,575	21,203	1,372	2,749	2,606	143	7,914	7,230	684
HINDU ...	423,909	213,315	210,594	66,446	56,322	10,124	357,463	156,993	200,470	59,033	49,503	9,530	20,887	19,574	1,313	2,389	2,308	81	7,302	6,980	322
0—10 ...	116,367	58,009	58,358	1,953	1,236	717	114,414	56,773	57,641	1,816	1,160	656	228	143	85	8	6	2	112	78	34
10—15 ...	51,872	27,155	24,717	6,307	4,621	1,686	45,565	22,534	23,031	6,008	4,409	1,599	741	581	160	53	46	7	391	333	58
15—20 ...	40,945	19,628	21,317	8,206	6,323	1,883	32,739	13,305	19,434	7,662	5,886	1,776	1,319	1,072	247	108	90	18	759	674	85
20 and over...	214,725	108,523	106,202	49,980	44,142	5,838	164,745	64,381	100,364	43,547	38,048	5,499	18,599	17,778	821	2,220	2,166	54	6,040	5,895	145
MUSALMAN ...	51,197	25,733	25,464	4,055	3,714	341	47,142	22,019	25,123	2,702	2,547	155	2,028	1,926	102	723	590	133	64	59	5
0—10 ...	14,688	7,325	7,363	104	77	27	14,584	7,248	7,336	66	55	11	33	26	7	18	7	11	3	3	...
10—15 ...	6,578	3,391	3,187	360	298	62	6,218	3,093	3,125	233	195	38	103	93	10	137	107	30	11	11	...
15—20 ...	4,752	2,304	2,448	467	409	58	4,285	1,895	2,390	312	284	28	164	157	7	114	86	28	17	17	...
20 and over...	25,179	12,713	12,466	3,124	2,930	194	22,055	9,783	12,272	2,091	2,013	78	1,728	1,650	78	454	390	64	33	28	5
CHRISTIAN ...	77,305	39,371	37,934	9,789	7,159	2,630	67,516	32,212	35,304	8,060	5,904	2,156	3,038	2,356	682	81	53	28	2,564	1,696	868
0—10 ...	23,134	11,282	11,902	333	205	128	22,851	11,077	11,774	297	181	116	49	35	14	...	...	...	102	58	44
10—15 ...	10,032	5,152	4,930	1,202	766	436	8,880	4,386	4,494	1,020	633	387	312	240	72	...	...	...	233	141	92
15—20 ...	7,637	3,629	4,038	1,454	919	535	6,213	2,710	3,503	1,252	799	453	432	309	123	7	4	3	390	192	198
20 and over ...	33,372	19,308	17,064	6,800	5,269	1,531	29,572	14,039	15,533	5,491	4,291	1,200	2,245	1,772	473	74	49	25	1,839	1,305	534

TABLE VIII.

Education.—QUILON DIVISION.

AGE.	Population. Total. Persons.	Population. Total. Males.	Population. Total. Females.	Population. Literate. Persons.	Population. Literate. Males.	Population. Literate. Females.	Population. Illiterate. Persons.	Population. Illiterate. Males.	Population. Illiterate. Females.	Literate in Malayalam. Persons.	Literate in Malayalam. Males.	Literate in Malayalam. Females.	Literate in Tamil. Persons.	Literate in Tamil. Males.	Literate in Tamil. Females.	Literate in Other Languages. Persons.	Literate in Other Languages. Males.	Literate in Other Languages. Females.	Literate in English. Persons.	Literate in English. Males.	Literate in English. Females.
1	2	3	4	5	6	7	8	9	10	11	12	13	14	15	16	17	18	19	20	21	22
All Religions.	*1,233,360*	*620,773*	*612,587*	*186,486*	*157,128*	*29,358*	*1,046,874*	*463,645*	*583,229*	*175,945*	*147,957*	*27,988*	*23,587*	*21,341*	*2,246*	*2,131*	*1,845*	*286*	*6,704*	*5,846*	*858*
0—10 ...	**327,569**	162,010	165,559	**5,070**	3,536	1,534	**322,499**	158,474	164,025	**4,844**	3,365	1,479	**453**	330	123	**33**	21	12	**161**	125	36
10—15 ...	**150,472**	77,802	72,670	**19,608**	14,351	5,257	**130,864**	63,451	67,413	**18,898**	13,859	5,037	**1,269**	961	308	**111**	77	34	**838**	620	218
15—20 ...	**117,236**	56,388	60,848	**24,941**	19,056	5,885	**92,295**	37,332	54,963	**23,780**	18,152	5,628	**2,233**	1,841	422	**262**	204	58	**1,411**	1,209	202
20 and over...	**638,083**	324,573	313,510	**136,867**	120,185	16,682	**501,216**	204,388	296,828	**128,425**	112,581	15,844	**19,602**	18,209	1,393	**1,725**	1,543	182	**4,294**	3,892	402
Hindu ...	*877,605*	*438,137*	*439,468*	*120,357*	*103,468*	*16,889*	*757,248*	*334,669*	*422,579*	*112,539*	*96,636*	*15,903*	*17,243*	*15,456*	*1,787*	*923*	*798*	*125*	*3,345*	*3,132*	*213*
0—10 ...	**224,655**	111,318	113,337	**3,056**	2,219	837	**221,599**	109,099	112,500	**2,875**	2,079	796	**368**	271	97	**12**	7	5	**63**	51	12
10—15 ...	**104,334**	53,918	50,416	**11,918**	9,090	2,828	**92,416**	44,828	47,588	**11,383**	8,738	2,645	**982**	718	264	**33**	21	12	**396**	333	63
15—20 ...	**83,046**	39,297	43,749	**15,702**	12,371	3,331	**67,344**	26,926	40,418	**14,917**	11,768	3,149	**1,589**	1,284	305	**106**	79	27	**630**	588	42
20 and over...	**465,570**	233,604	231,966	**89,631**	79,788	9,893	**375,889**	153,816	222,073	**83,364**	74,051	9,313	**14,304**	13,183	1,121	**772**	691	81	**2,256**	2,160	96
Musalman ...	*89,750*	*46,209*	*43,541*	*8,457*	*8,018*	*439*	*81,293*	*38,191*	*43,102*	*6,737*	*6,444*	*293*	*2,908*	*2,783*	*125*	*1,015*	*893*	*122*	*115*	*112*	*3*
0—10 ...	**25,601**	12,663	12,938	**113**	84	29	**25,488**	12,579	12,909	**82**	60	22	**47**	31	16	**21**	14	7	**1**	1	...
10—15 ...	**11,355**	5,911	5,444	**482**	422	60	**10,873**	5,489	5,384	**361**	321	40	**159**	138	21	**63**	47	16	**7**	7	...
15—20 ...	**8,593**	4,304	4,289	**849**	773	76	**7,744**	3,531	4,213	**658**	598	60	**228**	208	20	**118**	101	17	**31**	28	3
20 and over...	**44,201**	23,331	20,870	**7,013**	6,739	274	**37,188**	16,592	20,596	**5,636**	5,465	171	**2,474**	2,406	68	**813**	731	82	**76**	76	...
Christian ...	*262,446*	*134,621*	*127,825*	*57,663*	*45,635*	*12,028*	*204,783*	*88,986*	*115,797*	*56,666*	*44,874*	*11,792*	*3,436*	*3,102*	*334*	*187*	*150*	*37*	*3,244*	*2,602*	*642*
0—10 ...	**76,283**	37,511	38,772	**1,901**	1,233	668	**74,382**	36,278	38,104	**1,887**	1,226	661	**38**	28	10	...	...	...	**97**	73	24
10—15 ...	**34,371**	17,755	16,616	**7,208**	4,839	2,369	**27,163**	12,916	14,247	**7,152**	4,800	2,352	**128**	105	23	**15**	9	6	**435**	280	155
15—20 ...	**25,286**	12,647	12,639	**8,390**	5,912	2,478	**16,895**	6,735	10,161	**8,205**	5,786	2,419	**446**	349	97	**38**	24	14	**750**	593	157
20 and over...	**126,506**	66,708	59,798	**40,164**	33,651	6,513	**86,342**	33,057	53,285	**39,422**	33,062	6,360	**2,824**	2,620	204	**134**	117	17	**1,962**	1,656	306

TABLE VIII.

Education.—KOTTAYAM DIVISION.

AGE.	POPULATION. Total. Persons.	Total. Males.	Total. Females.	Literate. Persons.	Literate. Males.	Literate. Females.	Illiterate. Persons.	Illiterate. Males.	Illiterate. Females.	LITERATE IN Malayalam. Persons.	Malayalam. Males.	Malayalam. Females.	Tamil. Persons.	Tamil. Males.	Tamil. Females.	Other Languages. Persons.	Other Languages. Males.	Other Languages. Females.	Literate in English. Persons.	Literate in English. Males.	Literate in English. Females.
1	2	3	4	5	6	7	8	9	10	11	12	13	14	15	16	17	18	19	20	21	22
ALL RELIGIONS.	*1,139,101*	*576,060*	*563,041*	*176,592*	*147,275*	*29,317*	*962,509*	*428,785*	*533,724*	*174,800*	*145,790*	*29,010*	*7,902*	*7,151*	*751*	*1,841*	*1,714*	*127*	*5,632*	*4,849*	*783*
0—10 ...	**312,732**	155,323	157,409	**5,403**	3,722	1,681	**307,329**	151,601	155,728	**5,341**	3,682	1,659	**206**	145	61	**12**	11	1	**142**	119	23
10—15 ...	**137,871**	72,286	65,585	**16,258**	11,771	4,487	**121,613**	60,515	61,098	**16,027**	11,631	4,396	**481**	352	129	**68**	52	16	**838**	641	197
15—20 ...	**103,897**	53,111	53,786	**23,533**	17,941	5,592	**83,364**	35,170	48,194	**23,257**	17,707	5,550	**803**	673	130	**183**	165	18	**1,510**	1,269	241
20 and over...	**581,601**	295,340	286,261	**131,398**	113,841	17,557	**450,203**	181,499	268,704	**130,175**	112,770	17,405	**6,412**	5,981	431	**1,578**	1,486	92	**3,142**	2,820	322
HINDU ...	*640,983*	*322,027*	*318,956*	*90,919*	*77,611*	*13,308*	*550,064*	*244,416*	*305,648*	*89,769*	*76,688*	*13,081*	*5,511*	*5,006*	*505*	*514*	*483*	*31*	*2,043*	*1,953*	*90*
0—10 ...	**170,227**	84,590	85,637	**2,721**	1,926	795	**167,506**	82,664	84,842	**2,676**	1,900	776	**160**	111	49	**3**	3	...	**57**	53	4
10—15 ...	**72,859**	38,460	34,399	**7,948**	5,997	1,951	**64,911**	32,463	32,448	**7,754**	5,879	1,875	**388**	286	102	**25**	21	4	**280**	256	24
15—20 ...	**59,479**	29,155	30,324	**11,687**	9,222	2,465	**47,792**	19,933	27,859	**11,493**	9,054	2,439	**580**	490	90	**66**	61	5	**494**	470	24
20 and over...	**338,418**	169,822	168,596	**68,563**	60,466	8,097	**269,855**	109,356	160,499	**67,846**	59,855	7,991	**4,383**	4,119	264	**420**	398	22	**1,212**	1,174	38
MUSALMAN ...	*67,061*	*34,935*	*32,126*	*5,853*	*5,422*	*431*	*61,208*	*29,513*	*31,695*	*5,463*	*5,067*	*396*	*970*	*909*	*61*	*865*	*785*	*80*	*61*	*59*	*2*
0—10 ...	**19,900**	9,955	9,945	**89**	69	20	**19,811**	9,886	9,925	**86**	67	19	**8**	4	4	**9**	8	1	**8**	8	...
10—15 ...	**8,610**	4,574	4,036	**370**	303	67	**8,240**	4,271	3,969	**363**	298	65	**41**	33	8	**36**	25	11	**6**	6	...
15—20 ...	**6,103**	3,223	2,883	**692**	641	51	**5,414**	2,582	2,832	**657**	607	50	**102**	92	10	**79**	68	11	**10**	10	...
20 and over...	**32,445**	17,183	15,262	**4,702**	4,409	293	**27,743**	12,774	14,969	**4,357**	4,095	262	**819**	780	39	**741**	684	57	**42**	40	2
CHRISTIAN ...	*428,706*	*217,874*	*210,832*	*79,760*	*64,192*	*15,568*	*348,946*	*153,682*	*195,264*	*79,509*	*63,986*	*15,523*	*1,421*	*1,236*	*185*	*456*	*440*	*16*	*3,527*	*2,836*	*691*
0—10 ...	**122,012**	60,468	61,544	**2,591**	1,727	864	**119,421**	58,741	60,680	**2,577**	1,715	862	**38**	30	8	...	...	...	**82**	63	19
10—15 ...	**56,101**	29,101	27,000	**7,933**	5,465	2,468	**48,168**	23,636	24,532	**7,903**	5,448	2,455	**52**	33	19	**7**	6	1	**552**	379	173
15—20 ...	**41,103**	20,636	20,467	**11,150**	8,075	3,075	**29,953**	12,561	17,392	**11,103**	8,043	3,060	**121**	91	30	**38**	36	2	**1,006**	789	217
20 and over...	**209,490**	107,669	101,821	**58,036**	48,925	9,161	**151,404**	58,744	92,660	**57,928**	48,780	9,146	**1,210**	1,082	128	**411**	398	13	**1,887**	1,605	282

TABLE VIII.

Education.—DEVIKULAM DIVISION.

AGE.	POPULATION.									LITERATE IN									LITERATE IN ENGLISH.		
	TOTAL.			LITERATE.			ILLITERATE.			MALAYALAM.			TAMIL.			OTHER LANGUAGES.					
	Persons.	Males.	Females.	Persons.	Males.	Females.	Persons.	Males.	Females.	Persons.	Males.	Females.	Persons.	Males.	Females.	Persons.	Males.	Females.	Persons.	Males.	Females.
1	2	3	4	5	6	7	8	9	10	11	12	13	14	15	16	17	18	19	20	21	22
ALL RELIGIONS.	*68,562*	*37,992*	*30,570*	*9,599*	*8,075*	*1,524*	*58,963*	*29,917*	*29,046*	*7,140*	*5,897*	*1,243*	*2,755*	*2,443*	*312*	*226*	*210*	*16*	*722*	*598*	*124*
0—10 ...	**14,912**	7,279	7,633	**233**	150	83	**14,679**	7,129	7,550	**183**	107	76	**69**	53	16	...	...	...	**21**	17	4
10—15 ...	**9,625**	4,727	4,898	**709**	504	205	**8,916**	4,223	4,693	**524**	357	167	**197**	159	38	**4**	3	1	**16**	12	4
15—20 ...	**8,119**	4,396	3,723	**1,193**	920	273	**6,923**	3.476	3,450	**858**	628	230	**351**	299	52	**9**	8	1	**60**	46	14
20 and over...	**35,906**	21,590	14,316	**7,464**	6,501	963	**28,442**	15,089	13,353	**5,575**	4,805	770	**2,138**	1,932	206	**213**	199	14	**625**	523	102
HINDU ...	*43,700*	*23,898*	*19,802*	*4,358*	*3,864*	*494*	*39,342*	*20,034*	*19,308*	*3,086*	*2,693*	*393*	*1,361*	*1,257*	*104*	*58*	*56*	*2*	*115*	*109*	*6*
0—10 ...	**8,763**	4,292	4,471	**72**	50	22	**8,691**	4,242	4,449	**52**	35	17	**20**	15	5	...	...	...	...	...	...
10—15 ...	**6,681**	3,183	3,498	**306**	234	72	**6,375**	2,949	3,426	**211**	158	53	**96**	77	19	**1**	1	...	...	...	...
15—20 ...	**5,483**	2,925	2,558	**547**	449	98	**4,936**	2,476	2,460	**379**	299	80	**170**	150	20	**4**	4	...	**5**	3	2
20 and over...	**22,773**	13,498	9,275	**3,433**	3,131	302	**19,340**	10,367	8,973	**2,444**	2,201	243	**1,075**	1,015	60	**53**	51	2	**110**	106	4
MUSALMAN ...	*3,758*	*2,192*	*1,566*	*586*	*544*	*42*	*3,172*	*1,648*	*1,524*	*369*	*352*	*17*	*254*	*226*	*28*	*136*	*127*	*9*	*4*	*4*	...
0—10 ...	**868**	434	434	**4**	4	...	**864**	430	434	**2**	2	...	**2**	2	...	...	...	...	...	...	...
10—15 ...	**390**	228	162	**31**	28	3	**359**	200	159	**11**	10	1	**21**	19	2	**3**	2	1	...	...	...
15—20 ...	**434**	245	189	**77**	73	4	**357**	172	185	**24**	24	...	**53**	49	4	**4**	4	...	**1**	1	...
20 and over...	**2,036**	1,285	781	**474**	439	35	**1,592**	846	746	**332**	316	16	**178**	156	22	**129**	121	8	**3**	3	...
CHRISTIAN ...	*18,633*	*10,629*	*8,004*	*4,641*	*3,654*	*987*	*13,992*	*6,975*	*7,017*	*3,682*	*2,849*	*833*	*1,136*	*956*	*160*	*24*	*20*	*4*	*603*	*485*	*118*
0—10 ...	**4,600**	2,201	2,399	**157**	96	61	**4,443**	2,105	2,338	**129**	70	59	**47**	36	11	...	...	...	**21**	17	4
10—15 ...	**2,254**	1,169	1,085	**372**	242	130	**1,882**	927	955	**302**	189	113	**80**	63	17	...	...	...	**16**	12	4
15—20 ...	**1,978**	1,120	858	**568**	397	171	**1,410**	723	687	**454**	304	150	**128**	100	28	**1**	...	1	**54**	42	12
20 and over...	**9,801**	6,139	3,662	**3,544**	2,919	625	**6,257**	3,220	3,037	**2,797**	2,286	511	**881**	757	124	**23**	20	3	**512**	414	98

TABLE VIII.

Education.—WESTERN NATURAL DIVISION.

AGE.	POPULATION.									LITERATE IN									LITERATE IN ENGLISH.		
	TOTAL.			LITERATE.			ILLITERATE.			MALAYALAM.			TAMIL.			OTHER LANGUAGES					
	Persons.	Males.	Females.	Persons.	Males.	Females.	Persons.	Males.	Females.	Persons.	Males.	Females.	Persons.	Males.	Females.	Persons.	Males.	Females.	Persons.	Males.	Females.
1	2	3	4	5	6	7	8	9	10	11	12	13	14	15	16	17	18	19	20	21	22
ALL RELIGIONS.	*1,976,154*	*994,326*	*981,828*	*307,715*	*254,771*	*52,944*	*1,668,439*	*739,555*	*928,884*	*263,868*	*218,526*	*45,342*	*79,550*	*68,938*	*10,612*	*6,129*	*5,511*	*618*	*18,953*	*16,584*	*2,369*
0—10 ..	**531,385**	264,310	267,075	**10,260**	6,812	3,448	**521,125**	257,498	263,627	**9,123**	6,124	2,999	**1,848**	1,249	599	**69**	43	26	**440**	322	118
10—15 .	**237,377**	123,024	114,353	**32,120**	22,549	9,571	**205,257**	100,475	104,782	**28,961**	20,551	8,410	**5,480**	3,844	1,636	**328**	246	82	**1,740**	1,330	410
15—20 .	**138,763**	91,410	97,353	**40,154**	30,121	10,033	**148,609**	61,289	87,320	**35,581**	26,946	8,635	**7,846**	5,925	1,921	**581**	463	118	**3,184**	2,656	528
20 and over .	**1,018,629**	515,582	503,047	**225,181**	195,289	29,892	**793,448**	320,293	473,155	**190,203**	164,905	25,298	**64,376**	57,920	6,456	**5,151**	4,759	392	**13,589**	12,276	1,313
HINDU .	*1,417,412*	*709,447*	*707,965*	*214,500*	*180,314*	*34,186*	*1,202,912*	*529,133*	*673,779*	*187,180*	*157,193*	*29,987*	*57,243*	*50,704*	*6,539*	*3,494*	*3,272*	*222*	*11,616*	*11,018*	*598*
0—10 ..	**371,801**	185,680	186,121	**6,808**	4,571	2,237	**364,993**	181,109	183,884	**6,210**	4,240	1,970	**1,224**	819	405	**23**	16	7	**205**	157	48
10—15	**166,315**	86,370	79,945	**21,832**	15,677	6,155	**144,433**	70,693	73,790	**20,270**	14,713	5,557	**3,564**	2,572	992	**97**	76	21	**927**	791	136
15—20	**134,560**	64,668	69,892	**27,566**	21,127	6,439	**106,994**	43,541	63,453	**25,138**	19,481	5,657	**5,105**	3,906	1,199	**265**	215	50	**1,701**	1,553	148
20 and over	**744,736**	372,729	372,007	**158,294**	138,939	19,355	**586,442**	233,790	352,652	**135,562**	118,759	16,803	**47,350**	43,407	3,943	**3,109**	2,965	144	**8,783**	8,517	266
MUSALMAN	*135,210*	*68,978*	*66,232*	*13,949*	*13,009*	*940*	*121,261*	*55,969*	*65,292*	*10,121*	*9,604*	*517*	*5,338*	*5,029*	*309*	*2,090*	*1,795*	*295*	*210*	*201*	*9*
0—10	**38,046**	18,893	19,153	**286**	215	71	**37,760**	18,678	19,082	**169**	136	33	**128**	92	36	**46**	27	19	**5**	5	..
10—15	**17,143**	8,892	8,251	**888**	757	131	**16,255**	8,135	8,120	**636**	551	85	**252**	223	29	**201**	151	50	**22**	22	..
15—20	**12,894**	6,297	6,597	**1,479**	1,335	144	**11,415**	4,962	6,453	**1,060**	975	85	**429**	389	40	**252**	207	45	**49**	46	3
20 and over	**67,127**	34,896	32,231	**11,296**	10,702	594	**55,831**	24,194	31,637	**8,256**	7,942	314	**4,529**	4,325	204	**1,591**	1,410	181	**134**	128	6
CHRISTIAN .	*419,818*	*213,955*	*205,863*	*79,236*	*61,420*	*17,816*	*340,582*	*152,535*	*188,047*	*66,544*	*51,706*	*14,838*	*16,968*	*13,204*	*3,764*	*533*	*434*	*99*	*7,125*	*5,363*	*1,762*
0—10 .	**120,724**	59,326	61,398	**3,166**	2,026	1,140	**117,558**	57,300	60,258	**2,744**	1,748	996	**496**	338	158	..	.	..	**230**	160	70
10—15 .	**53,518**	27,555	25,963	**9,400**	6,115	3,285	**44,118**	21,440	22,678	**8,055**	5,287	2,768	**1,664**	1,049	615	**30**	19	11	**791**	517	274
15—20	**40,957**	20,291	20,666	**11,109**	7,659	3,450	**29,848**	12,632	17,216	**9,383**	6,490	2,893	**2,312**	1,630	682	**64**	41	[illegible]	**1,434**	1,057	377
20 and over .	**204,619**	106,783	97,836	**55,561**	45,620	9,941	**149,058**	61,163	87,895	**46,362**	38,181	8,181	**12,496**	10,187	2,309	**439**	374	[illegible]	**4,670**	3,629	1,041

TABLE VIII.

Education.—EASTERN NATURAL DIVISION.

AGE.	POPULATION.									LITERATE IN									Literate in English.		
	Total.			Literate.			Illiterate.			Malayalam.			Tamil.			Other Languages.					
	Persons.	Males.	Females.	Persons.	Males.	Females.	Persons.	Males.	Females.	Persons.	Males.	Females.	Persons.	Males.	Females.	Persons.	Males.	Females.	Persons.	Males.	Females.
1	2	3	4	5	6	7	8	9	10	11	12	13	14	15	16	17	18	19	20	21	22
All Religions..	***1,452,821***	*737,037*	*715,784*	***205,334***	*174,178*	*31,156*	***1,247,487***	*562,859*	*684,628*	***189,251***	*159,757*	*29,494*	***28,973***	*26,295*	*2,678*	***2,002***	*1,843*	*159*	***7,297***	*6,340*	*957*
0—10 ..	**393,809**	194,086	199,723	**5,155**	3,625	1,530	**388,654**	190,461	198,193	**4,793**	3,364	1,432	**676**	475	201	**9**	6	3	**172**	135	37
10—15 ..	**179,991**	93,471	86,520	**18,784**	14,016	4,768	**161,207**	79,455	81,752	**17,589**	13,065	4,524	**2,042**	1,643	399	**91**	70	21	**885**	674	211
15—20 .	**138,152**	68,525	69,627	**26,922**	20,684	6,238	**111,230**	47,841	63,389	**25,373**	19,447	5,926	**2,888**	2,396	492	**174**	147	27	**1,644**	1,366	278
20 and over .	**740,869**	380,955	359,914	**154,473**	135,853	18,620	**586,396**	245,102	341,294	**141,493**	123,881	17,612	**23,367**	21,781	1,586	**1,728**	1,620	108	**4,596**	4,165	431
Hindu ..	***865,205***	*436,064*	*429,141*	***110,343***	*96,590*	*13,753*	***754,862***	*339,474*	*415,388*	***99,812***	*86,866*	*12,946*	***20,161***	*18,552*	*1,609*	***704***	*659*	*45*	***2,856***	*2,745*	*111*
0—10 ..	**225,852**	110,975	114,877	**2,594**	1,896	698	**223,258**	109,079	114,179	**2,400**	1,740	660	**437**	320	117	**4**	4	..	**51**	48	3
10—15 ...	**103,717**	53,753	49,964	**9,337**	7,399	1,938	**94,360**	46,354	48,026	**8,576**	6,772	1,804	**1,444**	1.181	263	**25**	20	5	**296**	270	26
15—20 ..	**82,060**	40,025	42,035	**13,584**	10,850	2,734	**68,476**	29,175	39,301	**12,727**	10,164	2,563	**1,853**	1,547	306	**53**	47	6	**516**	488	28
20 and over..	**453,576**	231,311	222,265	**84,828**	76,445	8,383	**368,748**	154,866	213,882	**76,109**	68,190	7,919	**16,427**	15,504	923	**622**	588	34	**1,993**	1,939	54
Musalman	***91,407***	*47,510*	*43,897*	***7,393***	*6,902*	*491*	***84,014***	*40,608*	*43,406*	***5,623***	*5,248*	*375*	***2,974***	*2,846*	*128*	***989***	*888*	*101*	***89***	*87*	*2*
0—10 .	**26,895**	13,382	13,513	**99**	72	27	**26,796**	13,310	13,486	**80**	58	22	**29**	19	10	**5**	2	3	**3**	3	
10—15 .	**11,539**	6,137	5.402	**514**	430	84	**11,025**	5,707	5,318	**403**	338	65	**171**	148	23	**60**	45	15	**7**	7	..
15—20 .	**8,359**	4,414	3,945	**833**	762	71	**7,526**	3,652	3,874	**643**	585	58	**316**	298	18	**84**	66	18	**22**	21	1
20 and over .	**44,614**	23,577	21,037	**5,947**	5,638	309	**38,667**	17,939	20,728	**4,497**	4,267	230	**2,458**	2,381	77	**840**	775	65	**57**	56	1
Christian ..	***484,050***	*247,210*	*236,840*	***87,526***	*70,625*	*16,901*	***396,524***	*176,585*	*219,939*	***83,756***	*67,593*	*16,163*	***5,832***	*4,891*	*941*	***300***	*288*	*12*	***4,351***	*3,507*	*844*
0—10 ..	**137,785**	68,039	69,746	**2,460**	1,657	803	**135,325**	66,382	68,943	**2,314**	1,566	748	**210**	136	74	...	.		**118**	84	34
10—15 .	**63,339**	32,861	30,478	**8,926**	6,181	2,745	**54,413**	26,680	27,733	**8,603**	5,949	2,654	**427**	314	113	**6**	5	1	**582**	397	185
15—20 ..	**46,609**	23,552	23.057	**12,500**	9,068	3,432	**34,109**	14,484	19,625	**11,998**	8,694	3,304	**719**	551	168	**37**	34	3	**1,106**	857	249
20 and over	**236,317**	122,758	113,559	**63,640**	53,719	9,921	**172,677**	69,089	103,638	**60,841**	51,384	9,457	**4,476**	3,890	586	**257**	249	8	**2,545**	2,160	376

TABLE VIII.

Education.—Part II. Towns.

TABLE VIII.

Education.—TOWNS.

TOWNS.	AGE.	POPULATION. Total. Persons.	Total. Males.	Total. Females.	Literate. Persons.	Literate. Males.	Literate. Females.	Illiterate. Persons.	Illiterate. Males.	Illiterate. Females.	LITERATE IN Malayalam. Persons.	Malayalam. Males.	Malayalam. Females.	Tamil. Persons.	Tamil. Males.	Tamil. Females.	Other Languages. Persons.	Other Languages. Males.	Other Languages. Females.	Literate in English. Persons.	Literate in English. Males.	Literate in English. Females.
	1	2	3	4	5	6	7	8	9	10	11	12	13	14	15	16	17	18	19	20	21	22
Nagercoil.	All Religions.	*29,883*	*14,553*	*15,330*	*6,236*	*4,855*	*1,381*	*23,647*	*9,698*	*13,949*	*1,871*	*1,605*	*266*	*5,350*	*4,062*	*1,288*	*309*	*262*	*47*	*898*	*793*	*105*
	0—10 ..	**7,291**	3,607	3,684	**270**	196	74	**7,021**	3,411	3,610	**92**	75	17	**236**	175	61	**3**	..	3	**16**	14	2
	10—15 .	**3,599**	1,777	1,822	**852**	513	339	**2,747**	1,264	1,483	**291**	214	77	**794**	478	316	**9**	6	3	**88**	83	5
	15—20 .	**3,002**	1,463	1,539	**1,039**	778	261	**1,963**	685	1,278	**345**	294	51	**996**	758	238	**24**	17	7	**238**	227	11
	20 and over .	**15,991**	7,706	8,285	**4,075**	3,368	707	**11,916**	4,338	7,578	**1,143**	1,022	121	**3,324**	2,651	673	**273**	239	34	**556**	469	87
Trivandrum.	All Religions.	*63,561*	*32,292*	*31,269*	*24,498*	*19,259*	*5,239*	*39,063*	*13,033*	*26,030*	*19,093*	*14,522*	*4,571*	*10,392*	*9,302*	*1,090*	*2,307*	*2,143*	*164*	*7,216*	*6,334*	*882*
	0—10 ..	**14,822**	7,195	7,627	**988**	548	440	**13,834**	6,647	7,187	**844**	460	384	**186**	121	65	**21**	12	9	**147**	85	62
	10—15 ..	**7,539**	3,849	3,690	**2,765**	1,838	927	**4,774**	2,011	2,763	**2,328**	1,494	834	**729**	582	147	**112**	97	15	**454**	353	101
	15—20 ..	**6,621**	3,333	3,288	**3,190**	2,267	923	**3,431**	1,066	2,365	**2,652**	1,854	798	**1,063**	850	213	**146**	116	30	**890**	662	228
	20 and over ..	**34,579**	17,915	16,664	**17,555**	14,606	2,949	**17,024**	3,309	13,715	**13,269**	10,714	2,555	**8,414**	7,749	665	**2,028**	1,918	110	**5,725**	5,234	491
Shencottah.	All Religions.	*10,309*	*4,905*	*5,404*	*1,387*	*1,324*	*63*	*8,922*	*3,581*	*5,341*	*532*	*519*	*13*	*1,339*	*1,284*	*55*	*37*	*36*	*1*	*239*	*235*	*4*
	0—10	**2,791**	1,410	1,381	**52**	50	2	**2,739**	1,360	1,379	**27**	26	1	**50**	49	1	**1**	1	..	**1**	1	..
	10—15 .	**1,225**	591	634	**160**	144	16	**1,065**	447	618	**80**	77	3	**159**	144	15	**1**	1	...	**20**	19	1
	15—20	**929**	446	483	**172**	155	17	**757**	291	466	**87**	82	5	**166**	152	14	**1**	..	1	**44**	41	3
	20 and over .	**5,384**	2,458	2,900	**1,003**	975	28	**4,381**	1,483	2,878	**338**	334	4	**964**	939	25	**34**	34	.	**174**	174	...
Quilon.	All Religions.	*18,839*	*9,649*	*9,190*	*3,746*	*2,863*	*883*	*15,093*	*6,786*	*8,307*	*3,456*	*2,697*	*759*	*952*	*818*	*134*	*221*	*184*	*37*	*1,043*	*866*	*177*
	0—10 .	**4,502**	2,087	2,415	**130**	73	57	**4,372**	2,014	2,358	**111**	62	49	**14**	8	6	**5**	3	2	**32**	26	6
	10—15	**2,171**	1,070	1,101	**411**	256	155	**1,760**	814	946	**364**	227	137	**52**	33	19	**10**	9	1	**110**	74	36
	15—20 .	**1,968**	965	1,003	**558**	400	158	**1,410**	565	845	**500**	358	142	**105**	85	20	**42**	35	7	**139**	100	39
	20 and over ..	**10,198**	5,527	4,671	**2,647**	2,134	513	**7,551**	3,393	4,158	**2,481**	2,050	431	**781**	692	89	**164**	137	27	**762**	666	96

TABLE VIII.

Education.—TOWNS.

TOWNS.	AGE.	POPULATION. Total. Persons.	Total. Males.	Total. Females.	Literate. Persons.	Literate. Males.	Literate. Females.	Illiterate. Persons.	Illiterate. Males.	Illiterate. Females.	LITERATE IN Malayalam. Persons.	Malayalam. Males.	Malayalam. Females.	Tamil. Persons.	Tamil. Males.	Tamil. Females.	Other Languages. Persons.	Other Languages. Males.	Other Languages. Females.	Literate in English. Persons.	Literate in English. Males.	Literate in English. Females.
	1	2	3	4	5	6	7	8	9	10	11	12	13	14	15	16	17	18	19	20	21	22
Kayankulam.	All Religions	*5,830*	*2,772*	*3,058*	*1,589*	*1,054*	*535*	*4,241*	*1,718*	*2,523*	*1,335*	*872*	*463*	*549*	*358*	*191*	*135*	*97*	*38*	*124*	*109*	*15*
	0—10	**1,429**	627	803	**171**	111	60	**1,258**	516	742	**128**	83	45	**72**	45	27	**1**	..	1	**1**	1	..
	10—15	**701**	336	365	**195**	109	86	**506**	227	279	**152**	88	64	**71**	43	28	**11**	6	5	**22**	21	1
	15—20	**580**	258	322	**247**	153	94	**333**	105	228	**200**	117	83	**98**	59	39	**31**	22	9	**32**	30	2
	20 and over	**3,120**	1,551	1,569	**976**	681	295	**2,144**	870	1,274	**855**	584	271	**308**	211	97	**92**	69	23	**69**	57	12
Tiruvalla.	All Religions	*7,969*	*4,268*	*3,701*	*2,803*	*2,185*	*618*	*5,166*	*2,083*	*3,083*	*2,667*	*2,056*	*611*	*146*	*136*	*10*	*24*	*24*	..	*337*	*323*	*14*
	0—10	**1,384**	991	893	**122**	98	24	**1,762**	893	869	**121**	97	24	**2**	2	.	..		..	**5**	5	.
	10—15	**910**	518	392	**393**	274	119	**517**	244	273	**393**	274	119	**1**	1	..	..	.	..	**68**	65	3
	15—20	**911**	487	424	**445**	308	137	**466**	179	287	**441**	306	135	**14**	12	2	**3**	3		**134**	130	4
	20 and over	**4,264**	2,272	1,992	**1,343**	1,505	338	**2,421**	767	1,654	**1,712**	1,379	333	**129**	121	8	**21**	21	.	**130**	123	7
Alleppey.	All Religions	*25,665*	*13,370*	*12,295*	*5,869*	*4,663*	*1,206*	*19,796*	*8,707*	*11,089*	*5,262*	*4,255*	*1,007*	*958*	*725*	*233*	*141*	*115*	*26*	*839*	*691*	*148*
	0—10	**5,906**	2,868	3,038	**473**	348	125	**5,433**	2,520	2,913	**455**	336	119	**38**	30	8	**2**	1	1	**55**	46	9
	10—15	**2,414**	1,258	1,156	**527**	402	125	**1,887**	856	1,031	**444**	363	81	**111**	60	51	**13**	8	5	**190**	151	39
	15—20	**2,562**	1,305	1,257	**734**	599	135	**1,828**	706	1,122	**676**	552	124	**140**	122	18	**12**	8	4	**206**	169	37
	20 and over	**14,783**	7,939	6,844	**4,135**	3,314	821	**10,648**	4,625	6,023	**3,687**	3,004	683	**669**	513	156	**114**	98	16	**388**	325	63
Kottayam.	All Religions.	*15,141*	*7,863*	*7,278*	*6,218*	*4,674*	*1,544*	*8,923*	*3,189*	*5,734*	*6,012*	*4,492*	*1,520*	*343*	*287*	*56*	*144*	*130*	*14*	*1,241*	*1,074*	*167*
	0—10	**4,100**	2,027	2,073	**224**	172	52	**3,876**	1,855	2,021	**220**	169	51	**11**	7	4	..	.	...	**33**	22	11
	10—15	**1,897**	1,017	880	**865**	604	261	**1,032**	413	619	**848**	587	261	**32**	26	6	**9**	9	.	**184**	156	28
	15—20	**1,587**	856	731	**1,015**	712	303	**572**	144	428	**995**	697	298	**67**	49	18	**37**	34	3	**423**	359	64
	20 and over	**7,557**	3,963	3,594	**4,114**	3,186	928	**3,443**	777	2,666	**3,949**	3,039	910	**233**	205	28	**93**	87	11	**601**	537	64

TABLE VIII.

Education.—TOWNS.

TOWNS.	AGE.	POPULATION.									LITERATE IN									LITERATE IN ENGLISH.		
		TOTAL.			LITERATE.			ILLITERATE.			MALAYALAM.			TAMIL.			OTHER LANGUAGES.					
		Persons.	Males.	Females.	Persons.	Males.	Females.	Persons.	Males.	Females.	Persons.	Males.	Females.	Persons.	Males.	Females.	Persons.	Males.	Females.	Persons.	Males.	Females.
	1	2	3	4	5	6	7	8	9	10	11	12	13	14	15	16	17	18	19	20	21	22
CHANGANACHERY.	ALL RELIGIONS.	***17,242***	*8,826*	*8,416*	***4,417***	*3,469*	*948*	***12,825***	*5,357*	*7,468*	***4,278***	*3,343*	*935*	***554***	*523*	*31*	***35***	*33*	*2*	***331***	*265*	*66*
	0—10 ..	**4,690**	2,329	2,361	**104**	63	41	**4,586**	2,266	2,320	**102**	61	41	**6**	5	1	..	..	..	**6**	3	3
	10—15 ..	**2,034**	1,083	981	**379**	249	130	**1,685**	834	851	**374**	245	129	**23**	20	3	.		...	**38**	28	10
	15—20 .	**1,646**	885	761	**655**	489	166	**991**	396	595	**640**	475	165	**35**	33	2		..	.	**90**	77	13
	20 and over .	**8,842**	4,529	4,313	**3,279**	2,668	611	**5,563**	1,861	3,702	**3,162**	2,562	600	**490**	465	25	**35**	33	2	**197**	157	40
ALWAYE.	ALL RELIGIONS.	***3,869***	*2,103*	*1,766*	***860***	*733*	*127*	***3,009***	*1,370*	*1,639*	***834***	*714*	*120*	***88***	*66*	*22*	***9***	*6*	*3*	***152***	*187*	*5*
	0—10 ..	**1,096**	562	534	**26**	17	9	**1,070**	545	525	**25**	17	8	**4**	3	1	.	..	.	.	..	..
	10—15 ..	**525**	307	218	**115**	100	15	**410**	207	203	**114**	99	15	**4**	2	2	**1**	1	.	**25**	23	2
	15—20 ..	**364**	218	146	**144**	123	21	**220**	95	125	**142**	121	21	**13**	10	3	.	..	..	**47**	47	...
	20 and over..	**1,884**	1,016	868	**575**	493	82	**1,309**	523	786	**553**	477	76	**67**	51	16	**8**	5	3	**120**	117	3
PARUR.	ALL RELIGIONS.	***13,782***	*7,067*	*6,715*	***2,488***	*1,968*	*520*	***11,294***	*5,099*	*6,195*	***2,392***	*1,897*	*495*	***445***	*382*	*63*	***40***	*37*	*3*	***309***	*297*	*12*
	0—10 ..	**3,805**	1,913	1,892	**80**	53	27	**3,725**	1,860	1,865	**79**	52	27	**17**	11	6	..	..	.	**2**	2	.
	10—15 ..	**1,659**	888	771	**346**	284	62	**1,313**	604	709	**343**	283	60	**38**	30	8	**2**	1	1	**24**	21	3
	15—20 ..	**1,404**	761	643	**425**	316	109	**979**	445	534	**417**	311	106	**82**	69	13	**4**	4	.	**58**	56	2
	20 and over..	**6,914**	3,505	3,409	**1,637**	1,315	322	**5,277**	2,190	3,087	**1,553**	1,251	302	**308**	272	36	**34**	32	2	**225**	218	7

TABLE IX.

Education by Selected Castes, Tribes or Races.

NOTE.—For the purposes of this Table, some of the castes shown separately in Table XIII. (Caste, Tribe and Race) have been grouped together.

(I). AMPALAVĀSI INCLUDES:

(a) Ampalavāsi (1,996),
(b) Atika*l* (9),
(c) Chākkiyār (120),
(d) Daivampāti (182),
(e) Kurukka*l* (1,374),
(f) Mūttatu (615),
(g) Nampiti (54),
(h) Nampiyār (828),
(i) Pilāppa*ll*i (73),
(j) Pishārati (581),
(k) Potuva*l* (117),
(l) Pushpakan (1,925),
(m) Tīyattunni (259),
and *(n)* Vāriyar (2,769).

(II). MALAYA*L*A BRAHMAN INCLUDES:

(a) Malaya*l*a Potti (5,220), and *(b)* Nampūtiri (5,105).

(III). OTHER BRAHMAN INCLUDES.

(a) Aryappattar (31),
(b) Canarese Brahman (291),
(c) Gauda Brahman (120),
(d) Maharatta Brahmans (603),
(e) Tamil Brahmans (40,335),
(f) Telugu Brahmans (916),
and *(g)* Tulu Brahmans (3,053).

(IV) KAMMĀ*L*AN INCLUDES:

(a) Āsāri (62,882),
(b) Chāyakkuruppu (83),
(c) Chemputatti (58),
(d) Kallāsāri (7,992),
(e) Kammā*l*an (16,805),
(f) Kannān (3,951),
(g) Kollan (26,659),
(h) Sitpāsāri (104),
(i) Tattān (21,350),
(j) Uravā*l*an (187),
(k) Va*l*an (525),
and *(l)* Vilkuruppu (986).

TABLE IX.

Education by Selected Castes, Tribes or Races.

CASTE, TRIBE OR RACE.	POPULATION.								
	TOTAL.			LITERATE.			ILLITERATE.		
	Persons.	Males.	Females.	Persons.	Males.	Females.	Persons.	Males.	Females.
1	2	3	4	5	6	7	8	9	10
HINDU.									
1 Ampalavāsi ...	10,852	5,448	5,404	3,161	2,485	676	7,691	2,963	4,728
2. Ampa*tt*an	21,826	10,996	10,830	2,504	2,233	271	19,322	8,765	10,559
3. Brahman (Malaya*la*)	10,325	5,841	4,484	4,671	3,667	1,004	5,654	2,174	3,480
4. Brahman (Others) ...	45,349	23,892	21,457	15,700	13,320	2,380	29,649	10,572	19,077
5 Chakkāla	13,074	8,937	9,137	1,809	1,529	280	13,255	7,408	8,857
6 Chānnān	166,195	84,638	81,557	9,206	8,821	385	156,989	75,817	81,172
7. Che*tt*i	20,881	10,535	10,346	3,497	3,271	226	17,384	7,264	10,120
8. Itayan .. .	6,835	3,408	3,427	651	628	23	6,184	2,780	3,404
9. Īzhavan	546,265	271,677	274,588	55,192	50,517	4,675	491,073	221,160	269,913
10. Kammā*l*an .. .	141,582	71,538	70,044	20,168	19,164	1,004	121,414	52,374	69,040
11. Ka*n*iyān	11,987	6,155	5,832	3,515	3,073	442	8,472	3,082	5,390
12. Konka*n*i	10,219	5,356	4,863	4,065	3,894	171	6,154	1,462	4,692
13 Krish*n*anvaka ...	10,429	5,309	5,120	1,958	1,705	253	8,471	3,604	4,867
14. Kudumi	8,207	4,363	3,844	445	387	58	7,762	3,976	3,786
15. Ku*r*avan	61,827	30,183	31,644	413	360	53	61,414	29,823	31,591
16. Ma*nn*ān	9,946	5,014	4,932	162	150	12	9,784	4,864	4,920
17. Marakkān	14,604	7,274	7,330	790	736	54	13,814	6,538	7,276
18. Mārān	29,318	14,661	14,657	5,719	4,585	1,134	23,599	10,076	13,523
19. Ma*r*avan	8,376	4,245	4,131	584	561	23	7,792	3,684	4,108
20. Nāyar	592,489	295,703	296,786	144,946	120,263	24,683	447,543	175,440	272,103
21. Pa*ll*an	11,222	5,205	6,017	290	212	78	10,932	4,993	5,939
22. Pantāram	13,784	7,015	6,769	1,473	1,348	125	12,311	5,667	6,644
23. Paravan	9,313	4,648	4,665	494	463	31	8,819	4,135	4,634
24. Paraiyan	70,554	35,131	35,423	947	861	86	69,607	34,270	35,337
25. Pulayan	185,314	93,335	91,979	1,496	1,446	50	183,818	91,889	91,929
26. Sāliyan	9,919	4,953	4,966	485	359	126	9,434	4,594	4,840
27. Tantān	21,641	10,836	10,805	947	732	215	20,694	10,104	10,590
28. Vālan	16,746	8,588	8,160	593	550	43	16,155	8,033	8,117
29. Vā*n*iyan	16,235	8,115	8,120	1,583	1,447	136	14,652	6,668	7,984
30. Vēlan	12,957	6,350	6,607	1,040	912	128	11,917	5,438	6,479
31. Ve*ll*āla	49,479	24,774	24,705	11,803	10,948	855	37,676	13,826	23,850
32. Velu*tt*edan ..	11,356	5,718	5,638	1,199	1,051	148	10,157	4,667	5,490
CHRISTIAN.									
1. Anglo-Indian .	1,750	911	839	1,174	631	543	576	280	296
2. European	399	250	149	359	234	125	40	16	24
3. Native Christian ..	901,719	460,004	441,715	165,229	131,180	34,049	736,490	328,824	407,656

TABLE IX.

Education by Selected Castes, Tribes or Races.

LITERATE IN									LITERATE IN ENGLISH.		
MALAYALAM.			TAMIL.			OTHER LANGUAGES.					
Persons.	Males.	Females.	Persons.	Males.	Females.	Persons.	Males.	Females.	Persons.	Males.	Females.
11	12	13	14	15	16	17	18	19	20	21	22
3,141	2,470	671	420	394	26	25	25	...	107	107	.
2,368	2,148	220	393	336	57	...	...	...	37	28	9
4,610	3,609	1,001	452	418	34	113	107	6	31	28	3
12,328	11,255	1,073	11,819	10,324	1,495	1,235	1,127	108	3,007	2,941	66
1,605	1,430	175	872	765	107	38	29	9	45	45	..
3,521	3,308	213	7,009	6,794	215	12	12	.	295	241	54
2,776	2,598	178	2,001	1,928	73	73	73	..	67	62	5
453	446	7	280	262	18	...	..	..	27	24	3
54,466	49,942	4,524	3,077	2,814	263	149	149	..	1,441	1,359	82
17,180	16,434	746	5,062	4,587	475	35	35	..	186	186	.
3,417	2,983	434	599	523	76	24	22	2	7	7	...
3,093	2,928	165	805	784	21	418	383	35	106	104	2
979	924	55	1,853	1,637	216	8	5	3	77	72	5
399	342	57	57	50	7	...	...	.	5	4	1
365	320	45	52	43	9	2	2	.	4	4	.
162	150	12	...	...	...	...	..	..	..	...	..
790	736	54	10	10	...	...	...	...	19	19	.
5,585	4,458	1,127	721	681	40	7	7	...	59	55	4
79	76	3	545	523	22	..	..	..	16	16	.
142,163	118,946	23,217	25,683	23,410	2,273	641	611	30	5,446	5,038	358
290	212	78	...	...	...	..	...	..	...	..	.
1,193	1,080	113	515	481	34	..	...	...	7	7	..
391	366	25	110	103	7	..	..	...	..	...	..
238	218	20	751	684	67	...	.	...	13	13	.
1,488	1,438	50	35	34	1	...	...	..	21	21	
281	197	84	204	162	42	..	...	...	.	.	.
947	733	215	...	...	...	...	..	.	..	.	.
593	550	43	2	2	...	...	..	..	1	1	.
937	836	101	934	890	44	1	1	...	24	24	..
1,028	901	127	41	39	2	...	...	..	..	...	...
6,575	5,903	672	9,596	8,759	837	47	37	10	955	936	19
1,180	1,037	143	55	50	5	2	2	..	8	7	1
879	431	448	177	129	48	75	45	30	988	553	435
48	25	23	115	69	46	30	19	11	359	234	125
149,373	118,843	30,530	22,508	17,897	4,611	728	658	70	10,123	8,033	2,016

TABLE X.

Language.—Part I. State and Divisions.

TABLE X.

Language.—ADMINISTRATIVE DIVISIONS.

LANGUAGE.	STATE TOTAL.			PADMANABHAPURAM.		
	Persons.	Males.	Females.	Persons.	Males.	Females
1	2	3	4	5	6	7
STATE. ...	***3,428,975***	*1,731,363*	*1,697,612*	***430,087***	*215,313*	*214,774*
A. Vernaculars of India .	***3,426,548***	*1,730,008*	*1,696,540*	***429,993***	*215,265*	*214,728*
I. VERNACULARS OF TRAVANCORE STATE...	***3,391,346***	*1,710,724*	*1,680,622*	***426,477***	*213,327*	*213,150*
1. Malayalam	**2,836,728**	1,432,139	1,404,589	**55,326**	29,670	25,656
2. Tamil	**554,618**	278,585	276,033	**371,151**	183,657	187,494
II. VERNACULARS OF MADRAS PRESIDENCY...	***33,938***	*18,612*	*15,326*	***3,508***	*1,930*	*1,578*
1. Canarese	**1,901**	1,053	848	**232**	131	101
2. Hindostani	**4,647**	2,614	2,033	**520**	284	236
3. Konkani	**11,052**	5,886	5,166	...	..	.
4. Marathi	**6,740**	3,651	3,089	**118**	56	62
5. Oriya	**1**	1	...	..	...	..
6. Patnuli	**1,383**	758	625	**1,354**	740	614
7. Telugu	**6,452**	3,460	2,992	**939**	512	477
8. Tulu...	**1,762**	1,189	573	**295**	207	88
III. VERNACULARS OF OTHER PROVINCES .	***1,264***	*672*	*592*	***8***	*8*	..
1. Bengali	**26**	22	4	**1**	1	..
2. Gujarati	**810**	407	403	..	...	..
3. Hindi . . .	**2**	2	..	...	.	...
4. Kachchi	**378**	202	176	..	..	...
5. Nagari	**27**	22	5	..	..	...
6. Panjabi	**1**	1	..		..	...
7. Sanskrit	**8**	5	3	..	..	.
8. Urdu	**12**	11	1	**7**	7	...
B. Vernaculars of Asiatic countries Beyond India.	***172***	*116*	*56*	***3***	*3*	..
1. Arabic	**136**	84	52	**2**	2	..
2. Chinese	**3**	3	..	..	.	.
3. Singhalese	**28**	24	4	**1**	1	.
4. Syriac	**5**	5	...	.	...	...
C. European Languages ..	***2,255***	*1,239*	*1,016*	***91***	*45*	*46*
1. Dutch	**2**	2	...	**2**	2	..
2. English	**2,167**	1,181	983	**71**	36	35
3. Flemish	**3**	...	3	**3**	.	3
4. French	**1**	1	..	..	...	..
5. German	**18**	11	7	**6**	4	2
6. Italian	**5**	3	2	**1**	1	..
7. Latin	**6**	6	..	..	..	...
8. Norwegian	**8**	2	6	**6**	2	4
9. Portuguese	**35**	31	4	..	..	..
10. Spanish	**3**	2	1	..	..	..
11. Swiss	**4**	...	4	**1**	.	1
12. Turkish	**2**	.	2	...	..	.
13. Welsh	**1**	.	1	**1**	..	1

TABLE X.

Language.—ADMINISTRATIVE DIVISIONS.

Trivandrum.			Quilon.			Kottayam.			Devikulam.		
Persons.	Males.	Females.	Persons.	Males.	Females.	Persons.	Males.	Females.	Persons.	Males.	Females.
8	9	10	11	12	13	14	15	16	17	18	19
557,865	*281,225*	*276,640*	***1,233,360***	*620,773*	*612,587*	***1,139,101***	*576,060*	*563,041*	***68,562***	*37,992*	*30,570*
556,923	*280,772*	*276,151*	***1,232,495***	*620,271*	*612,224*	***1,138,819***	*575,903*	*562,916*	***68,318***	*37,797*	*30,521*
550,961	*277,221*	*273,740*	***1,220,160***	*613,807*	*606,353*	***1,127,110***	*569,529*	*557,581*	***66,638***	*36,840*	*29,798*
491,702	246,744	244,958	**1,151,586**	579,403	572,183	**1,104,461**	557,271	547,190	**33,653**	19,051	14,602
59,259	30,477	28,782	**68,574**	34,404	34,170	**22,649**	12,258	10,391	**32,985**	17,789	15,196
5,671	*3,397*	*2,274*	***11,428***	*5,973*	*5,455*	***11,657***	*6,359*	*5,298*	***1,674***	*953*	*721*
531	305	226	**379**	213	166	**415**	204	211	**344**	200	144
1,856	1,107	749	**1,568**	833	735	**534**	283	251	**169**	107	62
337	182	155	**2,957**	1,427	1,530	**7,751**	4,270	3,481	**7**	7	..
474	279	195	**3,938**	2,185	1,753	**2,173**	1,124	1,049	**7**	7	...
..	..	...	..	..	..	...	..	..	**1**	1	...
19	10	9	**10**	8	2	..	..	...	..	..	..
1,754	1,039	715	**2,194**	1,100	1,094	**390**	194	196	**1,125**	617	508
700	475	225	**352**	207	145	**394**	286	108	**21**	14	7
291	*154*	*137*	***907***	*491*	*416*	***52***	*15*	*37*	***6***	*4*	*2*
10	6	4	**15**	15		..					..
185	90	95	**590**	307	283	**31**	7	24	**4**	3	1
2	2		..								
92	54	38	**273**	143	130	**13**	5	8			
..	...	..	**22**	22	..	**5**		5			
1	1			..			..				
...	..	..	**5**	2	3	**3**	3				
1	1		**2**	2	..	..	..		**2**	1	1
4	*3*	*1*	***44***	*28*	*16*	***89***	*56*	*33*	***32***	*26*	*6*
2	1	1	**35**	22	13	**84**	51	33	**13**	8	5
	..		**3**	3	..						
2	2	...	**6**	3	3				**19**	18	1
..	..	..	..	..		**5**	5		..		
938	*450*	*488*	***821***	*474*	*347*	***193***	*101*	*92*	***212***	*169*	*43*
925	447	478	**792**	450	342	**178**	86	92	**201**	162	39
..	..	..	...					..		..	
6	3	3	**6**	4	2		..	..	**1**	1	
2		2	**2**	2			..		...	..	
...	...	..			..		..	..	..	..	
2		2			..	**6**	6				
..			**21**	18	3	**7**	7	...	**7**	6	1
..	..	..	..			**2**	2	..	**1**		1
3	...	3	..			...					
..	..	..					..		**2**		2
	..	..			..					..	

TABLE X.

Language.—NATURAL DIVISIONS.

LANGUAGE.	STATE TOTAL.			WESTERN NATURAL DIVISION			EASTERN NATURAL DIVISION		
	Persons.	Males.	Females.	Persons.	Males.	Females.	Persons.	Males.	Females.
1	2	3	4	5	6	7	8	9	10
STATE ..	*3,428,975*	*1,731,363*	*1,697,612*	*1,976,154*	*994,326*	*981,828*	*1,452,821*	*737,037*	*715,784*
A. Vernaculars of India .	*3,426,548*	*1,730,008*	*1,696,510*	*1,974,297*	*993,386*	*980,911*	*1,452,251*	*736,622*	*715,629*
I. VERNACULARS OF TRAVANCORE STATE ..	*3,391,346*	*1,710,724*	*1,680,622*	*1,946,621*	*978,154*	*968,467*	*1,444,725*	*732,570*	*712,155*
1. Malayalam ...	**2,836,728**	1,432,139	1,404,589	**1,591,964**	800,624	791,340	**1,244,764**	631,515	613,249
2. Tamil .. .	**554,618**	278,585	276,033	**354,657**	177,530	177,127	**199,961**	101,055	98,906
II. VERNACULARS OF MADRAS PRESIDENCY	*33,938*	*18,612*	*15,326*	*26,460*	*14,598*	*11,862*	*7,478*	*4,014*	*3,464*
1. Canarese .. .	**1,901**	1,053	848	**1,189**	653	536	**712**	400	312
2. Hindostani .	**4,647**	2,614	2,033	**3,577**	1,953	1,624	**1,070**	661	409
3. Konkani	**11,052**	5,886	5,166	**9,463**	5,118	4,345	**1,589**	768	821
4. Marathi .. .	**6,740**	3,651	3,089	**5,967**	3,264	2,703	**773**	387	386
5. Oriya	**1**	1	...	.	.	...	**1**	1	...
6. Patnuli . .	**1,383**	758	625	**1,381**	756	625	**2**	2	..
7. Telugu	**6,452**	3,460	2,992	**3,574**	1,966	1,608	**2,878**	1,494	1,384
8. Tulu	**1,732**	1,189	573	**1,309**	888	421	**453**	301	152
III. VERNACULARS OF OTHER PROVINCES.	*1,264*	*672*	*592*	*1,216*	*634*	*582*	*48*	*38*	*10*
1. Bengali	**26**	22	4	**25**	21	4	**1**	1	...
2. Gujarati	**810**	407	403	**800**	398	402	**10**	9	1
3. Hindi	**2**	2	...	**2**	2	...	...	...	.
4. Kachchi	**373**	202	176	**373**	202	176	..	...	..
5. Nagari	**27**	22	5	...	...	...	**27**	22	5
6. Panjabi	**1**	1	...	**1**	1	...	...	...	...
7. Sanskrit	**8**	5	3	...	...	..	**8**	5	3
8. Urdu	**12**	11	1	**10**	10	...	**2**	1	1
B. Vernaculars of Asiatic countries Beyond India .	*172*	*116*	*56*	*74*	*43*	*31*	*98*	*73*	*25*
1. Arabic	**136**	84	52	**71**	40	31	**65**	44	21
2. Chinese	**3**	3	..	**1**	1	...	**2**	2	..
3. Singhalese ..	**28**	24	4	**2**	2	...	**26**	22	4
4. Syriac	**5**	5	...	..	..	.	**5**	5	...
C. European Languages ..	*2,255*	*1,239*	*1,016*	*1,783*	*897*	*886*	*472*	*342*	*130*
1. Dutch	**2**	2	.	...	...	.	**2**	2	...
2. English	**2,167**	1,181	986	**1,712**	852	860	**455**	329	126
3. Flemish .. .	**3**	...	3	**3**	...	3	..	...	...
4. French	**1**	1	..	..	...	.	**1**	1	...
5. German	**18**	11	7	**18**	11	7	...	...	.
6. Italian	**5**	3	2	**5**	3	2	...	...	...
7. Latin	**6**	6	...	**6**	6	...	...	...	..
8. Norwegian ..	**8**	2	6	**8**	2	6	...	..	..
9. Portuguese ..	**35**	31	4	**26**	23	3	**9**	8	1
10. Spanish	**3**	2	1	...	...	..	**3**	2	1
11. Swiss	**4**	...	4	**4**	...	4	...	...	..
12. Turkish	**2**	...	2	...	...	...	**2**	...	2
13. Welsh	**1**	...	1	**1**	...	1	...	...	...

TABLE X.

Language.—Part II. Town:

TABLE X.

Language.—TOWNS.

LANGUAGE.	Nagercoil.			Trivandrum.			Shencottah.			Quilon.		
	Persons.	Males.	Females.	Persons.	Males.	Females.	Persons.	Males.	Females.	Persons.	Males.	Females.
1	2	3	4	5	6	7	8	9	10	11	12	13
Total ..	*29,883*	*14,553*	*15,330*	*63,561*	*32,292*	*31,269*	*10,309*	*4,905*	*5,404*	*18,839*	[illegible]	*9,190*
A. Vernaculars of India..	*29,846*	*14,535*	*15,311*	*62,837*	*31,966*	*30,871*	*10,308*	*4,904*	*5,404*	*18,619*	[illegible]	*9,080*
I. Vernaculars of Travancore State .	*27,627*	*13,378*	*14,249*	*57,943*	*29,074*	*28,869*	*9,859*	*4,686*	*5,173*	*17,566*	*8,978*	*8,588*
1. Malayalam ..	**489**	278	211	**36,960**	18,196	18,764	**70**	55	15	**15,099**	7,688	7,411
2. Tamil ..	**27,138**	13,100	14,038	**20,983**	10,878	10,105	**9,783**	4,631	5,159	**2,467**	1,290	1,177
II. Vernaculars of Madras Presidency	*2,211*	*1,149*	*1,062*	*4,615*	*2,750*	*1,865*	*449*	*218*	*231*	*970*	*509*	*461*
1. Canarese ...	**40**	25	15	**375**	206	169	**11**	3	8	**63**	37	26
2 Hindostani	**288**	136	152	**1,514**	900	614	**85**	48	37	**152**	73	79
3. Konkani .	...	..	...	**277**	157	120	...	..	...	**468**	224	244
4. Marathi .	**61**	30	31	**431**	256	175	..	...	...	**99**	45	54
5 Oriya ..	.	..	...	..	...	...	..	..	..	...	.	..
6 Patnuli ..	**1,352**	739	614	**19**	10	9	..	..	..	..	.	..
7. Telugu	**447**	205	242	**1,514**	870	644	**353**	167	186	**171**	113	58
8. Tulu .	**23**	15	8	**485**	351	134	..	...	.	**17**	17	.
III. Vernaculars of Other Provinces .	*8*	*8*	...	*279*	*142*	*137*	..	...	.	*83*	*52*	*31*
1. Bengali ..	**1**	1	...	**10**	6	4	...	..	...	**12**	12	..
2. Gujarati .	...	...	..	**182**	87	95	...	..	.	**66**	38	28
3. Hindi ..	...	...	...	**2**	2	...	...	...	..	...	...	.
4. Kachchi ...	.	...	..	**84**	46	38	..	...	..	**3**	...	3
5. Nagari ..	..	...	.	...	...	..	..	...	..	...	...	.
6 Panjabi .	.	...	..	..	..	..	...	...	...	...	...	..
7. Sanskrit .	...	..	..	..	..	...	...	...	...	..	...	..
8. Urdu .	**7**	7	...	**1**	1	..	...	...	...	**2**	2	...
B. Vernaculars of Asiatic Countries beyond India	*2*	*2*	..	..	..	.	...	...	..	*6*	*5*	*1*
1 Arabic .	**1**	1	...	..	...	.	..	..	..	**5**	4	1
2. Chinese .	..	..	...	..	...	...	...	...	...	**1**	1	...
3. Singhalese .	**1**	1	...	..	..	...	...	...	...	..	...	.
4. Syriac .	...	..	...	..	..	...	..	...	...	...	..	..
C. European languages .	*35*	*16*	*19*	*724*	*326*	*398*	*1*	*1*	..	*214*	*105*	*109*
1. Dutch .	...	...	...	.	..	..	..	...	..	..	..	.
2. English .	**23**	11	12	**711**	323	388	**1**	1	...	**212**	103	109
3. Flemish .	..	..	..	.	..	...	..	..	..	...	...	.
4. French	.	...	...	..	...	...	..	..	...	..	...	..
5. German .	**4**	2	2	**6**	3	3	..	.	..	...	..	..
6. Italian .	**1**	1	...	**2**	...	2	...	..	..	**2**	2	.
7. Latin .	..	..	..	...	.	..	...	...	...	...	...	
8. Norwegian .	**6**	2	4	**2**	..	2	..	...	.	...	..	..
9 Portuguese ..	...	.	...	...	...	...	..	...	..	..	.	.
10. Spanish	..	..	..	...	...	..	.	...	.	.	.	..
11. Swiss ..	**1**	...	1	**3**	.	3	...	..	.	..	..	..
12. Turkish .	..	...	...	..	..	..	..	...	..	..	..	..
13. Welsh .	..	...	..	.	...	...	..	...	..	.	...	..

TABLE X.

Language.—TOWNS.

Kayankulam.			Tiruvalla.			Alleppey.			Kottayam.		
Persons.	Males.	Females.	Persons.	Males.	Females.	Persons.	Males.	Females.	Persons.	Males.	Females.
14	15	16	17	18	19	20	21	22	23	24	25
5,830	*2,772*	*3,058*	***7,969***	*4,268*	*3,701*	***25,665***	*13,370*	*12,295*	***15,141***	*7,863*	*7,278*
5,825	*2,769*	*3,056*	***7,969***	*4,268*	*3,701*	***25,360***	*13,196*	*12,164*	***15,098***	*7,837*	*7,261*
5,030	*2,377*	*2,653*	***7,852***	*4,208*	*3,644*	***21,694***	*11,067*	*10,627*	***14,771***	*7,675*	*7,096*
4,652	2,179	2,473	**7,366**	3,955	3,411	**19,009**	9,658	9,351	**14,135**	7,308	6,827
378	198	180	**486**	253	233	**2,685**	1,409	1,276	**606**	337	269
788	*386*	*402*	***117***	*60*	*57*	***2,892***	*1,736*	*1,156*	***315***	*155*	*160*
7	3	4	**1**	1	...	**15**	9	6	**1**	1	..
20	12	8	**1**	1	...	**824**	422	402	**16**	7	9
13	8	5	**105**	54	51	**944**	496	448	**259**	123	136
730	354	376	..	...	...	**956**	723	233	**26**	16	10
..	.	...	...	..	.	.	.	.	.	.	..
.	...	.	..			.		.	.	..	.
15	8	7	**4**	2	2	**141**	78	63	**13**	8	5
3	1	2	**6**	2	4	**12**	8	4	.	.	.
7	*6*	*1*	..	...	..	***774***	*393*	*381*	***12***	*7*	*5*
.	...	...	..	...	...	..	..	...	.	.	.
.	...	...	...	...	..	**515**	260	255	**4**	4	...
..	.	.	...	..	..	..				.	..
7	6	1	.	...	..	**259**	133	126	.		.
..	.	..	...	..	.	..		.	**5**	.	5
.	...	...	...	..	.	..	.	...	.	.	
..	..	.	..	.	..	..	..		**3**	3	..
..	..	.	..	.	.	..	.	.	.	.	
.	..	..	..	..	...	***14***	*10*	***4***	***16***	*16*	..
.	..	.	..	.		**14**	10	4	**16**	16	.
.	.	..	..	..		.		.		.	.
...	..	..	..	.	...	..	..	..	..	..	.
5	*3*	*2*	...	...	...	***291***	*164*	*127*	***27***	*10*	*17*
5	3	2	..	.	...	**270**	146	124	**25**	8	17
..	...	.	...	...	.	..	..	.			
..	..	..	..	...	..	.	..	.		.	
..	...	..	...	..	..	.	..	..	.		
...	...	..	..	...	..	.	..	.	...	.	
..	...	..	...	...	...	..	...	.	.		
...	...	..	...	...	...	.	.	.	.	..	
..	...	.	...	...	...	**21**	18	3	**2**	2	
...	...	..	..	...	...	...	.	..	.		
..	..	..	.	..		..	..	.	..	.	
.	..	.	.	..	..	.	...	..	..	...	
..	..	.	.	.	.	..	.	..	..	.	.

TABLE X.

Language.—TOWNS (*Concluded*).

LANGUAGE.	CHANGANACHERRY.			ALWAYE.			PARUR.		
	Persons	Males.	Females.	Persons.	Males.	Females.	Persons	Males.	Females.
1	26	27	28	29	30	31	32	33	34
TOTAL ..	***17,242***	*8,826*	*8,416*	***3,869***	*2,103*	*1,766*	***13,782***	*7,067*	*6,715*
A. Vernaculars of India .	***17,234***	*8,818*	*8,416*	***3,863***	*2,100*	*1,763*	***13,749***	*7,046*	*6,703*
I. VERNACULARS OF TRAVANCORE STATE ..	***16,913***	*8,664*	*8,249*	***3,571***	*1,967*	*1,604*	***12,033***	*6,116*	*5,917*
1. Malayalam ...	**15,236**	7,990	7,246	**3,217**	1,819	1,393	**10,140**	4,770	5,370
2. Tamil ..	**1,677**	674	1,003	**354**	148	206	**1,893**	1,346	547
II. VERNACULARS OF MADRAS PRESIDENCY	***321***	*154*	*167*	***292***	*133*	*159*	***1,715***	*929*	*786*
1. Canarese ..	**4**	4	...	...	...	...	**11**	4	7
2. Hindostani ..	**7**	7	...	**27**	14	13	**62**	26	36
3. Konkani .	**238**	103	135	**110**	62	48	**1,541**	839	702
4. Marathi ..	...	...	...	**149**	51	98	**55**	30	25
5. Oriya .	...	...	...	...	...	...	...	...	...
6. Patnuli ..	...	...	...	...	...	...	...	...	...
7. Telugu ..	**70**	38	32	**6**	6	...	**18**	10	8
8. Tulu ...	**2**	2	...	...	...	...	**28**	20	8
III. VERNACULARS OF OTHER PROVINCES ..	...	...	...	...	...	...	***1***	*1*	...
1. Bengali ..	...	...	...	...	...	...	...	...	...
2. Gujarati ..	...	...	...	...	...	...	**1**	1	...
3. Hindi ...	...	...	...	...	...	...	...	...	...
4. Kachchi ...	...	...	...	...	...	...	...	...	...
5. Nagari ..	...	...	...	...	...	...	...	...	...
6. Panjabi ..	...	...	...	...	...	...	...	...	...
7. Sanskrit ...	...	...	...	...	...	...	...	...	...
8. Urdu ...	...	...	...	...	...	...	...	...	...
B.—Vernaculars of Asiatic Countries Beyond India .	***8***	*8*	...	...	...	...	...	...	...
1. Arabic ...	**8**	8	...	...	...	...	...	...	...
2. Chinese ..	...	...	...	...	...	...	...	...	...
3. Singhalese ..	...	...	...	...	...	...	...	...	...
4. Syriac ...	...	...	...	...	...	...	...	...	...
C.—European Languages...	...	...	...	***6***	*3*	*3*	***33***	*21*	*12*
1. Dutch ..	...	...	...	...	...	...	...	...	...
2. English ..	...	...	...	**6**	3	3	**28**	16	12
3. Flemish ..	...	...	...	...	...	...	...	...	...
4. French ..	...	...	...	...	...	...	...	...	...
5. German ..	...	...	...	...	...	...	...	...	...
6. Italian .	...	...	...	...	...	...	...	...	...
7. Latin ...	...	...	...	...	...	...	...	...	...
8. Norwegian ...	...	...	...	...	...	...	...	...	...
9. Portuguese ..	...	...	...	...	...	...	**5**	5	...
10. Spanish ..	...	...	...	...	...	...	...	...	...
11. Swiss ..	...	...	...	...	...	...	...	...	...
12. Turkish ...	...	...	...	...	...	...	...	...	...
13. Welsh ...	...	...	...	...	...	...	...	...	...

TABLE XI.

Birth-Place.

TABLE XI.

Birth-Place.

DISTRICT, STATE, PROVINCE OR COUNTRY WHERE BORN.	WHERE ENUMERATED.								
	STATE TOTAL.			PADMANABHAPURAM.		TRIVANDRUM.		QUILON.	
	Persons.	Males.	Females.	Males.	Females.	Males.	Females.	Males.	Females.
1	2	3	4	5	6	7	8	9	10
State..	***3,428,975***	*1,731,363*	*1,697,612*	*215,313*	*·214,774*	*281,225*	*276,640*	*620,773*	*612,587*
A.—Divisions within Travancore.	***3,367,810***	*1,700,525*	*1,667,285*	*212,132*	*210,876*	*276,739*	*273,251*	*615,728*	*605,993*
Padmanabhapuram ..	**424,105**	213,124	210,981	209,981	208,326	2,528	2,176	310	267
Trivandrum	**550,421**	275,833	274,588	1,701	2,315	271,112	269,687	2,305	2,097
Quilon	**1,224,534**	618,216	606,318	315	165	2,232	1,157	611,177	601,188
Kottayam	**1,131,022**	573,070	557,952	134	70	867	231	1,931	2,430
Devikulam	**37,728**	20,282	17,446	1	...	...	...	5	11
Western Natural Division ...	***1,980,135***	*998,205*	*981,930*	...	...	...	...	...	...
Eastern Natural Division ...	***1,387,675***	*702,320*	*685,355*	...	...	...	...	...	...
B. Provinces, Districts or States in India beyond Travancore.	***60,613***	*30,493*	*30,120*	*3,143*	*3,839*	*4,427*	*3,339*	*4,970*	*6,561*
MADRAS PRESIDENCY.	***59,466***	*29,745*	*29,721*	*3,096*	*3,818*	*4,278*	*3,271*	*4,792*	*6,438*
BRITISH TERRITORY.	***49,511***	*25,211*	*24,300*	*3,028*	*3,770*	*3,966*	*3,072*	*4,293*	*5,997*
Contiguous	***39,548***	*19,505*	*20,043*	*2,725*	*3,603*	*2,670*	*2,298*	*3,388*	*5,317*
Anjengo	**62**	36	26	...	...	26	10	8	16
Coimbatore	**2,982**	1,643	1,339	8	8	114	68	16	20
Madura	**4,568**	2,509	2,059	53	51	102	70	52	107
Tinnevelly	**31,936**	15,317	16,619	2,664	3,544	2,428	2,150	3,312	5,174
Non-Contiguous	***9,963***	*5,706*	*4,257*	*303*	*167*	*1,296*	*774*	*905*	*630*
Anantapur	**1**	...	1	...	...	...	1	...	..
Bellary	**26**	15	11	..	..	7	6	7	5
Chingleput	**720**	357	363	1	...	13	4	2	6
Cuddapah	**16**	14	2	...	...	1	2	...	..
Ganjam	**12**	8	4	...	...	4	...	...	2
Godavari	**30**	25	5	4	..	3	3	4	..
Guntur	**1**	1	...	...	...	1	...	..	..
Kistna	**5**	3	2	...	...	3	2	...	..
Kurnool	**41**	33	8	...	..	15	5	..	1
Madras	**603**	320	283	27	16	121	107	35	40
Malabar .. .	**3,216**	1,761	1,455	29	19	342	224	450	378
Nellore	**42**	18	24	.	..	5	10	1	3
Nilgiris	**252**	139	113	3	1	5	4	2	2
North Arcot	**316**	167	149	..	..	21	16	.	.
Ramnad	**731**	371	360	..	.	..	..	2	2
Salem	**367**	211	156	7	7	19	19	6	11
South Arcot	**160**	92	68	2	1	25	17	6	10
South Canara	**1,670**	1,222	448	175	65	473	180	261	102
Tanjore	**728**	416	312	48	47	163	111	82	71
Trichinopoly	**999**	515	484	7	10	65	57	45	46
Vizagapatam	**27**	18	9	..	1	10	6	2	1
FEUDATORY STATES .	***9,955***	*4,534*	*5,421*	*68*	*48*	*312*	*199*	*400*	*441*
Contiguous. COCHIN	***9,946***	*4,527*	*5,419*	*68*	*48*	*306*	*198*	*499*	*440*
Non-Contiguous. PUDUKOTTAI	***9***	*7*	*2*	..	.	*6*	*1*	.	*1*
Other Provinces and States.	***1,147***	*748*	*399*	*47*	*21*	*149*	*68*	*178*	*123*
BENGAL PRESIDENCY.	***123***	*100*	*23*	*20*	*6*	*7*	*4*	*53*	*7*
BRITISH TERRITORY .	***6***	*4*	*2*	...	..	..	..	..	
Hazaribag . ..	**1**	1	..	..	..	.	.	.	..

TABLE XI.

Birth-Place.—(Continued).

WHERE ENUMERATED.									
KOTTAYAM.		DEVIKULAM.		WESTERN NATURAL DIVISION.			EASTERN NATURAL DIVISION.		
Males.	Females.	Males.	Females.	Persons.	Males.	Females.	Persons.	Males.	Females.
11	12	13	14	15	16	17	18	19	20
576,060	*563,041*	*37,992*	*30,570*	***1,976,154***	*994,326*	*981,828*	***1,452,821***	*737,037*	*715,784*
571,366	*557,388*	*24,560*	*19,777*	***1,957,281***	*985,101*	*972,180*	***1,410,529***	*715,424*	*695,105*
196	142	109	70	...	...	...	...	...	...
492	381	223	108	..	...	...	...	...	...
3,633	[illegible],260	859	548	..	...	..	...	...	...
567,033	553,596	3,105	1,625	..	...	...	..	..	.
12	9	20,264	17,426	...	..	..	...	..	..
..	.	..	...	***1,940,895***	*978,589*	*962,306*	***39,240***	*19,616*	*19,624*
..	...	.	..	***16,386***	*6,512*	*9,874*	***1,371,289***	*695,808*	*675,481*
4,669	*5,650*	*13,284*	*10,731*	***18,630***	*9,099*	*9,531*	***41,983***	*21,394*	*20,589*
4,539	*5,592*	*13,040*	*10,602*	***18,113***	*8,762*	*9,351*	***41,353***	*20,983*	*20,370*
1,857	*1,286*	*12,067*	*10,175*	***12,479***	*6,584*	*5,895*	***37,032***	*18,627*	*18,405*
802	*535*	*9,920*	[illegible]	***8,030***	*3,960*	*4,070*	***31,518***	*15,545*	*15,973*
	.	2	.	**44**	24	20	**18**	12	6
235	158	1,270	1,085	**357**	209	148	**2,625**	1,434	1,191
54	37	2,248	1,794	**335**	164	171	**4,233**	2,345	1,888
513	840	6,400	5,411	**7,294**	3,563	3,731	**24,642**	11,754	12,883
1,055	*751*	*2,147*	*1,885*	***4,449***	*2,624*	*1,825*	***5,514***	*3,082*	*2,432*
.	.	...	..	**1**	..	1	..	..	.
..	.	1	.	**23**	12	11	**3**	3	..
1	2	310	351	**23**	17	11	**692**	340	352
1	..	12	.	**3**	1	2	**13**	13	..
3	2	1	..	**6**	4	2	**6**	4	2
1	2	13	.	**17**	12	5	**13**	13	.
.	..	.	..	.	..	.	**1**	1	..
	.	...	..	**5**	3	2	.		.
1	.	17	2	**21**	15	6	**20**	18	2
16	9	121	111	**314**	170	144	**239**	150	189
583	560	357	274	**1,953**	1,066	897	**1,263**	605	568
..	..	12	11	**18**	5	13	**24**	13	11
12	1	117	105	**9**	6	3	**243**	133	110
1	..	145	133	**36**	20	16	**280**	147	133
1	..	368	358	**3**	1	2	**728**	370	358
26	18	153	101	**68**	30	38	**299**	181	118
3	7	56	33	**59**	32	27	**101**	60	41
309	99	4	2	**1,197**	853	344	**473**	369	104
74	35	49	43	**472**	270	202	**256**	146	110
19	15	379	356	**195**	94	101	**804**	421	383
4	1	2	..	**21**	13	8	**6**	5	1
2,682	*4,306*	*973*	*427*	***5,634***	*2,178*	*3,456*	***4,321***	*2,356*	*1,965*
2,682	*4,306*	*972*	*427*	***5,626***	*2,172*	*3,451*	***4,320***	[illegible]	*1,965*
.	...	*1*	.	***8***	*6*	*2*	***1***	*1*	.
130	*58*	*244*	*129*	***517***	*337*	*180*	***630***	*411*	*219*
6	*2*	*13*	*4*	***91***	*77*	*14*	***32***	*23*	*9*
1	.	*3*	*2*	***1***	*1*	.	***5***	*3*	*2*
.	..	1	.		..		**1**	1	.

TABLE XI.

Birth-Place.—*(Continued)*.

DISTRICT, STATE PROVINCE OR COUNTRY WHERE BORN.	WHERE ENUMERATED.								
	State Total.			Padmanabhapuram.		Trivandrum.		Quilon.	
	Persons.	Males.	Females.	Males.	Females	Males.	Females.	Males	Females.
1	2	3	4	5	6	7	8	9	10
Midnapur	2	1	1	...	...	.	..	...	...
Orissa	1	1	..	...	.	.	.	..	..
24 Parganas	2	1	1	.	.	.	..		..
Districts Unspecified	*117*	*96*	*21*	*20*	*6*	*7*	*4*	*53*	*7*
BOMBAY PRESIDENCY	*197*	*92*	*105*	*7*	*1*	*13*	*11*	*55*	*81*
British Territory	*36*	*17*	*19*	..	.	...	.	*15*	*17*
Ahmedabad	2	.	2	..	.	...	...	..	.
Dharwar	1	1	...	..	..	...	.		.
Poona	9	5	4	.	...	...	...	5	4
Ratnagiri	1	1	...	..	...	..	.	.	..
Satara	23	10	13	...	..		...	10	18
Feudatory States	*26*	*11*	*15*	...	...	..	...	*10*	*15*
Cutch	18	5	13	...	...	...	...	5	13
Kathiawar	4	4	...	...	...	...	...	3	.
Kolhapur	4	2	2	...	...	..	...	2	2
Districts Unspecified	*135*	*64*	*71*	*7*	*1*	*13*	*11*	*30*	*49*
BURMA ...	*22*	*11*	*11*	...	...	*1*	..	*1*	..
CENTRAL PROVINCES AND BERAR	*41*	*36*	*5*	...	..	*33*	*4*	...	...
Mandla	1	...	1	...	..	...	...	..	...
Districts Unspecified	*40*	*36*	*4*	..	...	*33*	*4*	..	...
COORG	*1*	...	*1*	...	...	...	*1*	...	...
EASTERN BENGAL AND ASSAM	*3*	*2*	*1*	...	...	...	...	*1*	...
Dacca	1	1	...	...	...	...	...	1	...
Districts Unspecified	*2*	*1*	*1*	...	...	...	...	...	...
NORTH WEST FRONTIER PROVINCE	*8*	*7*	*1*	...	...	*7*	*1*	...	..
PUNJAB	*39*	*19*	*20*	*1*	*1*	*8*	*1*	*1*	...
British, Territory	*9*	*8*	*1*	*1*	...	...	*1*	...	..
Delhi	1	1	...	...	...	...	...	...	...
Ferozepur	1	1	...	...	...	..	...	...	...
Gujrat	7	6	1	1	...	...	1	...	...
Feudatory States.	*1*	*1*	...	..	...	...	...	..	...
Bashahr	1	1	...	...	...	...	...	...	...
Districts Unspecified	*29*	*10*	*19*	...	*1*	*8*	..	*1*	..
UNITED PROVINCES OF AGRA AND OUDH	*59*	*37*	*22*	*3*	*3*	*5*	*2*	*20*	*4*
Allahabad	4	3	1	..	...	...	...	2	1
Benares	12	10	2	1	...	5	2	4	...
Saharanpur	1	1	...	...	...	...	...	...	...
Districts Unspecified	*42*	*23*	*19*	*2*	*3*	...	...	*14*	*3*

TABLE XI.

Birth-Place.—*(Continued)*.

WHERE ENUMERATED.									
KOTTAYAM.		DEVIKULAM.		WESTERN NATURAL DIVISION.			EASTERN NATURAL DIVISION.		
Males.	Females.	Males.	Females.	Persons.	Males.	Females.	Persons.	Males.	Females.
11	12	13	14	15	16	17	18	19	20
...	.	1	1	...	...	...	2	1	1
1	...	..	...	1	1	...	...	...	..
...	...	1	1	...	...	...	2	1	1
7	2	9	2	90	76	14	27	20	7
12	6	5	6	99	36	63	98	56	42
...	...	2	2	...	...	...	36	17	19
...	...	..	2	...	...	...	2	...	2
...	...	1	...	...	...	...	1	1	..
..	...	...	...	..	...	...	9	5	4
.	...	1	...	...	...	...	1	1	..
...	...	...	...	...	...	...	23	10	13
1	...	...	...	18	5	13	8	6	2
...	...	..	...	18	5	13	...	...	...
1	...	...	..	...	...	...	4	4	..
...	...	...	...	...	...	...	4	2	2
11	6	3	4	81	31	50	34	33	21
...	...	9	11	2	2	...	20	9	11
...	...	3	1	37	33	4	4	3	1
...	...	...	1	...	...	...	1	...	1
...	...	3	...	37	33	4	3	3	...
...	...	...	...	1	...	1	...	...	...
...	...	1	1	1	1	...	2	1	1
...	...	...	...	1	1	...	...	...	...
...	...	1	1	...	...	...	2	1	1
...	...	...	...	8	7	1	...	...	...
...	...	14	18	6	6	1	33	14	19
...	...	7	...	1	1	...	8	7	1
...	...	1	...	...	...	...	1	1	...
...	...	1	...	...	...	...	1	1	..
...	...	5	...	1	1	...	6	5	1
...	...	1	...	...	...	...	1	1	...
...	...	1	...	...	...	...	1	1	...
...	...	6	18	5	4	1	24	6	18
1	...	8	13	16	12	4	43	25	18
1	...	...	...	4	3	1	...	...	...
...	...	...	..	6	6	...	6	4	2
...	...	1	...	...	...	...	1	1	...
...	...	7	13	6	3	3	36	20	16

TABLE XI.

Birth-Place.—*(Continued).*

DISTRICT, STATE PROVINCE OR COUNTRY WHERE BORN.	WHERE ENUMERATED								
	STATE TOTAL.			PADMANABHAPURAM.		TRIVANDRUM.		QUILON.	
	Persons.	Males.	Females.	Males.	Females.	Males	Females.	Males.	Females.
1	2	3	4	5	6	7	8	9	10
FEUDATORY STATES AND AGENCIES ...	*369*	*227*	*142*	*15*	*8*	*73*	*43*	*27*	*25*
BARODA ...	4	2	2	..	.	1	1	1	1
CENTRAL INDIA AGENCY. Indore	1	1	..	.	..	..	..	.	..
HYDERABAD	67	44	23	6	1	11	4	15	13
KASHMIR	1	1		.	.	..	..	1	
MYSORE ...	281	171	110	7	5	60	85	10	11
RAJPUTANA AGENCY.	*15*	*8*	*7*	*2*	*2*	*1*	..	.	..
Jaipur	2	1	1	1	1		.	..	..
UNSPECIFIED	13	7	6	1	1	1		..	.
FRENCH SETTLEMENTS	*85*	*49*	*36*	..	.	*1*	*1*	*1*	.
Mahe	53	34	19		..	.	..	..	.
Pondichery ...	32	15	17	...	..	1	1	1	..
PORTUGUESE SETTLEMENTS.									
Goa ...	*65*	*57*	*8*	..	..	*6*	...	*19*	*6*
INDIA UNSPECIFIED	*135*	*111*	*24*	*1*	*2*	...	..	..	..
C. Countries in Asia Beyond India	*229*	*146*	*83*	*16*	*22*	*22*	*17*	*31*	*10*
Afghanistan	6	3	3	..	.	1		2	3
Arabia ...	7	6	1	.		3	1	3	..
Ceylon	206	127	79	16	22	16	16	19	7
China	1	1	..	...	.	.	.	1	..
Japan ...	1	1	.	..	...	.	.	1	..
Nepal ...	1	1	..	.	.	.	.	...	..
Straits Settlements	2	2	..	...	..	2	.	...	..
Turkey in Asia	5	5	..	.	..	..	.	5	...
D. Countries in Europe. ...	*312*	*191*	*121*	*19*	*34*	*35*	*33*	*44*	*23*
UNITED KINGDOM	*237*	*160*	*77*	*11*	*15*	*29*	*19*	*38*	*16*
England and Wales	174	118	56	9	12	21	15	26	10
Scotland	48	35	13	2	2	7	4	10	..
Ireland ...	15	7	8	..	1	1	..	2	6
Austria-Hungary	3	2	1	..	..	2	1	...	..
Belgium	21	5	16	2	16	3	...	...	..
Denmark	2	..	2	..	..	..	...	...	..
France	2	1	1	..	..	..	..	.	.
Germany	11	4	7	2	..	..	4	..	3
Holland	1	1	..	..	.	.	..	..	..
Iceland	1	1	.	.	...	.		...	..
Italy	5	4	1	1		1	1	2	
Norway ...	2	..	2	..	.	.	2	..	..
Portugal ...	2	2	...	..	..	..	..	..	..
Spain	1	1	.	...	..	..	..	..	..
Sweden	3	1	2	1	2	..	..	...	.
Switzerland	9	...	9	..	1	..	6		2
EUROPE UNSPECIFIED	12	9	3	2	..	.	.	4	2
E. Africa ...	*1*	*1*	..	..	..	..	...	..	..
F America	*9*	*6*	*3*	*3*	*3*	*1*	...	.	..
G Australasia	*1*	*1*	..	..	.	*1*	..	.	..
H. At Sea	...	...		..	..	.	.	.	..

TABLE XI.

Birth-Place.—(*Concluded*).

WHERE ENUMERATED									
Kottayam.		Devikulam.		Western Natural Division.			Eastern Natural Division.		
Males.	Females.	Males.	Females	Persons.	Males.	Females.	Persons.	Males.	Females.
11	12	13	14	15	16	17	18	19	20
6	*1*	*106*	*65*	***142***	*85*	*57*	***227***	*142*	*85*
..	..	.	..	**2**	1	1	**2**	1	1
	.	1	.	...	...	..	**1**	1	..
1	..	11	5	**28**	19	9	**39**	25	14
..	.	..	.	**1**	1	..	..	.	.
5	1	89	55	**108**	62	46	**173**	109	61
..	...	*5*	*5*	***3***	*2*	*1*	***12***	*6*	*6*
..	..	.	.	**2**	1	1	.	..	..
.	.	5	5	**1**	1	...	**12**	6	6
40	*25*	*7*	*10*	***20***	*16*	*4*	***65***	*33*	*32*
32	19	2	.	**17**	14	8	**36**	20	16
8	6	5	10	**3**	2	1	**29**	18	16
32	*2*	...	...	***40***	*33*	*7*	***35***	*25*	*1*
31	*22*	*79*	...	***54***	*30*	*24*	***81***	*81*	...
11	...	*66*	*34*	***75***	*48*	*32*	***154***	*103*	*51*
..	...	.	...	**8**	8	8	.	.	..
.	..	.	..	**6**	5	1	**1**	1	
11	..	65	84	**59**	81	28	**147**	93	51
..	..	..	..	**1**	1	..	.	..	..
..	..	.	..	**1**	1	.	..	.	..
..	.	1	.	..	..	..	**1**	1	..
.	...	...	...	**2**	2	..	..	..	..
...	...	...	..	...	..	..	**5**	5	..
14	*3*	*79*	*28*	***160***	*78*	*82*	***152***	*113*	*39*
6	*2*	*76*	*25*	***98***	*56*	*42*	***139***	*104*	*35*
6	2	56	17	**70**	40	30	**104**	78	26
...	..	16	7	**20**	14	6	**28**	21	7
...	..	4	1	**8**	2	6	**7**	5	2
...	..	...	...	**3**	2	1	..	.	...
...	..		..	**19**	3	16	**2**	2	...
.	...	.	2	..		..	**2**	.	2
	.	1	1	.	..	.	**2**	1	1
2	.	..	..	**11**	4	7	...	.	...
1	..	.	.	**1**	1	.	..	..	...
...		1	..	..	..	.	**1**	1	..
..	...	...	...	**5**	4	1	...	...	...
..	..	..	..	**2**	..	2	...	..	...
2	..	...	.	**2**	2	.	.	..	..
1	.	.	.	..	..	.	**1**	1	..
.	.	..	.	**3**	1	2		..	...
.	..	..		**9**	.	9	..	...	..
2	1	1	..	**7**	5	2	**5**	4	1
..	...	*1*	..	...	..	.	***1***	*1*	..
..	...	*2*	..	***7***	*4*	*3*	***2***	*2*	...
...	..	...	.	***1***	*1*	..	...	..	...
...	..	...	..	...	..	.	...	..	..

TABLE XII.

Infirmities.—Part I. Distribution by Age.

TABLE XII.

Infirmities.—Distribution by Age.

AGE.	POPULATION AFFLICTED.															AFFECTED WITH ELEPHANTIASIS.		
	TOTAL.			INSANE.			DEAF-MUTES.			BLIND.			LEPERS.					
	Persons	Males.	Females.	Persons.	Males.	Females.	Persons.	Males.	Females.	Persons.	Males.	Females	Persons.	Males.	Females.	Persons.	Males.	Females.
1	2	3	4	5	6	7	8	9	10	11	12	13	14	15	16	17	18	19
TOTAL	*3,953*	*2,508*	*1,445*	*628*	*349*	*279*	*993*	*588*	*405*	*1,217*	*724*	*493*	*1,115*	*847*	*268*	*4,217*	*2,393*	*1,824*
0—1	**8**	2	6			.	**1**	..	1	**8**	1	5	**1**	1	..		.	..
1—2	**15**	7	8				**3**	2	1	**10**	4	6	**2**	1	1	.	. .	.
2—3	**18**	10	8				**5**	3	2	**11**	6	5	**2**	1	1		. .	
3—4	**23**	15	11	**1**	1		**12**	5	7	**9**	7	2	**4**	2	2	.		.
4—5	**31**	20	11	**1**	1	.	**17**	12	5	**9**	5	4	**4**	2	2	..		
Total 0—5	*98*	*54*	*44*	*2*	*2*	.	*38*	*22*	*16*	*45*	*23*	*22*	*13*	*7*	*6*	.	..	.
5—10	**203**	121	82	**10**	7	3	**93**	50	43	**92**	56	36	**8**	8	..	**16**	10	6
10—15	**247**	142	105	**8**	5	3	**117**	66	51	**87**	44	43	**35**	27	8	**50**	23	27
15—20	**287**	171	116	**22**	15	7	**130**	79	51	**81**	47	34	**54**	30	24	**199**	101	98
20—25	**328**	218	110	**41**	28	13	**115**	79	36	**89**	56	33	**83**	55	28	**353**	188	165
25—30	**425**	266	159	**72**	39	33	**128**	71	57	**88**	60	28	**137**	96	41	**475**	268	207
30—35	**377**	231	146	**83**	47	89	**64**	39	25	**91**	53	38	**103**	82	24	**444**	239	205
35—40	**395**	260	135	**99**	53	46	**74**	43	31	**93**	59	34	**129**	105	24	**604**	387	217
40—45	**373**	242	131	**87**	47	40	**52**	34	18	**94**	51	43	**140**	110	30	**516**	305	211
45—50	**325**	219	107	**70**	32	38	**51**	30	21	**82**	55	27	**123**	102	21	**408**	213	195
50—55	**264**	175	89	**39**	20	19	**47**	27	20	**80**	53	27	**93**	75	23	**475**	261	214
55—60	**221**	159	62	**23**	16	12	**29**	21	8	**79**	52	27	**85**	70	15	**293**	160	133
60—65	**200**	127	73	**30**	18	12	**25**	13	12	**92**	51	41	**53**	45	8	**222**	123	99
65—70	**95**	51	44	**13**	7	9	**12**	5	7	**41**	20	21	**25**	19	7	**101**	69	32
70 and over	**144**	82	62	**13**	13	5	**18**	9	9	**83**	44	39	**25**	16	9	**61**	46	15

TABLE XII.

Infirmities.—Part II. Distribution by Divisions.

TABLE XII.

Infirmities.—Distribution by Divisions.

DIVISION.	POPULATION AFFLICTED.															AFFECTED WITH ELEPHANTIASIS.		
	TOTAL.			INSANE.			DEAF-MUTES.			BLIND.			LEPERS.					
	Persons.	Males.	Females.	Persons.	Males.	Females.	Persons.	Males.	Females.	Persons.	Males.	Females.	Persons.	Males.	Females.	Persons.	Males.	Females.
1	2	3	4	5	6	7	8	9	10	11	12	13	14	15	16	17	18	19
STATE ...	***3,953***	***2,508***	***1,445***	***628***	***349***	***279***	***993***	***588***	***405***	***1,217***	***724***	***493***	***1,115***	***847***	***268***	***4,217***	***2,393***	***1,824***
I. PADMANABHAPURAM ...	**582**	367	215	**72**	30	42	**155**	89	66	**200**	119	81	**155**	129	26	..	..	..
II. TRIVANDRUM ...	**749**	509	240	**210**	130	80	**147**	93	54	**155**	90	65	**237**	196	41	**5**	2	3
III. QUILON ...	**1,239**	783	456	**172**	91	81	**332**	196	136	**343**	205	138	**392**	291	101	**236**	142	94
IV. KOTTAYAM ...	**1,307**	789	518	**163**	89	74	**334**	190	144	**497**	292	205	**313**	218	95	**3,973**	2,246	1,727
V. DEVIKULAM ...	**76**	60	16	**11**	9	2	**25**	20	5	**22**	18	4	**18**	13	5	**3**	3	...
A.-Western Natural Division ..	***2,156***	*1,425*	*731*	***376***	*214*	*162*	***501***	*298*	*203*	***548***	*337*	*211*	***731***	*576*	*155*	***4,192***	*2,378*	*1,814*
B.-Eastern Natural Division ...	***1,797***	*1,083*	*714*	***252***	*135*	*117*	***492***	*290*	*202*	***669***	*387*	*282*	***384***	*271*	*113*	***25***	*15*	*10*

TABLE XII A.

Infirmities by Castes, Tribes or Races.

TABLE XII A.

Infirmities by Castes, Tribes or Races.

CASTE, TRIBE OR RACE.	POPULATION DEALT WITH.			POPULATION AFFLICTED.												AFFECTED WITH ELEPHANTIASIS.		
				INSANE.			DEAF-MUTES.			BLIND.			LEPERS.					
	Persons.	Males.	Females.	Persons.	Males.	Females.	Persons.	Males.	Females.	Persons.	Males.	Females.	Persons.	Males.	Females.	Persons.	Males.	Females.
1	2	3	4	5	6	7	8	9	10	11	12	13	14	15	16	17	18	19
HINDU.	*2,188,467*	*1,097,452*	*1,091,015*	*370*	*211*	*159*	*658*	*396*	*262*	*850*	*479*	*371*	*690*	*527*	*163*	*3,040*	*1,694*	*1,346*
Alavan	870	448	422	...	...	...	...	..	...	4	4	..	...	..	...	...	...	..
Ampattan	21,823	10 996	10,830	2	..	2	13	11	2	6	3	3	6	3	3	23	16	10
Asāri	62,882	31,804	31,078	12	10	2	23	15	8	26	14	12	24	19	5	59	27	32
Brahman Malayala Potti	5,220	2,979	2,241	9	7	2	4	1	3	14	7	7	.	...	.	2	1	1
,, Tamil	40,335	20,769	19,566	14	12	2	23	16	7	17	11	6	10	8	2	16	11	5
,, Telugu	916	485	431	1	1	..	...	.	...	..	..	..	..	..	..	..	...	...
,, Tulu	3,053	2,058	995	1	1	...	.	.	..	.	.		..	...	..	..	...	...
Chakkāla	18,074	8,937	9,137	..	...	..	6	3	3	10	9	1	8	7	1	3	1	2
Chānnān	168,195	84,638	81,557	39	22	17	59	39	20	69	39	30	35	31	4	...	..	...
Cheṭṭi	20,881	10,535	10,346	4	2	2	11	10	1	7	3	4	4	3	1	9	..	9
Gosayi	209	123	86	2	2	...	..	.	..	..	..	..	..	..	...	...	..	.
Ilayatu	4,349	2,284	2,065	1	..	1	3	1	2	1	1	..	...	..	..	1	1	..
Īṭayan	6,835	3,408	3,427	1	1	..	2	1	1		.	...	4	3	1	..	..	.
Īzhavan	546,235	271,677	274,588	108	52	56	144	84	60	159	76	83	153	119	34	1,931	1,083	873
Īzhavatti	6,671	3,211	3,460	2	2	.	.		...	1	...	1	3	2	1	...	...	...
Kākkalan	830	451	409	...	...	.		.	.	..	.	...	...	..	..	1	..	1
Kallan	1,039	633	406	.	.	..	.	.	..		...		3	3	..	.	..	...
Kallāsāri	7,992	4,051	3,941	...	..	..	2	.	2	6	3	3	4	4	.	.	.	..
Kammalan	16,805	8,516	8,289	2	1	1	9	7	2	7	1	6	10	10			..	...
Kaniyān	11,987	6,155	5,832	1	..	1	3	2	1	6	3	3	3	3	...	49	7	42
Kannan	3,951	2,057	1,894	.	.	...	2	.	2	.	.	.	1	..	1	.	.	.
Kāvati	5,943	3,055	2,891	1	..	1	5	3	2	2	2		.		..	.	.	.
Kollan	23,659	13,387	13,272	2	1	1	9	5	4	23	18	5	9	5	4	39	14	25
Konkani	10,219	5,356	4,833	5	2	3	2	2		1	1	...	2	2		.	.	
Krishnanvaka	10,429	5,309	5,120	2	1	1	5	3	2	1	1	..	7	7	.	.		..

TABLE XII A.

Infirmities by Castes, Tribes or Races.—(*Continued*).

CASTE, TRIBE OR RACE.	POPULATION DEALT WITH.			POPULATION AFFLICTED.												AFFECTED WITH ELEPHANTIASIS.		
				INSANE.			DEAF-MUTES.			BLIND.			LEPERS.					
	Persons.	Males.	Females.	Persons.	Males.	Females.	Persons.	Males.	Females.	Persons.	Males.	Females	Persons.	Males.	Females	Persons.	Males.	Females.
1	2	3	4	5	6	7	8	9	10	11	13	13	14	15	16	17	18	19
Kshatriya	**1,165**	532	633	.		.				**1**	1		.			.	..	.
Kudumi	**8,207**	4,363	3,844	.	..		.						.			**29**	22	7
Kuravan	**61,827**	30,183	31,644	**2**	1	1	**10**	6	4	**21**	10	11	**27**	14	13	**4**	4	.
Kurukkal	**1,374**	711	663	..		..	.	...	..	.				.		**1**	1	...
Mannān	**9,946**	5,014	4,932	**1**	1	.	**1**	1		**3**	2	1	**3**	2	1	**6**	2	4
Marakkān	**14,604**	7,274	7,330	.		.	**3**	2	1	**5**	4	1	**5**	3	2	**29**	17	12
Mārān	**29,318**	14,661	14,657	**2**	1	1	**4**	3	1	**13**	8	5	**7**	5	2	**12**	7	5
Nāikkan . ..	**2,729**	1,459	1,270	..		.	**1**	1					..		.		.	...
Nampiyār . ..	**828**	422	406	**1**	1		**1**	1					..		.	..		..
Nāyar	**592,489**	295,703	296,786	**97**	64	33	**175**	100	75	**244**	151	90	**203**	168	35	**479**	274	205
Pānan	**3,316**	1,679	1,637	**1**	1	.	**1**		1						.	**2**	2	..
Pantāram	**13,784**	7,015	6,769	..	.		**5**	1	4	**1**		1	**1**	1		**1**	1	..
Paravan .. .	**9,313**	4,648	4,665	**5**	2	3	**3**	2	1	**5**	3	2	**1**	1	..		..	..
Parayan .. .	**70,554**	35,131	35,423	**13**	5	8	**25**	14	11	**36**	16	20	**16**	11	5	**11**	5	6
Pilāppalli .	**73**	34	39	..			.				.		.		...	**4**	4	..
Pulayan	**185,314**	93,335	91,979	**18**	6	12	**42**	22	20	**88**	46	42	**81**	49	32	**51**	33	13
Pushpakan ..	**1,925**	1,012	913	.			**2**	1	1	**1**	.	1	**1**	.	1	**1**	1	.
Sāliyan	**9,919**	4.953	4,966	...	.	.	**4**	2	2	**3**	2	1	**3**	3	.	**58**	33	25
Talavan	**1,889**	931	958	**1**		1	**1**	1		.	..		**2**	2				
Tantān	**21,641**	10,836	10,805	**2**	1	1	**7**	6	1	**5**	4	1	**10**	10			.	
Tattān	**21,350**	10,718	10,632	**5**	4	1	**7**	5	2	**10**	7	3	**5**	4	1	**14**	10	4
Ullātan . ..	**3,974**	2,129	1,845	..			**5**	2	3	**2**	1	1				**20**	12	8
Vairāvi	**1,455**	704	751				**1**	1			..		.			.		..
Valan	**16,748**	8,588	8,160	.			**1**		1	**1**	.	1			.	**52**	31	21
Vālan	**525**	275	250	**1**	.	1	**6**	4	2	**12**	10	2	**7**	2	5	**2**	1	1
Valluvan	**982**	505	477	..			..	..	..	**4**	4	..		.			.	.
Vāniyan	**16,235**	8,115	8,120	.			**6**	4	2	**2**		2	**5**	5		**13**	9	4
Vannān	**2,690**	1,272	1,418	**1**	1		..			**1**		1	,	.	.	.	.	...
Vāriyar	**2,769**	1,411	1,358	**2**	1	1			.	**4**	2	2	**3**	2	1	**1**	1	..
Vēlan	**12,957**	6,350	6,607	**1**	..	1	**3**	1	2	**2**		2	**3**	1	2	**41**	38	3
Vēlān	**5,782**	2,931	2,851	..	.		**3**	3	.	**6**		6	**2**	2		.		..
Vellāla .. .	**49,479**	24,774	24,705	**6**	4	2	**10**	5	5	**15**	6	9	**16**	12	4	**17**	4	13

TABLE XII A.

Infirmities by Castes, Tribes or Races.—(*Concluded*).

CASTE, TRIBE OR RACE.	POPULATION DEALT WITH.			POPULATION AFFLICTED.												AFFECTED WITH ELEPHANTIASIS.		
				INSANE.			DEAF-MUTES.			BLIND.			LEPERS.					
	Persons.	Males.	Females.	Persons.	Males.	Females	Persons.	Males.	Females.	Persons.	Males.	Females.	Persons.	Males.	Females.	Persons.	Males.	Females.
1	2	3	4	5	6	7	8	9	10	11	12	13	14	15.	16	17	18	19
Veluttedan	**11,358**	5,718	5,638	**2**	1	1	**6**	5	1	**4**	3	1	**3**	1	2	**26**	11	15
Vettuvan	**1,482**	744	738	...	..	..	...	...	...	**1**	..	1	.	.	...	.	.	
MUSALMAN ...	***205,362***	***104,952***	***100,410***	***30***	***18***	***12***	***63***	***33***	***30***	***68***	***46***	***22***	***79***	***58***	***21***	***201***	***119***	***82***
Ārab	**94**	52	42	...	..	...	..	..	..	**1**	1	..	**1**	1	.	..	.	.
Jōnakan	**57,031**	29,415	27,616	**8**	8	.	**15**	12	3	**18**	8	10	**19**	13	6	**125**	69	56
Kach	**325**	187	138	...	..	..	**1**	1	...	**1**	1	.	..		.		.	...
Khān	**182**	106	76	**1**	1	...	...	..	...	**2**	2	...	**1**	1	..	**5**	2	3
Labbai	**14,694**	7,281	7,413	...	..	..	...	..	...	...	..	..	...	..	..	**1**	1	.
Mēttan	**66,864**	33,768	33,096	**5**	3	2	**15**	7	8	**17**	13	4	**25**	18	7	**44**	31	13
Mughal	**483**	272	211	...	.	..	**1**	...	1	.	.	..	..	..	.		...	...
Osta	**1,029**	528	501	...	..	..	..	..	..	...	..	..	**1**	1	..	..	.	...
Shiekh	**3,565**	1,926	1,639	**4**	...	4	**6**	4	2	**7**	5	2	**11**	8	3	**24**	14	10
Tulukkan	**61,095**	31,417	29,678	**12**	6	6	**25**	9	16	**22**	16	6	**21**	16	5	**2**	2	...
CHRISTIAN ..	***903,469***	***460,915***	***442,554***	***225***	***119***	***106***	***261***	***156***	***105***	***294***	***198***	***96***	***326***	***251***	***75***	***972***	***576***	***396***
Anglo-Indian	**1,750**	911	839	...	...	...	**3**	2	1	...	.	...	**1**	1	..	**4**	1	3
Indian Christian ...	**901,719**	460,004	441,715	**225**	119	106	**258**	154	104	**294**	198	96	**325**	250	75	**968**	575	393
ANIMISTIC ...	***12,694***	***6,558***	***6,136***	***3***	***1***	***2***	***11***	***3***	***8***	***5***	***1***	***4***	***20***	***11***	***9***	***3***	***3***	...
Kānikkāran ...	**4,034**	2,166	1,868	**1**	..	1	**5**	1	4	**3**	...	3	**11**	7	4	..	..	..
Malankuravan ...	**997**	514	483	...	..	...	..	..	..	...	..	...	...	...	.	**3**	3	.
Malayarayan ..	**2,612**	1,294	1,318	**2**	1	1	**6**	2	4	**2**	1	1	**5**	1	4	.	..	
Malavētan	**5,051**	2,584	2,467	...	...	...	...	...	...	...	...	...	**4**	3	1	..	.	.
JEW	***73***	***53***	***20***	...	...	...	...	...	..	...	..	...	...	...	...	***1***	***1***	..

TABLE XIII.

Castes, Tribes, Races or Nationalities.
Part A.—Hindu.

TABLE XIII.

Castes, Tribes, Races or Nationalities. Part A.—Hindu.

CASTE. TRIBE, RACE OR NATIONALITY.	State Total.			Padmanabhapuram.		Trivandrum.		Quilon.	
	Persons.	Males.	Females.	Males.	Females.	Males.	Females.	Males.	Females.
1	2	3	4	5	6	7	8	9	10
HINDU ..	*2,282,617*	*1,145,511*	*1,137,106*	*148,134*	*148,286*	*213,315*	*210,594*	*438,137*	*439,468*
1. Ampattan	**21,828**	10,996	10,830	1,226	1,175	2,595	2,666	3,907	4,008
2. Āsāri	**62,882**	31,804	31,078	2,422	2,406	7,192	7,087	12,324	12,094
3. Brahman Gauda ..	**120**	86	34	3	2	62	16	8	8
4. ,, Kanarese ..	**291**	148	143	8	8	132	126	5	9
5. ,, Maharatta...	**603**	332	271	31	26	231	193	55	82
6. ,, Malayala Potti.	**5,220**	2,979	2,241	91	40	480	408	1,784	1,404
7 ,, Namputiri .	**5,105**	2,862	2,243	4	5	75	12	122	91
8. ,, Tamil ..	**40,335**	20,769	19,566	3,654	3,991	6,335	5,941	6,105	5,566
9. ,, Telugu .	**916**	485	431	125	134	205	174	128	107
10. ,, Tulu ...	**3,053**	2,058	995	272	72	629	363	584	307
11. Chakkāla	**18,074**	8,937	9,137	1,712	1,816	2,242	2,289	4,519	4,589
12. Chānnān (Shanan) ...	**166,195**	84,639	81,557	63,412	61,785	18,691	17,293	1,435	1,542
13. Chavalakkāran ..	**1,661**	802	859	383	508	13	17	178	191
14. Chāyakkāran	**3,294**	1,690	1,604	427	439	425	363	722	721
15. Chetti	**20.881**	10,535	10,346	2,551	2,724	1,649	1,686	4,156	4,243
16. Ilavāniyan	**6,116**	3,055	3,061	293	268	343	357	2,248	2,377
17. Ilayatu	**4.349**	2,284	2,065	3	..	22	19	755	718
18. Itayan	**6,835**	3,408	3,427	1,905	1,968	437	504	908	870
19. Īzhavan	**546 235**	271 677	274.588	3,034	2,934	42,475	42,527	113,942	114,992
20. Īzhavātti	**6,671**	3,211	3,460	34	35	751	851	1,522	1,671
21. Kallasāri	**7,992**	4,051	3,941	67	54	79	64	1,558	1,406
22. Kammālan	**16,805**	8,516	8,289	3,741	3,920	3,766	3,454	840	806
23. Kaniyān	**11,937**	6,155	5,832	143	123	679	657	2,647	2,547
24. Kannān	**3,951**	2,057	1,894	105	130	209	178	1,066	1,005
25. Kavati	**5,946**	3,055	2,891	2,577	2,466	475	423	3	2
26. Kollan	**26,659**	13,387	13.272	533	479	948	928	5,263	5,131
27. Konkani	**10,219**	5,356	4,863	2	...	117	99	2,270	2,194
28. Krishnanvaka	**10,429**	5,309	5,120	5,217	5,082	90	68	..	..
29. Kshatriya (Malayala)	**2,025**	1,067	958	..	...	98	43	529	495
30. Kudumi	**8,207**	4,363	3,844	..	...	135	99	807	657
31. Kuravan	**61.827**	30,183	31,644	154	146	7,283	7,674	22,383	23,426
32. Kurukkal	**1.374**	711	663	51	54	258	250	263	274
33. Kusavan	**3,307**	1,703	1,604	573	556	293	305	488	451

TABLE XIII.

Castes, Tribes, Races or Nationalities. Part A.—Hindu. *(Continued).*

Kottayam.		Devikulam.		Western Natural Division.			Eastern Natural Division.		
Males.	Females.	Males.	Females	Persons.	Males.	Females.	Persons.	Males.	Females.
11	12	13	14	15	16	17	18	19	20
322,027	*316,956*	*23,898*	*19,803*	***1,417,412***	*703,447*	*707,965*	***865,205***	*436,064*	*429,141*
3,074	2,796	194	185	**11,510**	5,751	5,759	**10,318**	5,245	5,071
9,573	9,210	288	281	**32,836**	16,642	16,194	**30,043**	15,162	14,884
13	8	...	...	**110**	80	30	**10**	6	4
3	.	..	...	**277**	144	133	**14**	4	10
13	18	2	2	**564**	315	249	**39**	17	22
601	380	14	..	**2,875**	1,670	1,205	**2,345**	1,309	1,036
2,686	2,124	25	11	**893**	541	352	**4,212**	2,321	1,891
4,596	4,008	79	40	**27,524**	14,221	13,303	**12,811**	6,548	6,263
18	16	9	.	**659**	349	310	**257**	136	121
573	258	..	...	**2,123**	1,433	689	**928**	622	306
431	407	83	36	**13,291**	6,584	6,707	**4,733**	2,358	2,430
33	12	1,017	935	**133,801**	68,254	65,547	**32,394**	16,384	16,010
77	77	151	66	**430**	204	276	**1,131**	598	583
88	78	28	9	**2,043**	1,049	994	**1,251**	641	610
1 488	1,258	741	440	**12,122**	5,989	6,133	**8,759**	4,543	4,213
7	6	167	53	**1,087**	548	539	**5,029**	2,507	2,522
1,469	1,318	35	10	**1,419**	747	672	**2,930**	1,537	1,393
46	67	27	18	**3,697**	1,790	1,907	**3,138**	1,618	1,520
110,353	112,655	1,843	1,480	**383,784**	189,394	194,390	**162,481**	82,283	80,198
904	908	...	...	**4,537**	2,139	2,398	**2,134**	1,072	1,062
2,307	2,404	40	13	**1,931**	1,005	926	**6,061**	3,046	3,015
163	106	6	3	**12,934**	6,479	6,455	**3,871**	2,037	1,834
2,627	2,459	59	46	**5,441**	2,841	2,600	**6,546**	3,314	3,232
660	536	17	..	**2,278**	1,163	1,115	**1,673**	894	779
...	...	...	...	**5,064**	2 ,607	2,457	**882**	448	434
6,374	6,471	263	263	**10,135**	5,046	5,089	**16,524**	8,341	8,183
2,967	2,570	...	..	**8,460**	4,407	4,053	**1,759**	949	810
2	...	..	..	**8,285**	4,267	4,018	**2,144**	1,042	1,102
445	420	..	..	**1,512**	816	696	**513**	251	262
3,416	3,074	5	4	**7,221**	3,827	3,394	**986**	536	450
427	372	36	26	**23,356**	12,982	13,674	**35,171**	17,201	17,970
103	73	16	7	**1,099**	550	539	**275**	151	124
325	275	24	17	**2,151**	1,101	1,050	**1,156**	602	554

TABLE XIII.

Castes, Tribes, Races or Nationalities. Part A.—Hindu. *(Continued).*

CASTE, TRIBE, RACE OR NATIONALITY	STATE TOTAL.			PADMANABHAPURAM.		TRIVANDRUM.		QUILON.	
	Persons.	Males.	Females.	Males.	Females.	Males.	Females.	Males.	Females.
1	2	3	4	5	6	7	8	9	10
34. Mannān	**9,946**	5,014	4,932	302	279	467	424	2,789	2,778
35 Marakkān	**14,604**	7,274	7,330	11	7	48	31	6,577	6,668
36. Mūvān	**29,318**	14,661	14,657	430	480	2,432	2,326	7,728	7,844
37. Marātti ...	**4,471**	2,770	1,701	51	50	77	84	2,392	1,482
38. Maravan	**8,376**	4,245	4,131	1,228	1,258	167	46	2,005	2,059
39. Mukkuvan	**1,742**	937	805	19	12	20	13	201	186
40. Nūkkan	**2,729**	1,459	1,270	127	88	140	153	554	527
41. Nāyar	**592,489**	295,703	296,786	14,572	14,485	68,368	68,510	131,280	135,393
42 Nulayan	**3,393**	1,764	1,629	482	474	1,187	1,142	95	13
43. Oddan	**1,801**	925	876	28	26	42	47	767	742
44 Pallan	**11,222**	5,205	6,017	683	686	139	137	1,336	1,623
45. Pānān	**3,316**	1,679	1,637	188	176	406	430	855	842
46. Pantāram	**13,784**	7,015	6,769	1,193	1,108	1,672	1,686	2,722	2,620
47. Paravan	**9,313**	4,648	4,665	570	565	1,094	1,175	674	660
48. Parayan	**70,554**	35,131	35,423	10,521	11,370	2,528	2,475	11,955	11,882
49. Patnūl	**3,292**	1,569	1,723	1,425	1,575	19	15	125	138
50 Pōntan	**2,390**	1,148	1,242	68	94	466	540	294	291
51. Pulayan	**185,314**	93,335	91,979	257	264	14,746	14,409	39,108	36,663
52. Pushpakan	**1,925**	1,012	913	41	28	134	101	362	334
53. Sāliyan (chaliya)	**9,919**	4,953	4,966	1,879	1,898	362	349	307	297
54. Talavan	**1,889**	931	958	1	...	304	315	626	648
55. Tantān	**21,641**	10,836	10,805	47	68	2,285	2,190	8,414	8,505
56 Tattān	**21,350**	10,718	10,632	758	825	1,630	1,710	4,215	3,977
57. Ullātan	**3,974**	2,129	1,845	...	..	15	16	399	378
58 Urāli	**5,758**	2,364	2,894	413	401	1,395	1,460	26	28
59 Vālan	**16,748**	8,588	8,160	...	...	...	..	680	693
60. Vāniyan	**16,235**	8,115	8,120	2,019	2,244	3,198	3,033	1,789	1,843
61. Vannān	**2,690**	1,272	1,418	423	511	371	422	387	402
62. Vāriyar	**2,739**	1,411	1,358	12	19	113	100	455	453
63. Vēlan	**13,457**	6,850	6,607	117	117	1,542	1,422	833	853
64. Vēlān	**5,782**	2,931	2,851	55	41	1,014	1,017	637	618
65. Vellāla	**49,479**	24,774	24,705	12,183	12,633	8,981	8,830	5,498	5,354
66. Veluttedan	**11,356**	5,718	5,638	168	187	875	956	2,672	2,584
67. Vettuvan	**1,482**	744	738	8	2	...	..	17	19
68 Others	**37,189**	19,014	18,175	2,990	3,125	2,715	2,881	5,828	6,207

TABLE XIII.

Castes, Tribes, Races or Nationalities. Part A.—Hindu. *(Concluded).*

Kottayam.		Devikulam.		Western Natural Division.			Eastern Natural Division.		
Males.	Females.	Males.	Females	Persons.	Males.	Females.	Persons.	Males.	Females.
11	12	18	14	15	16	17	18	19	20
1,429	1,405	27	46	**6,263**	3,164	3,099	**3,683**	1,850	1,833
643	624	.	.	**14,599**	7,271	7,328	**5**	3	2
3,972	3,987	99	70	**15,490**	7,674	7,816	**13,828**	6,987	6,841
62	46	188	89	**672**	433	239	**3,799**	2,337	1,462
6	2	839	766	**1,491**	830	661	**6,885**	3,415	3,470
516	455	181	139	**1,193**	628	565	**549**	309	240
317	302	321	200	**810**	414	396	**1,919**	1,045	874
78,516	76,088	2,967	2,310	**362,185**	180,444	181,741	**230,304**	115,259	115,045
.	.	.	.	**3,232**	1,641	1,591	**161**	123	38
10	5	78	56	**93**	50	43	**1,708**	875	833
...	.	3,047	3,571	**1,083**	547	536	**10,139**	4,658	5,481
220	189	10		**1,989**	984	1,005	**1,327**	695	632
1,291	1,216	137	139	**6,676**	3,472	3,204	**7,108**	3,543	3,565
2,310	2,265	...		**4,408**	2,184	2,224	**4,905**	2,464	2,441
6,659	6,360	3,468	3,336	**28,819**	14,219	14,600	**41,735**	20,912	20,823
	.	.	.	**3,291**	1,568	1,723	**1**	1	.
320	317	.	.	**1,871**	884	987	**519**	264	255
37,876	39,752	1,348	891	**100,643**	51,104	49,539	**84,671**	42,231	42,440
468	450	7		**1,370**	725	645	**555**	287	268
2,405	2,422	...	...	**9,390**	4,704	4,686	**529**	249	280
	...	.	..	**620**	305	315	**1,269**	626	643
36	32	54	15	**19,955**	9,929	10,026	**1,686**	907	779
4,014	4,034	101	86	**12,157**	6,120	6,037	**9,193**	4,598	4,595
1,170	1,148	545	318	**1,349**	680	669	**2,625**	1,449	1,176
687	742	343	263	**3,516**	1,733	1,783	**2,242**	1,131	1,111
7,687	7,243	221	224	**14,874**	7,646	7,228	**1,874**	942	932
1,063	947	46	53	**12,594**	6,382	6,212	**3,641**	1,733	1,908
91	83	..	...	**2,138**	994	1,144	**552**	478	474
828	781	3	.	**1,035**	538	497	**1.734**	873	861
3,768	4,106	90	109	**5,874**	2,828	3,046	**7,083**	3,522	3,561
1,207	1,162	18	13	**1,772**	917	855	**4,010**	2,014	1,996
2,736	2,645	381	233	**26,430**	13,287	13,143	**23,049**	11,487	11,[illegible]62
1,883	1,930	125	81	**5,692**	2,844	2,848	**5,664**	2,874	2,790
724	717	.	..	**1,400**	701	699	**82**	43	39
3,346	3,098	4,135	2,864	**13,637**	6,655	6,982	**23,552**	12,359	11,193

TABLE XIII.

Castes, Tribes, Races or Nationalities.
Parts B to E.—Other

TABLE XIII.

Castes, Tribes, Races or Nationalities. Parts B to E.—Other Religionists.

CASTE, TRIBE, RACE OR NATIONALITY.	STATE TOTAL.			PADMANABHAPURAM.		TRIVANDRUM.		QUILON.	
	Persons	Males.	Females.	Males	Females.	Males.	Females.	Males.	Females.
1	2	3	4	5	6	7	8	9	10
B. MUSALMAN	***226,617***	*116,488*	*110,129*	*7,419*	*7,432*	*25,733*	*25,464*	*46,209*	*43,541*
1. Jōnakan	**57,031**	29,415	27,616	.	.	970	544	4,192	4,199
2. Labbai	**14,694**	7,281	7,413	616	666	5,365	5,522	955	936
3. Māppila	**4,624**	2,545	2,079	4	2	4	.	44	28
4. Mēttan	**66,864**	33,768	33,096	1,657	1,750	6,592	7,124	24,352	23,263
5. Pathān	**3,853**	2,330	1,523	84	47	689	528	1,125	593
6. Rāvuttan	**1,202**	684	518	58	50	18	12	96	88
7. Sayyid	**10,425**	5,319	5,106	416	394	708	667	2,850	2,665
8. Sheikh	**3,565**	1,926	1,639	205	195	428	386	404	308
9. Tulukkan	**61,095**	31,417	29,678	4,215	4,210	10,532	10,309	11,408	10,789
10. Others	**3,264**	1,808	1,461	164	118	427	372	788	672
C. CHRISTIAN	***903,868***	*461,165*	*442,703*	*58,670*	*58,108*	*39.371*	*37,934*	*134,621*	*127,825*
1. Anglo-Indian	**1,750**	911	839	20	4	378	439	393	311
2. European	**399**	250	149	24	40	50	41	47	24
3. Indian Christian	**901,719**	460,004	441,715	58,626	58,064	38,943	37,454	134,181	127,490
D. ANIMISTIC	***15,773***	*8,123*	*7,650*	*1,090*	*948*	*2,794*	*2,644*	*1,793*	*1,750*
1. Kānikkaran	**4,034**	2,166	1,868	1,090	948	873	775	.	.
2. Malaukuravan	**397**	514	483		.	485	471	.	.
3. Malayarayan	**2,612**	1,294	1,318	.	..	4	6	449	477
4 Malavētan	**5,051**	2,584	2,467	.	..	1,258	1,243	1,198	1,121
5. Mannān	**1,239**	647	592	.	.	.	.	.	.
6. Others	**1,840**	918	922	.	.	174	149	146	152
E. OTHERS	***100***	*76*	*24*	...	..	*12*	*4*	*13*	*8*
1. Jew	**73**	53	20	..	.	11	4	5	..
2. Jain	**11**	8	3	.	.	...	..	8	3
3. Buddhist	**16**	15	1	...	..	1	.	.	...

TABLE XIII.

Castes, Tribes, Races or Nationalities. Parts B to E.—Other religionists.

Kottayam.		Devikulam.		Western Natural Division.			Eastern Natural Division.		
Males.	Females.	Males.	Females.	Persons.	Males.	Females.	Persons.	Males.	Females.
11	12	13	14	15	16	17	18	19	20
34,935	*32,126*	*2,192*	*1,566*	***135,210***	*68,978*	*66,232*	***91,407***	*47,510*	*43,897*
23,412	22,259	841	614	**16,678**	8,545	8,133	**40,353**	20,870	19,483
261	245	84	44	**12,301**	6,074	6,227	**2,393**	1,207	1,186
2,498	2,049	..	..	**4,617**	2,510	2,077	**7**	5	2
874	747	293	210	**58,089**	29,311	28,778	**8,775**	4,457	4,318
392	345	40	10	**2,392**	1,400	992	**1,461**	930	531
464	359	48	9	**252**	131	121	**950**	553	397
1,196	1,258	143	122	**6,022**	3,073	2,949	**4,403**	2,246	2,157
867	748	22	2	**2,665**	1,425	1,240	**900**	501	399
4,582	3,829	685	541	**29,862**	15,213	14,649	**31,233**	16,204	15,029
394	287	30	12	**2,332**	1,266	1,066	**932**	537	395
217,874	*210,832*	*10,629*	*8,004*	***419,818***	*213,955*	*205,863*	***484,050***	*247,210*	*236,810*
74	85	46	..	**1,513**	750	763	**237**	161	76
15	5	114	39	**193**	96	97	**203**	154	52
217,785	210,742	10,469	7,965	**418,112**	213,109	205,003	**483,607**	246,895	236,712
1,187	*1,111*	*1,259*	*1,197*	***3,631***	*1,886*	*1,745*	***12,142***	*6,237*	*5,905*
203	145	.	.	**2,184**	1,161	1,023	**1,850**	1,005	845
.	..	29	12	.	.	.	**997**	514	483
275	256	566	579	**10**	4	6	**2,602**	1,290	1,312
105	83	23	20	**1,083**	524	539	**3,988**	2,060	1,928
6	6	641	586	..	..	..	**1,239**	647	593
598	621	.	..	**374**	197	177	**1,466**	721	745
37	*16*	*14*	*1*	***83***	*60*	*23*	***17***	*16*	*1*
37	16	...	.	**71**	51	20	**2**	2	.
...	..	.	.	**11**	8	3	...	..	.
..	..	14	1	**1**	1	.	**15**	14	1

TABLE XIII.

Castes, Tribes, Races or Nationalities.—(Others). *

CASTE, TRIBE, RACE OR NATIONALITY.	Males.	Females.	CASTE, TRIBE, RACE OR NATIONALITY.	Males.	Females.	CASTE, TRIBE, RACE OR NATIONALITY.	Males.	Females.
			Hindu.					
1. Ahir ..	8	4	35. Kaikkalavan ...	412	417	69. Patyān ...	9	7
2. Akamutayān ..	4	11	36. Kākkālan .	451	409	70. Pilāppalli ...	34	39
3. Alavan ..	448	422	37. Kallan .	633	406	71. Pishārati .	230	301
4. Ampalakkāran ..	30	21	38. Kalluli ..	64	74	72. Potuvā. ...	55	62
5. Ampalavāsi ...	943	1,053	39. Kamma ..	170	182	73. Pulluvan .	960	779
6 Āri ..	53	70	40. Kannadian .	31	91	74. Purha... .	9	15
7. Āryappattar .	14	17	41. K[illegible] ..	28	28	75. Rājput .	165	139
8. Ātichchan ..	59	[illegible]	42. Kattikkāran ...	143	158	76. Rāju ..	132	141
9 [illegible] ...	2	7	43. Kāvalkkāran ..	24	25	77. Reddi ..	390	443
10. Atiyōti ..	6	7	44. Kavarai ..	278	294	78. Sādhu .	23	31
11. Balija ..	76	66	45. Koli ...	171	125	79. Saivakkurukkal ...	24	25
12. Bania ...	154	124	46. Kōmatti ...	72	125	80. Sakkiliyan ..	1,001	668
13. Besta ...	17	15	47. Konnan ...	14	7	81. Sāmantan ...	368	365
14. Bōya ...	292	191	48. Kotippattan ...	72	48	82. Silpāsāri ...	55	49
15. Chākkiyār ...	46	74	49. Kaundan ..	365	325	83. Singalese .	3	1
16. Chamar ..	13	27	50. Kshatriya ...	532	633	84. Sujali ..	13	14
17. Chāyakkuruppu ..	38	45	51. Kudumbo ...	9	11	85. Sunois ..	11	14
18. Chemmān ..	464	476	52. Kuluvan ...	132	155	86. Talayan ..	212	213
19. Chemputatti ..	82	26	53. Kumbi ...	65	60	87. Telugu ..	15	10
20. Cholayan ..	35	35	54. Kuruppu ..	379	444	88. Tiyyāttunni ...	124	135
21. Chūntappattan .	19	11	55. Kūttati ..	2	5	89. Totliyan ...	358	234
22. Daivampāti ..	75	107	56. Malanāyar .	57	45	90. Udāsi ..	18	15
23. Dhangar ..	41	37	57. Māli ...	16	18	91. Uppāra ..	75	83
24. Dāsi ..	208	353	58. Marvati ..	31	30	92. Uravālan ...	92	95
25. Dhōbi ..	51	31	59. Mochchi ...	6	8	93. Vairāvi ...	704	751
26. Gadaria ..	4	2	60. Mutali ..	289	266	94. Vaisyan ...	231	195
27 Gauda ...	173	86	61. Mūttatu ...	361	254	95. Vālan ..	275	250
28. Gōsāyi ..	123	86	62. Naidu ...	671	675	96. Valluvan ...	505	477
29. Gujarāti ..	10	7	63. Nampiti ..	22	32	97. Vatukan ...	539	537
30. Hindustani ..	168	160	64. Nampiyār ...	422	406	98. Vilkuruppu ...	513	473
31. Holia ...	28	21	65. Nāyāti ...	18	13	99. Not Returned ...	3	1
32. Kachchi ...	126	144	66. Ōchchan ...	243	272			
33. Kadiya ...	4	3	67. Panchaman ...	1,600	1,427			
34. Kahar ...	8	9	68. Panikkan ...	323	395	***Total*** ...	***19,014***	***18,175***
			Musalman.					
1. Afghan ...	1	1	14. Kach ...	187	138	27. Salya ...	41	7
2. Alima ...	1	1	15. Khan ...	106	76	28. Sākhi ..	4	2
3. Ambi ...	4	1	16. Malabari ..	6	10	29. Shāribha ...	15	16
4. Arab ...	52	42	17 Māli ..	4	5	30. Sikh ...	2	2
5. Ashabi ...	70	64	18. Maula ...	10	13	31. Sindh ..	59	65
6. Borah ...	4	7	19. Mèmman ...	197	167	32. Sunèshian ...	7	3
7. Chinese ...	11	8	20. Maghal ...	272	211	33. Tangal ...	12	13
8. Fakir ..	27	28	21. Mutali ...	19	11	34. Tarakan ...	2	1
9. Hamdei ..	1	1	22. Osta ..	528	501	35. Wais ..	7	8
10. Hindi ..	1	...	23. Tailmān ...	7	5			
11. Islam ...	72	8	24. Pannayār ...	10	7			
12. Ismail ...	11	2	25. Pilātti ...	6	2	***Total*** ...	***1,803***	***1,461***
13. Jemat ...	45	43	26. Rājas Baniya ...	2	2			
			Animistic.					
1. Kātan ..	19	22	6 Malavèlan ...	209	178	11. Nāyāti ...	22	19
2. Kāttālan ...	51	64	7. Mala-Ullātan ..	68	73	12. Vettuvan ...	2	2
3. Malankuti ...	98	103	8 Mala-Urāli ..	169	197			
4. Malappantāram ...	59	45	9. Mutuvān ...	195	184			
5. Malappulayan ...	17	28	10. Nāti ...	9	7	***Total*** ...	***918***	***922***

* This statement gives the castes which are included under the head 'others' in the main Table.

TABLE XIV.

Civil Condition by age for Selected Castes and Races.

TABLE XIV.

Civil Condition by Age for Selected Castes and Races.

CASTE, TRIBE OR RACE.	SEX.	Population dealt with.	UNMARRIED.						
			TOTAL.	0—5	5—12	12—15	15—20	20—40	40 and over.
1	2	3	4	5	6	7	8	9	10
HINDU.									
1. Ampalavāsi	Male	**5,448**	**2,999**	782	858	519	348	432	60
	Female	**5,404**	**2,350**	795	782	505	158	59	51
2. Ampa*tt*an	Male	**10,996**	**6,326**	1,585	2,359	915	772	631	64
	Female	**10,830**	**4,450**	1,398	1,661	726	411	209	45
3. Brahman (Malayala)	Male	**5,841**	**2,865**	433	795	531	505	512	89
	Female	**4,484**	**1,525**	458	636	219	131	51	30
4. Brahman (Others)	Male	**23,892**	**12,743**	3,517	4,263	1,068	1,909	1,913	78
	Female	**21,457**	**7,[illegible]30**	3,446	3,359	222	279	113	71
5. Chakkāla	Male	**8,937**	**4,596**	1,163	1,151	367	942	937	36
	Female	**9,137**	**3,240**	1,075	1,064	244	578	265	14
6. Chānnān	Male	**84,638**	**50,179**	12,638	17,782	4,953	7,553	6,998	260
	Female	**81,557**	**39,688**	12,574	15,749	3,981	4,996	2,104	284
7. Che*tt*i	Male	**10,535**	**5,716**	1,251	2,098	783	820	679	85
	Female	**10,346**	**4,[illegible]82**	1,242	1,877	723	398	169	78
8. Itayan	Male	**3,408**	**1,718**	418	555	327	237	141	40
	Female	**3,427**	**1,516**	424	509	298	186	51	48
9. Izhavan	Male	**271,677**	**155,051**	33,270	54,801	21,280	24,307	20,728	665
	Female	**274,588**	**127,768**	34,222	52,564	18,913	14,093	7,352	624
10. Kammā*l*an	Male	**71,538**	**38,669**	9,193	14,702	2,488	6,525	5,516	245
	Female	**70,044**	**31,049**	9,488	14,576	3,039	2,045	1,612	294
11. Ka*n*iyān	Male	**6,155**	**3,114**	547	915	269	743	609	31
	Female	**5,832**	**2,479**	628	854	282	363	312	40
12. Konka*n*i	Male	**5,356**	**2,657**	546	728	250	653	462	18
	Female	**4,863**	**1,314**	355	566	120	156	106	11
13. Krish*n*anvaka	Male	**5,309**	**2,953**	537	907	303	551	638	17
	Female	**5,120**	**1,486**	432	752	202	87	11	2
14. Kudumi	Male	**4,363**	**2,293**	677	686	269	339	311	11
	Female	**3,844**	**1,777**	642	646	257	125	97	10
15. Kuravan	Male	**30,183**	**15,037**	4,974	5,272	1,482	2,089	1,164	56
	Female	**31,644**	**12,905**	4,529	5,134	2,193	592	402	55
16. Ma*nn*ān	Male	**5,014**	**2,406**	625	549	185	511	459	77
	Female	**4,932**	**1,865**	684	604	169	235	103	70
17. Marakkān	Male	**7,274**	**3,611**	938	1,250	417	623	360	23
	Female	**7,330**	**3,125**	988	1,150	450	310	207	20
18. Mārān	Male	**14,661**	**7,628**	2,104	3,005	1,136	719	630	44
	Female	**14,657**	**6,423**	2,149	2,273	1,090	513	356	42

TABLE XIV.

Civil Condition by Age for Selected Castes and Races.

Married.							Widowed.						
Total.	0—5	5—12	12—15	15—20	20—40	40 and over.	Total.	0—5	5—12	12—15	15—20	20—40	40 and over.
11	12	13	14	15	16	17	18	19	20	21	22	23	24
2,097	.	..	2	85	1 004	916	**352**	..	1	2	3	100	237
2,030	..	11	37	329	1,167	486	**1,024**	...	...	3	24	196	801
4,109	.	1	2	168	2,035	1,903	**561**	..	...	4	5	184	368
4,304	.	2	59	897	2,987	859	**1,576**	...	2	9	83	294	1,238
2,625	..	...	1	114	1,287	1,223	**351**	...	1	5	4	102	239
1,955	...	16	63	235	1,146	495	**1,004**	..	...	1	13	217	773
9,756	...	24	166	195	5,849	3,582	**1,393**	..	9	25	32	279	1,048
9,402	. ..	318	719	1,640	4,811	1,914	**4,565**	...	12	18	93	954	3,488
3,648	.	7	10	59	1,864	1,708	**693**	..	1	3	8	111	570
3,994	.	9	36	654	2,754	541	**1,903**	..	...	17	58	348	1,480
30,933	.	23	35	625	15,889	14,361	**3,526**	...	3	16	56	854	2,597
29,934	..	114	252	2,350	22,195	5,023	**11,935**	..	3	29	112	3,125	8,666
4,135	.	15	25	169	2,121	1,805	**684**	..	2	5	10	146	521
4,169	.	29	66	558	2,403	1,110	**1,695**	..	7	16	29	391	1,252
1,568	.	...	2	31	849	686	**122**	..	...	1	5	31	85
1,493	...	14	58	176	946	299	**413**	...	...	8	9	119	287
104,475	...	31	121	1,580	60,622	42,121	**12,151**	..	6	31	168	4,213	7,733
104,095	...	201	1,165	11,515	70,416	20,798	**42,725**	...	28	112	697	12,987	28,901
29,749	..	65	95	440	15,336	13,813	**3,120**	...	5	26	42	988	2,059
29,353	..	85	464	3,928	18,083	6,798	**9,642**	...	10	35	124	2,569	6,904
2,774	..	2	12	51	1,643	1,066	**267**	..	...	3	6	74	184
2,611	...	6	37	341	1,326	901	**742**	...	...	4	15	211	512
2,591	..	6	13	44	1,455	1,078	**103**	...	1	3	7	28	69
2,494	...	13	114	271	1,161	935	**1,055**	.	3	16	34	285	717
2,138	...	1	2	37	1,184	914	**218**	.	1	1	2	53	161
2,945	...	9	76	472	1,648	740	**689**	..	...	5	21	209	454
1,916	..	1	2	33	1,026	854	**154**	...	...	..	...	59	95
1,647	..	3	25	234	1,034	351	**420**	...	...	3	10	121	286
13,614	...	7	22	219	6,987	6,379	**1,532**	...	1	3	9	498	1,026
13,552	...	33	160	2,534	8,342	2,483	**5,187**	...	3	13	71	972	4,128
2,340	...	...	1	52	1,345	942	**268**	...	...	...	...	79	189
2,216	...	7	33	335	1,309	532	**851**	...	...	7	27	183	634
3,356	...	...	1	77	1,838	1,440	**307**	..	...	...	1	75	231
3,259	...	9	45	587	2,012	606	**946**	...	2	6	39	289	610
6,627	...	1	2	164	3,574	2,886	**406**	...	1	5	5	86	309
6,898	...	12	56	1,138	4,124	1,566	**1,338**	...	3	9	44	378	904

TABLE XIV.

Civil Condition by Age for Selected Castes and Races.

CASTE, TRIBE OR RACE.	SEX.	Population dealt with	UNMARRIED						
			TOTAL.	0—5	5—12	12—15	15—20	20—40	40 and over
1	2	3	4	5	6	7	8	9	10
19. Maravan	Male ...	**4,245**	**2,029**	564	661	277	268	238	21
	Female .	**4,131**	**1,426**	450	558	249	139	27	3
20. Nayar	Male ...	**295,703**	**168,545**	37,915	50,851	22,777	24,592	31,071	1,339
	Female ..	**296,786**	**131,389**	42,363	47,206	19,513	14,201	6,791	1,315
21. Pallan	Male ...	**5,205**	**2,592**	561	806	207	506	493	19
	Female .	**6,017**	**2,599**	547	804	373	493	370	14
22. Pantāram	Male .	**7,015**	**3,588**	771	1,074	331	718	630	49
	Female .	**6,709**	**2,812**	726	1,033	305	405	294	49
23. Paravan	Male ..	**4,648**	**2,388**	603	926	271	320	228	40
	Female .	**4,665**	**2,122**	586	1,019	267	133	78	89
24. Parayan	Male ..	**35,131**	**18,280**	3,965	5,300	2,617	2,982	3,334	62
	Female .	**35,423**	**15,886**	4,008	5,173	2,435	2,775	805	95
25. Pulayan	Male ..	**93,335**	**46,383**	12,860	15,423	4,680	6,264	6,969	237
	Female ..	**91,979**	**38,452**	12,663	15,327	4,334	3,600	2,187	341
26. Sāliyan ..	Male .	**4,953**	**2,489**	692	862	210	368	332	25
	Female .	**4,966**	**2,255**	690	950	240	275	68	23
27. Tantān . .	Male .	**10,336**	**5,257**	1,206	1,978	791	598	572	112
	Female .	**10,605**	**4,505**	1,255	2,265	450	275	154	106
28. Vālan	Male ..	**8,588**	**4,114**	1,265	1,643	435	498	217	56
	Female	**8,160**	**3,699**	1,270	1,671	472	174	60	52
29. Vāniyan ..	Male ..	**8,115**	**4,338**	849	1,607	627	706	530	19
	Female ..	**8,120**	**3,218**	840	1,542	427	233	137	39
30. Vel[illegible]n .. .	Male	**6,350**	**2,939**	703	1,016	455	409	365	41
	Female .	**6,607**	**2,390**	767	1,000	402	279	200	33
31. Vellāla . .	Male ..	**24,774**	**12,757**	3,117	3,655	1,453	2,218	2,225	89
	Female .	**24,705**	**8,982**	3,133	4,240	1,142	210	169	83
32. Veluttedan	Male ...	**5,718**	**3,038**	774	1,059	462	480	271	42
	Female .	**5,633**	**2,494**	703	1,098	316	168	86	33
CHRISTIAN.									
1. Angolo-Indian .. .	Male ..	**911**	**612**	93	163	112	109	119	16
	Female	**839**	**502**	48	207	74	93	56	19
2. Indian Christian .	Male ..	**430,004**	**237,722**	62,355	84,979	38,659	31,555	19,128	1,043
	Female ..	**441,715**	**193,902**	66,023	72,112	41,761	12,655	5,818	1,008

Note.—For this Table, some castes shown separately in Table XIII (Castes, Tribes, Races or Nationalities) have

TABLE XIV.

Civil Condition by Age for Selected Castes and Races.

Married.							Widowed.						
Total.	0—5	5—12	12—15	15—20	20—40	40 and over.	Total.	0—5	5—12	12—15	15—20	20—40	40 and over.
11	12	13	14	15	16	17	18	19	20	21	22	23	24
1,927	.	.	1	36	1,037	853	**283**		.	..	2	78	209
1,620	..	6	35	194	1,124	261	**1,035**	.	..	8	49	284	744
112,795	..	51	115	1,113	60,207	51,309	**14,363**	...	5	29	161	5,218	8,950
110,855	...	174	1,459	13,712	71,468	24,042	**54,542**	.	31	136	820	13,728	39,832
2,446	...	5	6	69	1,275	1,091	**167**	..	...	1	3	45	118
2,409	.	5	37	259	1,215	898	**1,009**	...	.	1	7	102	800
2,756	...	...	5	47	1,383	1,321	**691**	..	..	4	2	137	548
2,573	..	8	39	278	1,310	983	**1,334**	...	2	9	54	357	962
1,985	.	.	13	33	1,027	912	**275**	...	..	2	3	75	195
1,915	...	2	28	211	1,196	478	**623**	...	1	5	23	210	334
15,310	..	27	36	329	7,964	6,954	**1,541**	.	1	9	18	425	1,088
15,271	.	61	181	2,894	8,678	3,457	**4,266**	...	3	13	57	1,100	3,093
44,098	.	5	32	831	26,531	16,649	**2,854**	.	3	16	46	911	1,878
43,771	...	137	697	5,380	30,290	7,267	**9,756**	.	4	21	156	2,397	7,178
2,197	...	1	3	72	1,225	896	**237**	...	...	2	2	53	210
2,136	..	4	58	286	1,220	598	**545**	..	...	3	27	199	316
5,245	..	1	2	133	4,045	1,064	**334**	..	..	2	2	71	259
4,887	..	17	66	938	2,767	1,099	**1,413**	.	..	6	25	804	983
3,903	.	1	1	65	2,257	1,579	**571**	..	..	...	5	169	397
3,441	.	22	184	547	1,915	773	**1,020**	.	..	5	13	283	769
3,333	..	2	3	54	1,733	1,494	**441**	..	..	1	2	75	363
3,303	.	25	179	594	1,876	629	**1,593**	..	1	6	18	363	1,206
3,044	..	5	4	86	1,593	1,351	**317**		1	2	3	94	217
2,846	.	16	69	244	1,596	921	**1,071**	..	..	7	19	275	770
10,490	..	18	34	128	5,824	4,486	**1,527**	.	3	9	9	827	1,179
10,713	...	67	224	979	6,075	2,468	**5,010**	.	4	13	55	1,053	3,883
2,232	..	4	8	41	1,346	898	**333**	..	.	2	2	56	278
2,100	..	15	66	272	1,258	494	**1,044**	..	..	9	23	248	764
256	.	...	3	11	108	134	**43**	..	..	.	6	12	25
233	.	...	7	13	129	84	**104**	..	..	...	10	18	76
205,277	.	232	1,058	11,971	120,044	71,977	**17,005**	.	11	99	181	3,713	13,001
197,794	.	986	6,184	30,575	120,533	39,516	**45,019**	.	42	122	861	9,138	35 356

been grouped together. The castes so grouped are those shown in the Note to Table IX.

TABLE XV.

Occupation or Means of Livelihood.
Part A.—General Table.

The Scheme of classification adopted in 1901 was a little too elaborate. It was also defective in certain respects. A new scheme based on that of Monsieur Bertillon was therefore recommended for this Census by the India Commissioner and has been adopted.

The occupations returned are now divided into four classes against 8 in 1901 and subdivided into 12 Sub-classes, 55 Orders and 169 Groups against 24 Orders, 79 Sub-orders and 520 Groups respectively.

Imperial Table XV is divided into five Parts —A, B, C, D and E.

Part A is complete in itself and deals with the entire population of the State by Administrative Divisions, to which is appended a Table of occupations by orders for the two Natural Divisions.

Part B details the Subsidiary Occupations of the actual workers among the agriculturists.

Part C shows for certain mixed occupations the number of persons who returned each of them as their (a) principal, and (b) subsidiary means of livelihood.

Part D classifies the occupational distribution of the entire population by religion. Separate figures for the total urban area are also given.

Part E gives information regarding industries. The details herein embodied were collected by means of a special schedule filled up by the owners, managers or agents of factories, mills, &c., in which not less than 20 persons were employed on the date of the Final Census —March 10, 1911. It is divided into four sub-parts. The first records information regarding each factory, mill &c., distinguishing those in which mechanical power is used from those in which it is not and classifies them according to the strength of the persons employed, while the second gives figures for the Administrative and Natural Divisions without these details. The caste and nationality of the owners and managers of certain important industries are embodied in the third and the fourth sub-parts.

TABLE XV.

Occupation or Means of Livelihood.—Part A. (General Table).

Number	OCCUPATION.	STATE.					
		TOTAL NO. OF WORKERS AND DEPENDANTS.	ACTUAL WORKERS.				DEPENDANTS
			Total.		Partially Agriculturists.		
			Males.	Females.	Males.	Females.	
	1	2	3	4	5	6	7
1	*Total* ..	*3,428,975*	*965,102*	*456,544*	*6,667*	*338*	*2,007.329*
2	CLASS A.—PRODUCTION OF RAW MATERIALS	**1,907,199**	**541,764**	**141,130**	**239**	**18**	**1,224,305**
3	**Sub-Class I.—Exploitation of the surface of the earth.**	**1,905,466**	**541,112**	**140,964**	**239**	**18**	**1,223,390**
4	ORDER I.—PASTURE AND AGRICULTURE .	*1,839,423*	*515,570*	*138,391*	*223*	*18*	*1,185,462*
5	*I (a). Ordinary cultivation*	**1,615,902**	**441,314**	**119,633**	**14**	...	**1,054,955**
6	1. Income from rent of agricultural land ..	95,761	21,408	4,963	..	..	69,390
7	(a) Non-cultivating landholder	91,305	20,358	4,673	..	..	66,274
8	(b) Non-cultivating tenant ..	4,456	1,050	290	...	..	3,116
9	2. Ordinary cultivators	1,288,041	345,150	55,260	..	..	887,631
10	(a) Cultivating landholder	1,163,974	310,961	50,866	.	.	802,147
11	(b) Cultivating tenant	124,067	34,189	4,394	..	.	85,484
12	3. Agents, managers of landed estates (not planters), clerks, rent collectors, etc. .	2,291	585	5	14	...	1,701
13	4. Farm servants and field labourers .	229,809	74,171	59,405	..	..	96,233
14	*I (b). Growers of special products and market gardening*	**208,856**	**68,164**	**16,256**	**84**	**11**	**122,436**
15	5. Tea, coffee, cinchona and indigo plantations	14,190	6,704	3,883	14	1	3,603
16	6. Fruit, flower, vegetable, betel, vine, areca nut, etc., growers.	192,666	61,460	12,373	70	10	118,833
17	*I (c). Forestry*	**6,466**	**1,646**	**1,664**	**76**	**4**	**3,156**
18	7. Forest officers, rangers, guards, etc. ..	1,734	575	..	4	...	1,159
19	8. Wood-cutters; firewood, lac, catechu, rubber, etc.,-collectors, and charcoal burners	4,732	1,071	1,664	72	4	1,997
20	*I (d). Raising of farm stock*	**10,196**	**4,443**	**833**	**49**	**3**	**4,915**
21	9. Cattle and buffalo breeders and keepers ..	884	284	79	8	1	521
22	10. Sheep, goat and pig breeders ...	509	161	64	2	..	284
23	11. Breeders of other animals (horses, mules, camels, asses, etc)	140	47	.	...	..	93
24	12. Herdsmen, shepherds, goatherds, etc. .	8,663	3,951	695	39	2	4,017
25	*I (e). Raising of small animals* (Group 13) Birds bees, silkworms, etc.	**3**	**3**	.	..	.	..
26	ORDER 2 —FISHING AND HUNTING	*66,043*	*25,542*	*2,573*	*16*	...	*37,929*
27	14. Fishing	65,978	25,519	2,571	16	...	37,888
28	15. Hunting	65	23	2	.	.	40
29	**Sub-Class II.—Extraction of minerals** .	**1,733**	**652**	**166**	..	..	**915**
30	ORDER 3.—MINES..	*1,295*	*502*	*133*	...	...	*660*
31	16. Coal mines and petroleum wells . .		.	..	.	...	..
32	17. Mines and metallic minerals (gold, iron, manganese, etc)	1,295	502	133	..	...	660
33	ORDER 4.—QUARRIES OF HARD ROCKS. (Group 18) Other minerals (jade, diamonds, limestone. etc.)	.	..	.	..	.	..
34	ORDER 5.—SALT, ETC.	*438*	*150*	*33*	..	.	*255*
35	19. Rock, sea and marsh salt	438	150	33	..	..	255
36	20. Extraction of saltpetre, alum and other substances soluble in water	.	..	...	..	.	...

TABLE XV.

Occupation or Means of Livelihood.—Part A. *(Continued).*

PADMANABHAPURAM.						TRIVANDRUM.						
Total No. of workers and dependants.	Actual Workers. Total. Males.	Actual Workers. Total. Females.	Partially agriculturists. Males.	Partially agriculturists. Females.	Dependants.	Total No. of workers and dependants.	Actual Workers. Total. Males.	Actual Workers. Total. Females.	Partially agriculturists. Males	Partially agriculturists. Females.	Dependants.	Number.
8	9	10	11	12	13	14	15	16	17	18	19	
430,087	*118,540*	*41,316*	*1,474*	*40*	*270,231*	*557,865*	*157,114*	*69,653*	*1,361*	*72*	*331,098*	1
211,608	**57,657**	**13,627**	**22**	**2**	**140,324**	**273,038**	**76,252**	**16,890**	**76**	**4**	**179,393**	2
211,184	**57,503**	**13,594**	**22**	**2**	**140,067**	**271,749**	**75,754**	**16,757**	**73**	**4**	**179,233**	3
193,728	*52,837*	*12 850*	*19*	*2*	*128,041*	*261,541*	*71,587*	*16,376*	*74*	*4*	*173,578*	4
172,781	**46,530**	**11,687**	**2**	.	**114,564**	**217,235**	**58,573**	**12,638**	**6**	..	**113,044**	5
9,475	2,414	631	...		6.430	14,017	3,178	910	.	..	9,929	6
8,347	2,151	536	.	..	5,660	13,414	3,016	872	.	..	9,526	7
1,128	263	95	..		770	603	162	33	.	..	403	8
144,285	39,035	3,971	.	.	101,229	181,581	46,333	7,371	...	..	127,877	9
125,499	33,716	3 291	.	..	88,492	167,502	41,633	6,811	...	...	119,058	10
18,786	5,369	680	...	.	13,787	14,079	4,700	560	.	...	8,819	11
231	58	.	2		173	902	203	.	6	.	693	12
18,790	4,973	7,035	...	.	6,732	20,755	6,856	4,357	..	..	9,512	13
17,251	**4,948**	**762**	**2**	**1**	**11,541**	**40,076**	**13,857**	**2,500**	**19**	**2**	**23,719**	14
271	125	25	...	.	121	350	130	66	..		154	15
16,980	4,823	737	2	1	11,420	39,726	13,727	2,434	19	2	23,565	16
1,005	**222**	**180**	**4**	**1**	**603**	**2,390**	**605**	**1,098**	**42**	**2**	**937**	17
202	60	..	.	.	142	300	105	..	1	.	195	18
803	162	180	4	1	461	2,390	500	1,098	41	2	792	19
2,691	**1,137**	**221**	**11**	..	**1,333**	**1,520**	**552**	**140**	**7**		**823**	20
225	76	18	2	..	136	174	47	14	1		113	21
98	29	10	...	.	54	128	40	14	1	.	74	22
50	17	.	.	.	33	49	15	.	.	.	34	23
2,323	1,015	198	9	..	1,110	1,160	450	112	5	..	607	24
..	...	...	.	..	..	..	.	..	..	..	..	25
17,436	*4,666*	*744*	*3*	.	*12,096*	*10,208*	*4,167*	*381*	*2*	..	*5,660*	26
17,436	4,666	744	3	.	12,035	10,186	4,161	380	2		5,645	27
.	.	.	.	.	..	22	6	1	.	.	15	28
444	**154**	**33**	.	.	**257**	**1,230**	**493**	**133**	.	..	**653**	29
6	*4*	..			*2*	*1,289*	*498*	*133*	..	.	*658*	30
	..	.	..	..	...	..	.	..	..	.	..	31
6	4	..	.		2	1,289	498	133	.	..	658	32
	...	.			.	.	..	..		..	.	33
438	*150*	*33*		.	*255*	...	...	..	.	..	.	34
438	150	33			255	.	..	..	.	.	..	35
..	. ..	..			..	...	..	..			.	36

TABLE XV.

Occupation or Means of Livelihood.—Part A. (General Table.)

Number	OCCUPATION.	QUILON. Total No. of workers and dependants.	Actual Workers. Total. Males.	Actual Workers. Total. Females.	Actual Workers. Partially Agriculturists. Males.	Actual Workers. Partially Agriculturists. Females	Dependants.
	1	20	21	22	23	24	25
1	*Total*	*1,233,360*	*351,336*	*177,288*	*2,027*	*119*	*704,736*
2	CLASS A.—PRODUCTION OF RAW MATERIALS	**712,588**	**206,102**	**61,211**	**78**	**9**	**445,275**
3	**Sub-Class I.—Exploitation of the surface of the earth**	**712,588**	**206,102**	**61,211**	**78**	**9**	**445,275**
4	ORDER I.—PASTURE AND AGRICULTURE	*691,511*	*197, 611*	*60,565*	*70*	*9*	*433,335*
5	*I (a). Ordinary cultivation*	**612,883**	**173,904**	**54,634**	**3**	..	**384,345**
6	1. Income from rent of agricultural land ..	37,714	7,561	1,994	..	...	28,159
7	(a) Non-cultivating landholder .. .	36,286	7,228	1,904	...	...	27,154
8	(b) Non-cultivating tenant	1,428	333	90	...	...	1,005
9	2. Ordinary cultivators	482,584	135,658	26,058	..	...	320,878
10	(a) Cultivating landholder	443,312	123,709	24,617	...	...	294,936
11	(b) Cultivating tenant	39,272	11,944	1,436	..	...	25,893
12	3. Agents, managers of landed estates (not planters), clerks, rent collectors, etc. ..	559	132	3	3	..	424
13	4. Farm servants and field labourers ..	92,026	30,558	26,584	..	...	34,884
14	*I (b). Growers of special products and market gardening*	**72,610**	**21,257**	**5,330**	**28**	**5**	**46,023**
15	5. Tea, coffee, cinchona and indigo plantations	827	401	204	2	...	222
16	6. Fruit, flower, vegetable, betel, vine, areca nut, etc., growers	71,783	20,856	5,126	26	5	45,801
17	*I (c). Forestry*	**1,649**	**444**	**287**	**18**	**1**	**918**
18	7. Forest officers, rangers, guards, etc. ..	683	221	..	2	..	462
19	8. Wood-cutters; firewood, lac, catechu, rubber, etc., collectors, and charcoal burners.	966	223	287	16	1	456
20	*I (d). Raising of farm stock*	**4,366**	**2,003**	**314**	**21**	**3**	**2,049**
21	9. Cattle and buffalo breeders and keepers ..	347	105	33	8	1	206
22	10. Sheep, goat and pig breeders	56	22	12	..	..	22
23	11. Breeders of other animals (horses, mules, camels, asses, etc.)	41	15	..	..	..	26
24	12. Herdsmen, shepherds, goatherds, etc. ..	3,922	1,861	266	18	2	1,795
25	*I (e) Raising of small animals* (Group 18) Birds, bees, silkworms, etc.	**3**	**3**	..	...	..	...
26	ORDER 2.—FISHING AND HUNTING	*21,077*	*8,491*	646	6	...	*11,940*
27	14 Fishing	21,064	8,486	646	6	..	11,932
28	15. Hunting	13	5	.	..	...	8
29	**Sub-Class II.—Extraction of minerals** .	...	...	..	...	..	..
30	ORDER 3.—MINES	...	...	..	...	..	...
31	16 Coal mines and petroleum wells	...	...	...	...	..	...
32	17. Mines and metallic minerals (gold, iron, manganese, etc.).	...	...	...	...	..	...
33	ORDER 4.—QUARRIES OF HARD ROCKS: (Group 18) Other minerals (jade, diamonds, limestone, etc.)	...	...	...	...	...	...
34	ORDER 5.—SALT, ETC.	..	...	...	..	.	..
35	19 Rock, sea and marsh salt	...	...	...	..	..	...
36	20. Extraction of saltpetre, alum and other substances soluble in water ...	...	...	..	...	..	...

TABLE XV.

Occupation or Means of Livelihood.—Part A. *(Continued).*

KOTTAYAM.						DEVIKULAM.						
Total No. of workers and dependants.	Actual Workers.				Dependants.	Total No. of workers and dependants.	Actual Workers.				Dependants.	Number.
	Total.		Partially Agriculturists.				Total.		Partially Agriculturists.			
	Males.	Females.	Males.	Females.			Males.	Females.	Males.	Females.		
26	27	28	29	30	31	32	33	34	35	36	37	
1,139,101	*315,327*	*155725*	*1,729*	*104*	*668,049*	*68,562*	*22,785*	*12,562*	*76*	*3*	*33,215*	1
658,635	**184,817**	**40,526**	**47**	**2**	**433,292**	**51,330**	**16,936**	**8,876**	**18**	**1**	**25,518**	2
658,635	**184,817**	**40,526**	**47**	**2**	**433,292**	**51,330**	**16,936**	**8,876**	**18**	**1**	**25,518**	3
641.342	*176,611*	*39,725*	*42*	*2*	*425,006*	*51,301*	*16,924*	*8,875*	*18*	*1*	*25,502*	4
582,171	**157,446**	**37,445**	**3**	...	**387,280**	**30,812**	**6,861**	**3,229**	...	...	**20,722**	5
32,996	8,110	1,402	..	.	23,484	1,559	145	26	..	..	1,388	6
31,816	7,843	1,338	...	.	22,635	1,442	120	23	..	.	1,299	7
1,180	267	64	.	.	849	117	25	3	...	...	89	8
454,318	118,493	15,772	..	..	320,053	25,273	5,586	2,093	...	.	17,594	9
403,590	106,627	14,153	..	...	282,810	24,071	5,276	1,994	..	...	16,801	10
50,728	11,866	1,619	...	...	37,243	1,202	310	99	...	...	793	11
490	167	...	8	...	323	109	22	2	...	..	85	12
94,367	30,676	20,271	...	...	43,420	3,871	1,108	1,108	...	..	1,655	13
56,869	**18,227**	**2,078**	**21**	**2**	**36,564**	**20,050**	**9,875**	**5,586**	**14**	**1**	**4,589**	14
114	14	7	...	...	93	12,628	6,034	3,581	12	1	3,013	15
56,755	18,213	2,071	21	2	36,471	7,422	3,841	2,005	2	...	1,576	16
913	**281**	**64**	**10**	..	**568**	**209**	**94**	**35**	**2**	..	**80**	17
483	142	...	1	...	341	66	47	..	...	...	19	18
430	189	64	9	..	227	143	47	35	2	..	61	19
1,339	**657**	**138**	**8**	..	**594**	**230**	**94**	**25**	**2**	..	**111**	20
116	47	13	2	..	56	22	9	3	..	.	10	21
219	66	27	1	..	120	13	4	1	...	..	8	22
...	...	..	..	...	...	...	...	...	..	..	..	23
1,054	544	98	5	...	412	105	81	21	2	..	93	24
...	...	...	...	...	...	...	...	...	..	..	...	25
17,293	*8,206*	*801*	*5*	...	*8,286*	*29*	*12*	*1*	..	..	*16*	26
17,287	8,203	801	5	..	8,283	5	3	...	...	...	2	27
6	3	...	...	...	3	24	9	1	..	.	14	28
...	...	..	...	...	...	...	...	...	.	...	...	29
...	...	.	...	...	...	...	...	...	..	...	...	30
...	...	...	..	...	...	...	...	...	.	..	...	31
...	...	...	...	...	...	...	..	..	.	...	...	32
...	...	..	..	.	...	..	...	..	...	...	...	33
...	...	...	...	...	...	...	...	..	...	...	...	34
...	...	...	...	...	...	...	...	...	...	..	...	35
..	...	..	.	..	...	...	...	.	.	...	...	36

TABLE XV.

Occupation or Means of Livelihood.—Part A. (General Table.)

Number.	OCCUPATION.	STATE.					
		TOTAL NO. OF WORKERS AND DEPENDANTS.	ACTUAL WORKERS.				DEPENDANTS
			Total.		Partially Agriculturists.		
			Males.	Females.	Males.	Females	
	1	2	3	4	5	6	7
37	CLASS B.—PREPARATION AND SUPPLY OF MATERIAL SUBSTANCES	**928,685**	**235,123**	**190,533**	**4,114**	**237**	**473,029**
38	**Sub-Class III.—Industry**	**588,410**	**138,332**	**120,615**	**2,311**	**107**	**299,463**
39	ORDER 6.—TEXTILES	*160,544*	*38,987*	*67,087*	*198*	*19*	*54,470*
40	21. Cotton ginning, cleaning and pressing ..	485	115	191	..	.	179
41	22. Cotton spinning, sizing and weaving ..	35,112	13,193	1,379	128	2	20,540
42	23. Jute spinning, pressing and weaving ...	.	.			.	
43	24. Rope, twine and string	110,750	23,874	57,955	66	16	28,921
44	25. Other fibres (cocoanut, aloes, flax, hemp, straw, etc)	13,627	1,709	7,313	4	1	4,605
45	26. Wool carders and spinners, weavers of woollen blankets, carpets, etc	..	..	.	.		..
46	27 Silk spinners and weavers. .. .	..	..	.	..		
47	28. Hair, camel and horse hair, bristles work, brush makers, etc.	195	62	.	..	.	133
48	29. Persons occupied with feathers	..	..	.	.		.
49	30. Dyeing, bleaching, printing, preparation and sponging of textiles.	85	24	10	..		51
50	31. Other (lace, crape, embroideries, fringes, etc.), and insufficiently described textile industries.	290	10	230			41
51	ORDER 7.—HIDES, SKINS AND HARD MATERIALS FROM THE ANIMAL KINGDOM. . ..	*119*	*55*	*3*		.	*88*
52	32. Tanners, curriers, leather dressers and dyers, etc.	63	28	3	...	.	32
53	33. Makers of leather articles, such as trunks, water bags, etc.	..	..	..	.	...	..
54	34. Furriers		..	..	.	..	..
55	35. Bone, ivory, horn, shell, etc., workers .	86	30	...	..	.	56
56	ORDER 8.—WOOD	*93,018*	*28,619*	*13,271*	*339*	*10*	*51,128*
57	36. Sawyers, carpenters, turners and joiners, etc.	61,005	20,729	778	301	7	39,498
58	37. Basket makers and other industries of woody material, including leaves. .	32,013	7,890	12,493	38	3	11,630
59	ORDER 9.—METALS	*35,391*	*11,801*	*603*	*132*	*3*	*22,987*
60	38. Forging and rolling of iron and other metals.	.	.	..	...	.	
61	39. Plough and agricultural implement makers.	.	..	.	...	.	...
62	40 Makers of arms, guns, etc. .. .	39	16	.	.		23
63	41. Other workers in iron and makers of implements and tools, principally or exclusively of iron.	28,269	9,463	549	116	3	18,257
64	42. Workers in brass, copper and bell metal .	6,456	2,093	52	16	.	4,311
65	43. Workers in other metals (tin, zinc, lead, quick-silver, etc).	540	202	2			33[illegible]
66	44. Workers in mints, die-sinkers, etc. ..	87	27	.	.	.	60
67	ORDER 10.—CERAMICS	*14,231*	*4,600*	*2,617*	*48*	*6*	*7,017*
68	45. Makers of glass and crystal ware .	.	.	...	.	.	
69	46 Makers of porcelain and crockery					.	
70	47. Potters and earthen pipe and bowl makers	8,029	2,656	2,012	44	6	3,360
71	48. Brick and tile makers .. .	6,203	1,914	605	4	.	3,657
72	49. Others (mosaic, talc, mica, alabaster, etc, workers).	...	.	..	..	.	..

TABLE XV.

Occupation or Means of Livelihood.—Part A. *(Continued).*

PADMANABHAPURAM.						TRIVANDRUM.						
Total No. of workers and dependants.	Actual Workers.				Dependants.	Total No. of workers and dependants.	Actual Workers.				Dependants.	Number.
	Total.		Partially Agriculturists.				Total.		Partially Agriculturists.			
	Males.	Females	Males.	Females.			Males.	Females.	Males.	Females.		
8	9	10	11	12	13	14	15	16	17	18	19	
174,292	**48,339**	**19,036**	**1,137**	**28**	**103,887**	**183,336**	**43,799**	**29,94[illegible]**	**72[illegible]**	**55**	**84,625**	37
117,417	**32,703**	**6,949**	**942**	**10**	**77,762**	**88,397**	**23,911**	**12,633**	**442**	**19**	**43,323**	38
12,360	*3,452*	*818*	*34*	.	*8,090*	*22,532*	*8,802*	*2,348*	*60*	*2*	*11,432*	39
..	..	..	..	..	..	..	..	..	..	...	..	40
11,425	8,105	480	82	..	7,750	11,119	4,680	172	47	1	6,267	41
.	.	...	...	..	.	.	..	.	...	.	..	42
509	199	103	2	..	207	10,562	8,828	1,907	12	1	4,742	43
127	31	28	..	..	65	837	277	178	1	..	382	44
.	...	.	..	..	.	.		.	.	..	...	45
..	.	.	..	.	.	..	.	..	..	.	...	46
23	6	.	..	.	23	33	13		.	..	25	47
.	.	.			.	..	.		.	.	.	48
38	10	7			21	26	9	1	..	.	16	49
233	8	200	.	.	25	..	.	...	...	...	...	50
8	*3*	.	.	.	*5*	*85*	*32*	*1*	..	..	*52*	51
8	3	.	..	..	5	27	10	1	..		16	52
...	.	.	...	..	...	.	..	..	.	.	..	53
...	.	.	..	..	.	.	..	..	.	.		54
	...	..	.	.	.	58	22		.	..	30	55
9,377	*2,642*	*607*	*43*	*1*	6,028	*18,879*	*6,208*	*2,352*	*94*	*1*	*10,339*	56
7,081	2,056	127	39	1	4,848	12,981	4,341	121	84	1	8,519	57
2,246	*538*	480	8	..	*1,180*	5,918	*1,867*	2,231	10	.	1,820	58
2,921	*822*	*28*	*9*	.	*2,071*	*5,970*	*2,169*	*56*	*27*	.	*3,715*	59
		.		.	..		.	..			.	60
	.	.					.	..	.	.	.	61
6	2	.			4	29	13		.		16	62
2,016	527	25	7	.	1,464	4,619	1,644	41	24		2,931	63
830	263	3	2	.	564	1,129	444	15	3		670	64
69	30	.	.		39	113	48				70	65
.		.	.	..		80	25		.		55	66
[illegible]	*771*	*247*	*6*		*1,175*	*[illegible]*	*[illegible]*	*609*	*13*	*2*	*1,482*	67
	.	.			.			.	.			68
		.	.					.	.			69
932	316	191	5	..	455	2,870	736	553	12	2	931	70
1,531	455	56	1		1,020	949	402	56	1	.	491	71
	.		.			.	.		.		.	72

TABLE XV.

Occupation or Means of Livelihood.—Part—A. (General Table.)

Number.	OCCUPATION.	QUILON.					
		TOTAL NO. OF WORKERS AND DEPENDANTS.	ACTUAL WORKERS.				DEPENDANTS.
			Total.		Partially Agriculturists.		
			Males.	Females.	Males.	Females.	
	1	20	21	22	23	24	25
37	CLASS B.—PREPARATION AND SUPPLY OF MATERIAL SUBSTANCES	**291,641**	**82,175**	**64,379**	**1,119**	**70**	**145,087**
38	**Sub-Class III.—Industry**	**171,866**	**46,360**	**41,801**	**664**	**36**	**83,705**
39	ORDER 6.—TEXTILES	*48,706*	*9,724*	*22,571*	*57*	*7*	*16,411*
40	21. Cotton ginning cleaning, and pressing ..	485	115	191	...	..	179
41	22. Cotton spinning, sizing and weaving ..	9,370	3,937	326	40	1	5,107
42	23. Jute spinning, pressing and weaving .	.	...	..	...	.	..
43	24. Rope, twine and string	35,905	5,107	20,869	16	6	9,923
44	25. Other fibres (cocoanut, aloes, flax, hemp, straw, etc.)	2,834	543	1,146	1	..	1,145
45	26. Wool carders and spinners, weavers of woollen blankets, carpets, etc.	...	...	..	.	...	..
46	27. Silk spinners and weavers	..	...	...	...	...	.
47	28. Hair, camel and horse hair, bristles work, brush makers, etc.	44	16	...	...	..	28
48	29. Persons occupied with feathers	.	..	.	...	..	.
49	30. Dyeing, bleaching, printing, preparation and sponging of textiles	11	4	..	..	...	7
50	31. Other (lace, crape, embroideries, fringes, etc.), and insufficiently described textile industries	57	2	39	...	..	16
51	ORDER 7.—HIDES, SKINS AND HARD MATERIALS FROM THE ANIMAL KINGDOM	*28*	*10*	..	..	...	*18*
52	32. Tanners, curriers, leather dressers and dyers, etc.	8	5	..	..	...	3
53	33. Makers of leather articles, such as trunks, water bags, etc.	.	..	..	..	..	...
54	34. Furriers	.	..	.	..		
55	35. Bone, ivory, horn, shell, etc., workers ...	20	5	.	..	..	15
56	ORDER 8.—WOOD	*34,674*	*10,546*	*5,214*	*109*	*4*	*18,914*
57	36. Sawyers, carpenters, turners and joiners, etc.	22,647	7,935	186	96	2	14,526
58	37. Basket makers and other industries of woody materials, including leaves ..	12,027	2,611	5,028	13	2	4,388
59	ORDER 9.—METALS	*14,027*	*4,663*	*271*	*52*	*2*	*9,093*
60	38. Forging and rolling of iron and other metals	..	...	..	...	.	..
61	39. Plough and agricultural implement makers	.	..	..	..	..	.
62	40. Makers of arms, guns, etc.	4	1	..	..	...	3
63	41. Other workers in iron and makers of implements and tools, principally or exclusively of iron	11,159	3,783	253	46	2	7,123
64	42. Workers in brass, copper and bell metal ..	2,701	825	18	6	..	1,858
65	43. Workers in other metals (tin, zink, lead, quick-silver, etc.)	156	52	.	..		104
66	44. Workers in mints, die-sinkers, etc. ..	7	2	..	.		5
67	ORDER 10.—CERAMICS	*4,540*	*1,225*	*740*	*1[illegible]*	*2*	*2,575*
68	45. Makers of glass and crystal ware	..	.	.			
69	46. Makers of porcelain and crockery .		.	.		.	.
70	47. Potters and earthen pipe and bowl makers.	2,445	775	614	1[illegible]	2	1,056
71	48. Brick and tile makers . ..	2 095	450	126	1		1,519
72	49. Others ([illegible], talc, mica, alabaster, etc.) workers	..	...	.			..

TABLE XV.

Occupation or Means of Livelihood.—Part A. *(Continued).*

KOTTAYAM.						DEVIKULAM.						
Total No. of workers and dependants.	Actual Workers. Total. Males.	Actual Workers. Total. Females.	Partially Agriculturists. Males.	Partially Agriculturists. Females.	Dependants.	Total No. of Workers and dependants.	Actual Workers. Total. Males.	Actual Workers. Total. Females.	Partially Agriculturists. Males.	Partially Agriculturists. Females.	Dependants.	Number.
26	27	28	29	30	31	32	33	34	35	36	37	
292,302	**82,917**	**76,272**	**1,119**	**84**	**133,113**	**7,084**	**2,893**	**874**	**16**	...	**3,317**	37
206,329	**58,456**	**58,655**	**752**	**42**	**89,218**	**4,401**	**1,899**	**547**	**11**	...	**1,955**	38
76,870	*16,999*	*41,348*	*47*	*10*	*18,523*	*26*	*10*	*2*	...	...	*14*	39
.	.	..	..	...	.	.	...	...	...	...	...	40
3,196	1,379	401	9	..	1,416	2	2	..	...	..	...	41
...	...	.	..	...	..	...	..	..	...	..	...	42
63,772	14,743	34,086	36	9	14,043	2	2	..	..	...	..	43
9.820	855	5,961	2	1	3,013	...	..	...	...	...	..	44
..	...	...	...	..	..	...	...	..	..	...	...	45
...	..	..	...	..	..	...	..	...	...	...	...	46
73	22	..	...	..	51	12	5	..	...	...	7	47
..	...	...	..	...	..	...	...	..	...	..	...	48
.	.	.	.	...	.	10	1	2	..	..	7	49
..	...	..	..	..	..	...	.	..	...	...	..	50
23	*9*	*2*	.	.	*12*	*5*	*1*	...	...	.	*1*	51
15	6	2	...	...	7	5	4	.	..	.	1	52
...	...	...	..	.	...		..			.	.	53
..	..	..	..	..	..	.	..	..		.	.	54
8	3	..	..	...	5	...	..			.	.	55
28,278	*8,076*	*4,947*	*80*	*4*	*15,255*	*1,890*	*1,117*	*131*	*5*	..	*592*	56
16,948	5,350	330	77	3	11,245	1,403	1,038	5	5	.	360	57
11.335	2,717	4,608	12	1	4,010	497	100	146	...	..	231	58
11,995	*3,994*	*248*	*14*	*1*	*7,753*	*478*	*153*	.	..	.	*325*	59
...	...	..	...	..	...	..	..	..	...	...	..	60
...	..	.	..	..	.	...	..	..	..	..	.	61
...	..	...	..	..	.	...	..	..	...	..	...	62
10,032	3,371	230	30	1	6,131	443	138	..	..	..	305	63
1,764	549	16	5	..	1,190	32	12	..	.	...	20	64
190	74	2	..	...	128	3	3	..	..	...	...	65
...	..	..	..	.	..	...	..	..	..	...	...	66
3,793	*1,352*	*993*	*15*	*2*	*1,148*	*189*	*124*	*28*	...	...	*37*	67
..	..	..	...	...	...	.	.	.	..	.	..	68
.	.	.	.	...	..	.	.	.	.		..	69
2,318	881	615	11	2	812	33	8	9	...	..	16	70
1,475	521	348	1	..	606	156	116	19	..	...	21	71
...	..	..	.	.	..	.	..	...	...	..	..	72

TABLE XV.

Occupation or Means of Livelihood.—Part A. (General Table.)

Number.	OCCUPATION.	STATE.					
		TOTAL NO. OF WORKERS AND DEPENDANTS.	ACTUAL WORKERS. Total.		ACTUAL WORKERS. Partially Agriculturists.		DEPENDANTS.
			Males.	Females.	Males.	Females.	
	1	2	3	4	5	6	7
73	ORDER 11.—CHEMICAL PRODUCTS PROPERLY SO CALLED, AND ANALOGOUS	*20,003*	*6,907*	*2,708*	*133*	*13*	*10,388*
74	50. Manufacture of matches and explosive materials	304	112	..	...	...	192
75	51. Manufacture of aerated and mineral waters.	192	90	...	..	...	102
76	52. Manufacture of dyes, paint and ink ..	169	43	19	...	..	107
77	53. Manufacture and refining of vegetable and mineral oils	19,223	6,626	2,680	133	13	9,917
78	54. Manufacture of paper, cardboard and papier machē	30	4	9	..	...	17
79	55. Others (soap, candles, lac, cutch, perfumes and miscellaneous drugs).	85	32	...	...	...	53
80	ORDER 12.—FOOD INDUSTRIES	*168,407*	*46,613*	*17,934*	*1,417*	*19*	*103,860*
81	56. Rice pounders and huskers and flour grinders	25,173	511	14,050	48	15	10,612
82	57. Bakers and biscuit makers	298	99	13	2	...	181
83	58. Grain parchers, etc.	248	25	120	..	...	103
84	59. Butchers	870	254	12	...	..	604
85	60. Fish curers	771	173	27	3	1	571
86	61. Butter, cheese and ghee makers ..	1,610	28	693	...	..	889
87	62. Makers of sugar, molasses and gur ..	4,997	105	2,879	2	3	2,013
88	63. Sweetmeat makers, preparers of jam and condiments, etc.	160	47	25	..	...	88
89	64. Brewers and distillers . . .	422	74	115	..	...	233
90	65. Toddy drawers	138,765	45,251	..	1,362	.	88,514
91	66. Manufacturers of tobacco, opium and ganja	98	46	.	...	...	52
92	ORDER 13.—INDUSTRIES OF DRESS AND THE TOILET.	*60,888*	*18,333*	*15,029*	*349*	*35*	*27,526*
93	67. Hat, cap and turban makers . ..	44	13	...	..	...	31
94	68. Tailors, milliners, dress-makers and darners, embroiderers on linen . ..	6,150	1,613	1,409	19	5	3,128
95	69. Shoe, boot and sandal makers ..	462	162	47	...	...	253
96	70. Other industries pertaining to dress-gloves, socks, gaiters, belts, buttons, umbrellas, canes, etc.	90	37	.	.	.	53
97	71. Washing, cleaning and dyeing . ..	26,556	7,468	9,614	89	17	9,474
98	72. Barbers, hairdressers and wig makers .	27,280	8,958	3,939	241	13	14,383
99	73. Other industries connected with the toilet (tattooers, shampooers, bath houses, etc.)	306	82	20	..	..	204
100	ORDER 14.—FURNITURE INDUSTRIES	*127*	*53*	...		..	*74*
101	74. Cabinet makers, carriage painters, etc. .	127	53	...	..	...	74
102	75. Upholsterers, tent makers, etc. .	.	...	..	...	.	..
103	ORDER 15.—BUILDING INDUSTRIES . .	*7,506*	*2,678*	*513*	*61*	...	*4,315*
104	76. Lime burners, cement workers . ..	2,060	703	355	7	...	1,002
105	77. Excavators, plinth builders and well-sinkers	519	159	20	...	..	340
106	78. Stone and marble workers, masons and bricklayers	4,118	1,605	138	51	...	2,705
107	79. Others (thatchers, building contractors, house painters, tilers, plumbers, locksmiths, etc.)	479	211	...	3	..	268
108	ORDER 16.—CONSTRUCTION OF MEANS OF TRANSPORT	*387*	*233*	...	*1*	..	*154*
109	80. Cart, carriage, palki, etc., makers and wheelwrights	...	..	...	..	..	...

TABLE XV.

Occupation or Means of Livelihood.—Part A. *(Continued).*

PADMANABHAPURAM.						TRIVANDRUM.						
TOTAL NO. OF WORKERS AND DEPENDANTS.	ACTUAL WORKERS.				DEPENDANTS.	TOTAL NO. OF WORKERS AND DEPENDANTS.	ACTUAL WORKERS.				DEPENDANTS.	Number.
	Total.		Partially Agriculturists.				Total.		Partially Agriculturists.			
	Males.	Females.	Males.	Females.			Males.	Females.	Males.	Females.		
8	9	10	11	12	13	14	15	16	17	18	19	
1,068	383	63	9	..	622	2,647	1,019	281	18	2	1,347	73
86	30	..	..	..	56	104	38	.	..	...	66	74
18	6	..	...	...	7	55	30	..	...	..	25	75
66	7	8	...	...	51	78	29	8	...	..	41	76
891	333	55	9	...	493	2,364	903	272	18	2	1,189	77
...	...	...	..	..	...	6	2	1	...	..	3	78
22	7	...	..	..	15	40	17	..	...	..	23	79
74,163	19,832	3,585	749	6	50,746	15,409	2,936	4,047	76	5	8,426	80
3,874	33	2,064	3	3	1,777	6,141	51	3,502	7	4	2,588	81
100	34	2	1	.	64	121	34	8	1	..	81	82
.	..	...	.	...	...	179	14	89	..	...	76	83
150	34	...	..	...	116	258	85	6	..	..	167	84
281	53	6	1	...	222	278	58	11	1	1	209	85
285	4	110	...	..	171	300	6	93	..	..	201	86
1,980	8	1,397	...	3	575	370	3	247	..	..	120	87
27	7	5	..	...	15	63	19	11	...	...	33	88
12	4	1	..	.	7	251	34	80	.	..	137	89
67,440	19,650	...	744	..	47,790	7,417	2,621	...	67	..	4,796	90
14	5	...	...	...	9	31	13	...	..	..	18	91
7,486	2,309	1,337	52	3	3,840	11,457	3,754	2,661	84	6	5,042	92
...	...	...	...	..	...	23	6	..	..	.	17	93
686	121	204	1	...	361	1,040	297	199	2	1	544	94
148	44	16	...	...	88	134	40	24	...	...	70	95
16	6	..	...	.	10	39	16	.	.	..	23	96
2,949	953	770	12	1	1,226	4,340	1,459	1,348	21	2	1,533	97
3,632	1,164	339	39	2	2,129	5,759	1,914	1,086	61	3	2,759	98
55	21	8	..	...	26	122	22	4	..	.	96	99
13	8	..	..	.	5	46	20	.	..	..	26	100
13	8	...	.	...	5	46	20	..	..	...	26	101
..	.	..	...	...	...	.	..	...	..	...	...	102
2,523	890	101	32	.	1,532	2,175	713	114	24	.	1,348	103
277	85	33	1	.	159	337	109	58	1	.	170	104
175	65	6	...	..	104	145	31	3	.	.	111	105
1,986	705	62	21	..	1,219	1,573	520	53	22	..	1,000	106
85	35	..	..	...	50	120	53	..	1	...	67	107
5	2	...	.	..	3	17	24	..	...	..	23	108
...	...	.	.	...	...	..	..	..	..	..	...	109

TABLE XV.

Occupation or Means of Livelihood.—Part A. (General Table.)

Number.	OCCUPATION.	QUILON. Total No. of workers and dependants.	Actual Workers. Total. Males.	Actual Workers. Total. Females.	Actual Workers. Partially Agriculturists. Males.	Actual Workers. Partially Agriculturists. Females.	Dependants.
	1	20	21	22	23	24	25
73	ORDER 11.—CHEMICAL PRODUCTS PROPERLY SO-CALLED, AND ANALOGOUS ..	*7,359*	*2,496*	*871*	*49*	*3*	*3,992*
74	50. Manufacture of matches and explosive materials	58	23	...	...	...	30
75	51. Manufacture of aerated and mineral waters.	76	33	...	.	...	43
76	52. Manufacture of dyes, paint and ink .	16	5	2	..	...	9
77	53. Manufacture and refining of vegetable and mineral oils	7,172	2,427	861	49	3	3,884
78	54. Manufacture of paper, card-board and papier maché	24	2	8	..	..	14
79	55. Others (soap, candles, lac, cutch, perfumes and miscellaneous drugs) ..	18	6	..	..	...	12
80	ORDER 12.—FOOD INDUSTRIES . .	*28,468*	*6,641*	*5,831*	*203*	*5*	*15,996*
81	56. Rice pounders and huskers and flour grinders	8,311	171	4,858	13	5	3,282
82	57. Bakers and biscuit makers . .	67	31	3	..	...	33
83	58. Grain parchers, etc. ..	67	11	31	...	...	25
84	59. Butchers	279	83	5	..	.	191
85	60. Fish curers	157	47	5	1	..	105
86	61. Butter, cheese and ghee makers .	352	5	152	..	..	195
87	62. Makers of sugar, molasses and gur .	1,615	59	735	1	...	821
88	63. Sweetmeat makers, preparers of jam and condiments, etc.	50	16	8	...	.	26
89	64. Brewers and distillers ...	150	34	34	..	.	82
90	65. Toddy drawers	17,380	6,162	...	188	...	11,218
91	66. Manufacturers of tobacco, opium and ganja	40	22	...	.	...	18
92	ORDER 13.—INDUSTRIES OF DRESS AND THE TOILET.	*23,303*	*7,233*	*5,795*	*132*	*13*	*10,275*
93	67. Hat, cap and turban makers	21	7	...	...	..	14
94	68. Tailors, milliners, dress-makers and darners, embroiderers on linen ..	2,649	728	669	10	2	1,252
95	69. Shoe, boot and sandal makers .	116	55	..	...	...	61
96	70 Other industries pertaining to dress-gloves, socks, gaiters, belts, buttons, umbrellas, canes, etc.	28	11	.	..	...	17
97	71. Washing, cleaning and dyeing ..	9,893	2,887	3,448	36	6	3,558
98	72 Barbers, hairdressers and wig makers .	10,543	3,527	1,672	86	5	5,344
99	73. Other industries connected with the toilet (tattooers, shampooers, bath houses, etc.)	53	18	6	..	...	29
100	ORDER 14.—FURNITURE INDUSTRIES ..	*56*	*20*	...	...	...	*36*
101	74. Cabinet makers, carriage painters, etc. ..	56	20	...	..	.	36
102	75. Upholsterers, tent makers, etc. ...	...	..	...	...	...	...
103	ORDER 15—BUILDING INDUSTRIES	*1,768*	*701*	*196*	*9*	...	*871*
104	76. Lime burners, cement workers ...	870	343	165	3	...	362
105	77. Excavators, plinth-builders and well-sinkers	144	45	8	...	...	91
106	78. Stone and marble workers, masons and brick-layers	597	238	23	5	...	336
107	79. Others (thatchers, building contractors, house painters, tilers, plumbers, locksmiths, etc)	157	75	..	1	...	82
108	ORDER 16.—CONSTRUCTION OF MEANS OF TRANSPORT . ..	*217*	*147*	..	*3*	..	*70*
109	80. Cart, carriage, palki, etc., makers and wheelrights	...	..	...	...	...	...

TABLE XV.

Occupation or Means of Livelihood.—Part A. *(Continued.)*

KOTTAYAM.						DEVIKULAM.						
Total No. of workers and dependants.	Actual Workers				Dependants.	Total No. of workers and dependants.	Actual Workers.				Dependants.	Number.
	Total.		Partially Agriculturists				Total.		Partially Agriculturists.			
	Males.	Females.	Males.	Females.			Males.	Females.	Males.	Females.		
26	27	28	29	30	31	32	33	34	35	36	37	
8,800	*2,976*	*1,477*	*57*	*8*	*4,347*	*129*	*33*	*16*	...	..	*80*	73
61	21	...	...	..	40	...	..	...	...	..	..	74
31	14	...	...	...	17	17	7	...	...	...	10	75
...	...	...	...	..	...	9	2	1	...	...	6	76
8,703	2,939	1,477	57	8	4,287	103	24	15	...	...	64	77
...	...	...	...	...	...	...	...	...	...	...	...	78
5	2	...	...	...	3	...	...	...	...	...	...	79
49,818	*17,130*	*4,308*	*388*	*3*	*28,380*	*549*	*74*	*163*	*1*	...	*312*	80
6,499	246	3,479	24	3	2,774	348	10	147	1	...	191	81
5	2	..	..	...	3	...	...	...	..	...	..	82
2	...	...	..	...	2	..	...	...	...	...	...	83
154	41	1	...	...	112	29	11	...	...	...	18	84
55	15	5	...	...	35	..	...	...	...	...	...	85
634	13	322	..	...	299	39	...	16	..	...	23	86
1,032	35	500	1	...	497	..	...	...	...	...	...	87
9	2	1	..	...	6	11	8	...	...	...	6	88
...	.	...	...	...	...	9	2	...	..	...	7	89
41,415	16,770	...	363	...	24,645	113	48	...	..	..	65	90
13	6	...	...	...	7	...	...	...	...	..	...	91
17,820	*4,791*	*5,068*	*76*	*13*	*7,961*	*822*	*246*	*168*	*5*	..	*408*	92
...	...	.	...	..	...	...	..	...	...	...	...	93
1,722	444	335	6	2	943	53	23	2	...	..	28	94
64	23	7	..	..	34	...	...	...	..	...	...	95
7	4	...	..	...	3	..	...	...	...	...	...	96
8,879	2,039	3,902	18	8	2,938	495	130	146	2	...	219	97
7,072	2,260	822	52	3	8,990	274	93	20	3	...	161	98
76	21	2	...	..	53	...	...	...	..	...	...	99
12	*5*	...	...	...	*7*	...	...	...	...	..	...	100
12	5	...	..	...	7	...	...	...	...	...	...	101
...	...	...	.	...	...	...	...	...	...	...	...	102
959	*351*	*96*	*6*	...	*512*	*81*	*23*	*6*	...	...	*52*	103
548	161	93	2	..	294	28	5	6	...	...	17	104
55	18	3	...	..	34	...	...	..	...	...	...	105
260	129	...	8	.	131	82	13	...	...	...	19	106
96	43	...	1	...	53	21	5	...	...	...	16	107
118	*60*	...	*1*	...	*58*	...	...	...	...	..	...	108
...	...	...	...	...	...	...	...	...	...	...	...	109

TABLE XV.

Occupation or Means of Livelihood.—Part A. (General Table).

Number.	OCCUPATION.	STATE.					
		Total No. of workers and dependants.	Actual Workers.				Dependants.
			Total.		Partially Agriculturists		
			Males.	Females.	Males.	Females.	
	1	2	3	4	5	6	7
110	81. Saddlers, harness-makers, whip and lash makers	37	13	...	..	..	24
111	82. Ship and boat builders...	350	220	..	4	.	130
112	ORDER 17.—PRODUCTION AND TRANSMISSION OF PHYSICAL FORCES (HEAT, LIGHT, ELECTRICITY, MOTIVE POWER, ETC.) (Group 83). Gas works, electric light and ice factories	*61*	*16*	.	..	...	*45*
113	ORDER 18.—INDUSTRIES OF LUXURY AND THOSE PERTAINING TO LITERATURE AND THE ARTS AND SCIENCES	*25,714*	*8,876*	*305*	*126*	*2*	*16,533*
114	84. Printers, lithographers, engravers, etc. ..	1,734	767	5	2	..	962
115	85. Newspaper and magazine managers and editors, journalists, etc.	95	28	.	1	...	67
116	86. Bookbinders and stitchers, envelope makers, etc.	492	168	..	1	..	324
117	87. Makers of musical instruments	23	9	.	.	..	14
118	88. Makers of watches and clocks and optical, photographic and surgical instruments .	76	23	..	...	...	53
119	89. Workers in precious stones and metals, enamellers, imitation jewellery makers, gilders, etc....	22,011	7,445	134	118	2	14,432
120	90. Makers of bangles, rosaries, bead and other necklaces, spangles, lingams and sacred threads	1,179	403	152	4	...	624
121	91. Toy, kite, cage, fishing tackle, etc., makers, taxidermists, etc.	54	13	14	.	...	27
122	92. Others, including managers, persons other than performers employed in theatres and other places of public entertainment, employes of public societies, race course service, huntsmen, etc.	50	20	...	...	.	30
123	ORDER 19.—INDUSTRIES CONCERNED WITH REFUSE MATTER. (Group 93) Sweepers, scavengers, dust and sweeping contractors	*1,981*	*558*	*545*	*4*	..	*878*
124	**Sub-Class IV.—Transport ... ..**	**54,942**	**22,724**	**5,921**	**100**	**2**	**23,237**
125	ORDER 20.—TRANSPORT BY WATER	*23,895*	*10,206*	*1,773*	*19*	..	*11,916*
126	94. Harbour works, dockyards and pilots ..	43	17	...	..	...	26
127	95. Ship owners and their employes, ship brokers, ships' officers, engineers, mariners and firemen	537	280	..	...	...	257
128	96. Persons employed on the maintenance of streams, rivers and canals (including construction)	6,463	2,811	1,773	3	.	1,879
129	97. Boat owners, boat men and tow men ..	16,852	7,098	..	16	...	9,754
130	ORDER 21.—TRANSPORT BY ROAD	*25,638*	*10,400*	*4,146*	*67*	*2*	*11,292*
131	98. Persons employed on the construction and maintenance of roads and bridges ..	4,019	1,722	777	4	...	1,520
132	99. Cart owners and drivers, coachmen, stable boys, tramway, mail carriage, etc., managers and employes (excluding private servants	7,583	3,741	...	58	2	3,842
133	100. Palki, etc., bearers and owners	107	42	..	.	..	65

TABLE XV.

Occupation or Means of Livelihood.—Part A. *(Continued.)*

PADMANABHAPURAM.						TRIVANDRUM.						
Total No. of workers and dependants	Actual Workers.				Dependants.	Total No. of workers and dependants.	Actual Workers.				Dependants.	Number.
	Total.		Partially Agriculturists.				Total.		Partially Agriculturists.			
	Males.	Females.	Males.	Females.			Males.	Females.	Males.	Females.		
8	9	10	11	12	13	14	15	16	17	18	19	
5	2	..	.		3	22	8		..	..	14	110
...	..		...	..	..	25	16	..	.	.	9	111
..	...	..	..	..	..	*61*	*16*	..	.	..	*45*	112
4,700	*1,493*	*60*	*18*	..	*3,147*	*5,330*	*1,937*	*81*	*44*	*1*	*3,321*	113
78	21	..	..	..	57	803	380	3	2	..	420	114
5	1	..	...	.	4	27	8	.	.	.	19	115
43	14	.		.	29	194	70	.	1	..	124	116
7	2	..	...	...	5	14	6	.	.	...	8	117
18	4	..	.	.	14	34	13	..	...	...	21	118
4,250	1,347	34	17	..	2,869	3,986	1,375	49	39	1	2,562	119
274	97	26	1	.	151	237	73	18	2	..	146	120
4	1	.	.	.	3	31	7	11	...	..	13	121
21	6	..	...	..	15	13	5	...	...	...	8	122
400	*99*	*103*	*1*	...	*198*	*461*	*153*	*113*	*2*	.	*195*	123
10,739	**4,583**	**2,215**	**17**	.	**3,941**	**7,929**	**3,676**	**535**	**31**	**2**	**3,718**	124
4,932	*2,208*	*1,508*	*3*	.	*1,216*	*2,203*	*912*	*45*	*2*	.	*1,246*	125
...	...	.	.	.	..	5	2	..	...	..	3	126
21	12	.	...	..	9	37	26	..	..	.	11	127
4,882	2,186	1,508	3	...	1,188	520	198	45	.	.	286	128
29	10	...	.	.	19	1,632	686	.	2		946	129
5,239	*2,165*	*707*	*13*	...	*2,367*	*4,727*	*2,470*	*489*	*25*	*2*	*1,763*	130
798	318	248	..	.	232	862	431	81	2	.	350	131
2,262	1,019	...	13	...	1,213	1,909	1,295	.	22	2	613	132
44	16	.	...	..	28	38	17	.	...	.	21	133

TABLE XV.

Occupation or Means of Livelihood.—Part A. (General Table.)

Number.	OCCUPATION.	QUILON.					
		TOTAL NO. OF WORKERS AND DEPENDANTS.	ACTUAL WORKERS.				DEPENDANTS
			TOTAL.		Partially Agriculturists.		
			Males.	Females.	Males.	Females.	
	1	20	21	22	23	24	25
110	81. Saddlers, harness-makers, whip and lash makers	10	3	...	..	...	7
111	82. Ship and boat-builders	207	144	...	3	..	63
112	ORDER 17.—PRODUCTION AND TRANSMISSION OF PHYSICAL FORCES (HEAT, LIGHT, ELECTRICITY, MOTIVE POWER, ETC.) (Group 83). Gas works, electric light and ice factories.	...	...	...	...	..	...
113	ORDER 18.—INDUSTRIES OF LUXURY AND THOSE PERTAINING TO LITERATURE AND THE ARTS AND SCIENCES	*7,975*	*2,754*	*85*	*35*	...	*5,136*
114	84. Printers, lithographers, engravers, etc. ..	393	170	...	..	...	223
115	85. Newspaper and magazine managers and editors, journalists, etc.	28	8	...	...	...	20
116	86. Bookbinders and stitchers, envelope makers, etc.	150	55	...	...	...	95
117	87. Makers of musical instruments	...	..	..	...	...	...
118	88. Makers of watches and clocks and optical, photographic and surgical instruments ...	13	2	...	...	...	11
119	89. Workers in precious stones and metals, enamellers, imitation jewellery makers, gilders, etc.	7,000	2,379	26	34	..	4,595
120	90. Makers of bangles, rosaries, bead and other necklaces, spangles, lingams and sacred threads	369	132	56	1	...	181
121	91. Toy, kite, cage, fishing tackle, etc., makers, taxidermists, etc.	19	5	3	..	...	11
122	92. Others including managers, persons other than performers employed in theatres and other places of public entertainment, employes of public societies, race course service, huntsmen, etc.... ..	3	3	..	..	...	..
123	ORDER 19.—INDUSTRIES CONCERNED WITH REFUSE MATTER (Group 93.) Sweepers, scavengers, dust and sweeping contractors	*745*	*200*	*227*	*1*	...	*318*
124	**Sub-class IV.—Transport**	**22,517**	**9,223**	**1,570**	**35**	..	**11,724**
125	ORDER 20.—TRANSPORT BY WATER	*12,302*	*5,232*	*126*	*10*	..	*6,944*
126	94. Harbour works, dockyards and pilots .	38	15	...	...	...	23
127	95. Ship owners and their employes, ship brokers, ships' officers, engineers, mariners and firemen.	471	234	...	..	...	237
128	96. Persons employed on the maintenance of streams, rivers and canals (including construction)	546	225	126	...	...	195
129	97. Boat owners, boat men and tow men ..	11,247	4,758	[illegible]	10	...	6,489
130	ORDER 21.—TRANSPORT BY ROAD	*8,297*	*3,133*	*1,443*	*20*	...	*3,721*
131	98. Persons employed on the construction and maintenance of roads and bridges ...	1,270	519	209	1	...	542
132	99. Cart owners and drivers, coachmen, stable boys, tramway, mail carriage, etc,. managers and employes (excluding private servants	2,175	944	...	17	...	1,231
133	100. Palki, etc., bearers and owners	25	9	...	...	...	16

TABLE XV.

Occupation or Means of Livelihood.—Part A. *(Continued).*

KOTTAYAM.						DEVIKULAM.						
Total No. of workers and dependants.	Actual Workers.				Dependants.	Total No. of workers and dependants.	Actual Workers.				Dependants.	Number.
	Total.		Partially Agriculturists.				Total.		Partially Agriculturists.			
	Males.	Females.	Males.	Females.			Males.	Females.	Males.	Females.		
26	27	28	29	30	31	32	33	34	35	36	37	
..	..	..		.	.	..	...	..	...	...	..	110
118	60	...	1	...	58	..	...	...	..	.	.	111
..	..	..	.	..		.	...	.	...	...	..	112
7,513	*2,617*	*76*	*29*	*1*	*4,820*	*187*	*75*	*3*	..	...	*109*	113
460	196	2	...		262	...	..	...	..	...	..	114
85	11	..	1	..	24	...	...	...	...	...	...	115
105	29	.	...	...	76	...	.	...	...	...	..	116
2	1	..	...	..	1	.	...	...	...	...	...	117
11	4	..	.	..	7	..	...	...	...	..	...	118
6,600	2,274	25	28	1	4,301	175	70	...	...	...	105	119
287	96	49	...	..	142	12	5	3	...	...	4	120
.	..	...	...	..	...	..	..	...	.	...	..	121
13	6	.	.	.	7	...	...	...	...	...	...	122
330	*96*	*92*	...	...	*142*	*45*	*10*	*10*	..	...	*25*	123
12,930	**4,899**	**1,516**	**17**	..	**6,515**	**827**	**343**	**85**	..	...	**399**	124
4,403	*1,834*	*84*	*4*	.	*2,485*	*55*	*20*	*10*	...	...	*25*	225
	..	..	..	..	..	..	..	...	...	...	...	126
8	8	..	...	...	...	..	..	...	...	...	..	127
451	182	84	.	...	185	55	20	10	...	...	25	128
3,944	1,644	...	4	..	2,300	...	.	...	..	..	.	129
6,996	*2,394*	*1,432*	*9*	...	*3,170*	*579*	*238*	*75*	...	...	*266*	130
939	397	201	1	.	341	150	57	38	...	...	55	131
1,107	391	...	6	..	716	131	62	...	...	.	69	13.
.	...	...	.	...	...	...	..	.	.	.	.	13:

TABLE XV.

Occupation or Means of Livelihood.—Part A. (General Table).

Number.	OCCUPATION.	STATE. Total No. of workers and dependants.	Actual Workers. Total. Males.	Females.	Partially Agriculturists. Males.	Females.	Dependants.
	1	2	3	4	5	6	7
134	101. Pack elephant, camel, mule, ass and bullock owners and drivers	603	272	..	3	..	336
135	102 Porters and messengers	13,521	4,623	3,369	2	..	5,529
136	Order 22.—Transport by rail .. .	*929*	*567*	..	*2*	...	*362*
137	103. Railway employes of all kinds other than construction coolies	751	481	...	2	...	270
138	104. Laboures employed on railway construction	178	86	.	...	..	92
139	Order 23 —Post Office Telegraph and Telephone Services . ..	*4,280*	*1,551*	*2*	*12*	..	*2,727*
140	105 Post Office, Telegraph and Telephone services.	4,280	1,551	2	12	.	2,727
141	(a) Do Do. Do. ...	913	545	2	...	..	366
142	(b) Anchal service (*Travancore*) ...	3,367	1,006	..	12	..	2,361
143	**Sub-Class V.—Trade ... ...**	**285,333**	**74,067**	**63,997**	**1,203**	**126**	**147,269**
144	Order 24.—Banks establishments of credit exchange, and insurance (Group 106.) Bank managers, money lenders exchange and insurance agents, money changers and brokers and employes ..	*9,446*	*1,887*	*861*	*44*	*4*	*6,698*
145	Order 25.—Brokerage commission and export. (Group 107). Brokers commission agents, commercial travellers warehouse owners and employes ..	*827*	*259*	*26*	*5*	...	*542*
146	Order 26.—Trade in Textiles (Group 108) Trade in piece-goods wool, cotton, silk, hair and other textiles ..	*45,221*	*12,436*	*9,957*	*143*	*11*	*22,828*
147	Order 27.—Trade in Skins, Leather and Furs (Group 109). Trade in skins, leathers, furs, feathers horn, etc. ..	*508*	*184*	*3*	*1*	..	*321*
148	Order 28 —Trade in Wood (Group 110). Trade in wool (not firewood) cork, bark etc.	*9,031*	*2,094*	*3,732*	*44*	*6*	*3,205*
149	Order 29.—Trade in Metals (Group. 111) Trade in metals, machinery, knife, tool, etc. sellers	*78*	*30*	..	.	.	*48*
150	Order 30 —Trade in Pottery (Group 112). Trade in pottery	*2,289*	*620*	*635*	*12*	..	*1,034*
151	Order 31.—Trade in Chemical Products (Group 113). Trade in chemical products (drugs dyes, paints, petroleum, explosives, etc.	*131*	*47*	.	.	.	*84*
152	Order 32.—Hotels, Cafes, Restaurants, Etc.	*23,413*	*6,871*	*5,427*	*100*	*38*	*11,205*
153	114. Vendors of wine, liquors, aerated waters, etc. .	20,218	5,944	4,685	89	38	9,589
154	115. Owners and managers of hotels, cookshops, sarais, etc, and their employes.	3,225	867	742	11	.	1,616
155	Order 33 —Other Trade in Food Stuffs	*163,703*	*42,185*	*39,647*	*587*	*49*	*86,871*

TABLE XV.

Occupation or Means of Livelihood.—Part A. *(Continued).*

PADMANABHAPURAM.						TRIVANDRUM.						
Total No. of workers and dependants.	Actual Workers.				Dependants	Total No of workers and dependants	Actual Workers.				Dependants.	Number.
	Total.		Partially Agriculturists.				Total.		Partially Agriculturists.			
	Males.	Females.	Males.	Females.			Males.	Females	Males.	Females.		
8	9	10	11	12	13	14	15	16	17	18	19	
26	10	.	.	.	16	98	39	..	1	..	59	134
2,109	772	459	..		878	1,921	633	403	.	.	725	135
.	..	..	..	.	..	..	...	..	.	...	..	136
..	...	..	..	.	.	...	..	...	..	.	..	137
..	..	..	..	...		..	..	.	..	...	...	138
568	*210*	.	*1*	.	*358*	*999*	*294*	*1*	*4*	...	*704*	139
568	210	.	1	.	358	999	294	1	4	..	704	140
141	80	..	..	.	61	154	89	1	..	..	64	141
427	130	..	1	.	297	845	205	.	4	..	640	142
46,136	**11,050**	**9,992**	**178**	**13**	**25,184**	**67,040**	**13,212**	**18,744**	**250**	**34**	**34,084**	143
2,423	*430*	*342*	*11*	*1*	*1,651*	*2,591*	*428*	*169*	*12*	..	*1,994*	144
130	*36*	..	*1*	..	*94*	*345*	*116*	*14*	*2*	..	*215*	145
3,972	*1,119*	*158*	*13*	..	*2,695*	*10,692*	*3,114*	*1,377*	*40*	*1*	*6,201*	146
83	*29*	*3*	..	..	*51*	*92*	*34*	..	...	..	*58*	147
704	*173*	*167*	*10*	.	*364*	*1,472*	*462*	*535*	*7*	*1*	*475*	148
22	*9*	.	.	.	*13*	*27*	*11*	..	..	...	*16*	149
333	*111*	*98*	*2*	.	*124*	*251*	*53*	*101*	*1*	.	*97*	150
28	*13*	.	.	.	*15*	*15*	*6*	.			*9*	151
2,409	*631*	*812*	*9*	*5*	*966*	*3,687*	*1,141*	*985*	*17*	*8*	*1,561*	152
2,088	592	729	8	5	767	2,838	883	803	14	8	1,152	153
381	99	83	1		199	849	258	182	3	.	400	154
31,400	*7,266*	*7,768*	*102*	*9*	*16,366*	*41,652*	*9,121*	*12,188*	*130*	*18*	*20,343*	155

TABLE XV.

Occupation or Means of Livelihood.—Part A. (General Table.)

Number.	OCCUPATION.	QUILON.					
		Total No. of workers and dependants.	Actual Workers.				Dependants.
			Total.		Partially Agriculturists.		
			Males.	Females.	Males.	Females.	
	1	20	21	22	23	24	25
134	101. Pack elephant, camel, mule, ass and bullock owners and drivers	242	110	...	1	..	132
135	102. Porters and messengers	4,585	1,551	1,234	1	...	1,800
136	Order 22.—Transport by rail	*535*	*320*	...	*1*	..	*215*
137	103. Railway employes of all kinds other than construction coolies ..	398	253	...	1	..	145
138	104. Labourers employed on railway construction	137	67	...	...	..	70
139	Order 23.—Post Office, Telegraph and Telephone Services	*1,383*	*538*	*1*	*4*	..	*844*
140	105. Post Office, Telegraph and Telephone services	1,383	538	1	4	...	844
141	(a) Do. Do. Do. .	360	211	1	..	..	148
142	(b) Anchal service *(Travancore)* .	1,023	327	...	4	..	696
143	**Sub-Class V.—Trade ... ..**	**97,258**	**26,592**	**21,008**	**420**	**34**	**49,658**
144	Order 24—Banks Establishments of credit exchange, and Insurance (Group 106) Bank managers, money-lenders exchange and insurance agents, money-changers and brokers and employes ...	*2,793*	*617*	*237*	*12*	*2*	*1,939*
145	Order 25.—Brokerage commission and export (Group 107.) Brokers commission agents, commercial travellers, warehouse owners and employes	*312*	*93*	*12*	*2*	..	*207*
146	Order 26—Trade in Textiles (Group 108.) Trade in piece-goods, wool, cotton, silk, hair and other textiles	*17,173*	*5,308*	*3,105*	*55*	*4*	*8,760*
147	Order 27.—Trade in skins, leathers and furs (Group 109.) Trade in skins, leathers, furs, feathers horn, etc. ...	*158*	*57*	..	*1*	..	*101*
148	Order 28.—Trade in Wood (Group 110.) Trade in wood (not fire-wood) cork bark etc.	*3,570*	*730*	*1,698*	*14*	*3*	*1,142*
149	Order 29—Trade in metals (Group 111). Trade in metals, machinery, knife, tool, etc. sellers	*20*	*7*	...	.	..	*13*
150	Order 30.—Trade in pottery (Group 112.) Trade in pottery	*844*	*228*	*214*	*4*	..	*402*
151	Order 31.—Trade in chemical products (Group 113.) Trade in chemical products (drugs, dyes, paints, petroleum, explosives, etc.	*39*	*15*	..	.	...	*24*
152	Order 32.—Hotels, cafes, restaurants, etc.	*4,942*	*1,763*	*1,081*	*27*	*2*	*2,092*
153	114. Vendors of wine, liquors, aerated waters, etc.	3,804	1,470	778	22	2	1,556
154	115. Owners and managers of hotels, cookshops, sarais, etc, and their employes ...	1,138	299	303	5	...	536
155	Order 33.—Other Trade in food stuffs ...	*52,216*	*15,286*	*13,547*	*200*	*14*	*30,383*

TABLE XV.

Occupation or Means of Livelihood.—Part A. *(Continued)*.

KOTTAYAM.						DEVIKULAM.						
Total No. of workers and dependants.	Actual Workers.				Dependants.	Total No. of workers and dependants.	Actual Workers.				Dependants.	Number.
	Total.		Partially Agriculturists.				Total.		Partially Agriculturists.			
	Males.	Females.	Males.	Females.			Males.	Females.	Males.	Females.		
26	27	28	29	30	31	32	33	34	35	36	37	
213	105	..	1	.	108	29	8	.	..	.	21	134
4,737	1,501	1,231	1	..	2,005	269	111	37	.	..	121	135
388	*246*	.	*1*	..	*142*	*6*	*1*	...	.	...	*5*	136
353	228	..	1	.	125	...	...	...	...	...	...	137
35	18	..	...	...	17	6	1	...	...	...	5	138
1.143	*425*	...	*3*	..	*718*	*187*	*84*	...	...	.	*103*	139
1,143	425	.	3	.	718	187	84	...	.	..	103	140
223	142	...	...	..	81	35	23	...	..	.	12	141
920	283	...	3	..	637	152	61	...	.	.	91	142
73,043	**19,562**	**16,101**	**350**	**42**	**37,380**	**1,856**	**651**	**242**	**5**	..	**963**	143
1,623	*409*	*112*	*9*	*1*	*1,102*	*16*	*3*	*1*	..	.	*12*	144
40	*14*	..	...	...	*26*	..	...	...	...	..	...	145
13,310	*2,876*	*5,317*	*35*	*6*	*5,117*	*74*	*19*	...	...	...	*55*	146
175	*64*	...	...	...	*111*	...	...	...	...	...	...	147
3,210	*697*	*1,311*	*12*	*2*	*1,202*	*75*	*32*	*21*	*1*	...	*22*	148
9	*3*	...	...	..	*6*	...	...	...	...	...	...	149
813	*213*	*210*	*5*	..	*390*	*48*	*15*	*12*	...	...	*21*	150
49	*13*	...	...	..	*36*	...	...	...	...	...	..	151
11,997	*3,090*	*2,495*	*45*	*23*	*6,412*	*348*	*120*	*54*	*2*	...	*174*	152
11,230	2,897	2,336	43	23	5,997	258	102	39	2	...	117	153
767	193	159	2	...	415	90	18	15	...	...	57	154
35,460	*10,165*	*6,029*	*153*	*8*	*10,266*	*975*	*347*	*115*	*2*	.	*513*	155

TABLE XV.

Occupation or Means of Livelihood.—Part A. (General Table.)

Number.	OCCUPATION.	STATE. Total No. of workers and dependants.	Actual Workers. Total. Males.	Actual Workers. Total. Females.	Partially Agriculturists. Males.	Partially Agriculturists. Females.	Dependants
	1	2	3	4	5	6	7
156	116. Fish dealers	50,021	10,817	19,748	76	10	19,456
157	117. Grocers and sellers of vegetable oil, salt and other condiments	27,448	7,937	8,062	181	9	16,449
158	118. Sellers of milk, butter, ghee, poultry, eggs, etc.	1,779	317	616	1	..	846
159	119. Sellers of sweetmeats, sugar, gur and molasses...	15,057	2,702	5,329	5	..	7,026
160	120. Cardamom, betel-leaf, vegetables, fruit and arecanut sellers	32,783	8,892	3,413	176	8	20,478
161	121. Grain and pulse dealers	26,528	7,447	4,490	88	14	14,591
162	122. Tobacco, opium, ganja, etc., sellers	9,717	2,764	1,053	53	6	5,900
163	123. Dealers in sheep, goats and pigs	42	13	3	.	...	26
164	124. Dealers in hay, grass and fodder	5,328	1,296	1,933	7	2	2,099
165	Order 34.—Trade in clothing and toilet articles. (Group 125) Trade in ready-made clothing and other articles of dress and the toilet (hats, umbrellas, socks, ready-made shoes, perfumes, etc.)	*64*	*25*	*4*	*1*	..	*35*
166	Order 35.—Trade in furniture ...	*3,281*	*834*	*412*	*20*	*6*	*2,035*
167	126 Trade in furniture, carpets, curtains and bedding	1,456	316	369	14	6	771
168	127. Hardware, cooking utensils, porcelain, crockery, glassware, bottles, articles for gardening, the cellar, etc.	1,825	518	43	6	.	1,264
169	Order 36.—Trade in building materials, (Group 128) Trade in building materials (stones, bricks, plaster, cement, sand, tiles, thatch, etc.)	*5,004*	*1,363*	*86[illegible]*	*21*	*4*	*2,779*
170	Order 37.—Trade in means of transport. (Group 129) Dealers and hirers of elephants, camels, horses, cattle, asses, mules, etc. sellers (not makers) of carriages, saddlery, etc.	*937*	*331*	*8*	*1*	..	*598*
171	Order 38.—Trade in fuel. (Group 130) Dealers in firewood, charcoal, coal, cow-dung, etc.	*4,032*	*1,025*	*1,448*	*2*	*1*	*1,609*
172	Order 39.—Trade in articles of luxury and those pertaining to letters and the arts and sciences	*1.415*	*457*	...	*13*	.	*958*
173	131. Dealers in precious stones, jewellery (real and imitation), clocks, optical instruments, etc.	719	208	...	13	...	511
174	132. Dealers in common bangles, bead necklaces, fans, small articles, toys, hunting and fishing tackle, flowers, etc....	209	83	..	..	..	126
175	133. Publishers, booksellers, stationers, dealers in music, pictures, musical instruments and curiosities	487	166	..	...	...	321
176	Order 40.—Trade in refuse matter (Group 134) Dealers in rags, stable refuse, etc...	*38*	*13*	...	..	.	*25*
177	Order 41.—Trade of other sorts...	*10,835*	*3,466*	*975*	*209*	*9*	*6,394*
178	135. Shopkeepers otherwise unspecified	7,300	2,187	668	130	8	4,450
179	136. Itinerant traders, pedlars, hawkers, etc.	83	31	...	..	..	52

TABLE XV.

Occupation or Means of Livelihood.—Part A. *(Continued.)*

PADMANABHAPURAM.						TRIVANDRUM.						
TOTAL NO. OF WORKERS AND DEPENDANTS.	ACTUAL WORKERS.				DEPENDANTS.	TOTAL NO. OF WORKERS AND DEPENDANTS.	ACTUAL WORKERS.				DEPENDANTS.	Number.
	Total.		Partially Agriculturists.				Total.		Partially Agriculturists.			
	Males.	Females.	Males.	Females.			Males.	Females.	Males.	Females.		
8	9	10	11	12	13	14	15	16	17	18	19	
9,038	1,719	3,280	14	1	4,039	11,767	2,272	4,814	13	8	4,681	156
5,071	1,313	686	31	2	3,072	6,553	1,828	1,220	46	4	3,505	157
238	42	84	...	.	112	456	103	174	1	...	174	158
3,659	586	1,272	1	..	1,801	4,005	654	1,555	1	..	1,796	159
7,227	1,706	1,209	33	3	4,312	6,646	1,423	1,325	29	3	3,898	160
4,158	1,400	605	16	2	2,152	7,414	1,563	1,917	23	6	3,934	161
1,045	317	161	6	1	567	2,348	605	269	14	2	1,474	162
32	10	2	...	..	20	.	..	..	.	.	...	163
932	173	468	1	..	291	2,463	668	914	3	..	881	164
24	*8*	*4*	*1*	..	*12*	*29*	*13*	.	...	..	*16*	165
722	*180*	*50*	*3*	*1*	*492*	*619*	*174*	*73*	*4*	*1*	*372*	166
226	50	45	2	1	131	234	47	62	3	1	125	167
496	130	5	1	..	361	385	127	11	1	.	247	168
1,063	*262*	*178*	*4*		*623*	*1,180*	*313*	*268*	*4*	*2*	*599*	169
236	*75*	...	..	..	*161*	*218*	*74*	*3*	.	.	*141*	170
821	*146*	*208*	..	.	*470*	*2,092*	*546*	*838*	*2*	*1*	*708*	171
413	*115*	...	*3*	.	*298*	*471*	*153*	..	*6*	.	*318*	172
283	66	..	3	.	217	263	79	...	6	..	184	173
56	22	...	.	..	34	103	36	..	.		67	174
74	27	...	.	..	47	105	38	..	.	..	67	175
19	*6*	..	..	...	*13*	*5*	*2*	..	..	.	*3*	176
1,271	*381*	*114*	*19*	*2*	*776*	*1,602*	*451*	*193*	*25*	*2*	*958*	177
914	262	103	13	2	579	1,045	273	121	16	2	648	178
17	7	.	...	...	10	35	13	..	..	..	22	179

TABLE XV.

Occupation or Means of Livelihood.—Part A. (General Table.)

Number.	OCCUPATION.	QUILON. Total No. of workers and dependants.	Actual Workers. Total. Males.	Actual Workers. Total. Females.	Actual Workers. Partially Agriculturists. Males.	Actual Workers. Partially Agriculturists. Females.	Dependants
	1	20	21	22	23	24	25
156	116. Fish dealers	18,121	4,028	8,014	28	4	6,079
157	117. Grocers and sellers of vegetable oil, salt and other condiments	8,662	2,484	702	54	2	5,476
158	118. Sellers of milk, butter, ghee, poultry, eggs, etc.	620	73	224	...	...	323
159	119. Sellers of sweetmeats, sugar, gur and molasses	4,728	785	1,871	2	...	2,072
160	120. Cardamom, betel-leaf, vegetables, fruit and arecanut sellers	12,695	3,817	574	68	2	8,304
161	121. Grain and pulse dealers	8,986	2,669	1,338	28	4	4,979
162	122. Tobacco, opium, ganja, etc., sellers ..	3,946	1,135	335	18	2	2,476
163	123. Dealers in sheep, goats, and pigs ...	5	.	1	.	..	4
164	124. Dealers in hay, grass and fodder ..	1,453	295	488	2	..	670
165	ORDER 34.—TRADE IN CLOTHING AND TOILET ARTICLES (Group 125.) Trade in ready-made clothing and other articles of dress and the toilet (hats, umbrellas, socks, ready-made shoes, perfumes etc.) ...	*11*	*4*	...	...	..	*7*
166	ORDER 35.—TRADE IN FURNITURE	*1,076*	*270*	*183*	*8*	*4*	*623*
167	126. Trade in furniture, carpets, curtains and bedding	601	122	174	6	4	305
168	127. Hardware, cooking utensils, porcelain, crockery, glassware, bottles, articles for gardening, the cellar, etc.	475	148	9	2	...	318
169	ORDER 36.—TRADE IN BUILDING MATERIALS (Group 128.) Trade in building materials (stone, bricks, plaster, cement, sand tiles, thatch, etc.)	*1,423*	*352*	*287*	*5*	*2*	*784*
170	ORDER 37.—TRADE IN MEANS OF TRANSPORT (Group 129.) Dealers and hirers of elephants, camels, horses, cattle, asses, mules, etc., sellers (not makers) of carriages, saddlery, etc.	*417*	*148*	*5*	*1*	...	*264*
171	ORDER 38.—TRADE IN FUEL (Group 130.) Dealers in fire-wood, charcoal, coal, cow-dung etc.	*948*	*252*	*379*	...	...	*317*
172	ORDER 39.—TRADE IN ARTICLES OF LUXURY AND THOSE PERTAINING TO LETTERS AND THE ART AND SCIENCES	*358*	*129*	...	*4*	...	*229*
173	131. Dealers in precious stones, jewellery, (real and imitation) clocks, optical instruments, etc.	120	42	...	4	...	78
174	132. Dealers in common bangles, bead, necklaces, fans, small articles, toys, hunting and fishing tackle, flowers, etc. ..	40	20	...	...	...	20
175	133. Publishers, book-sellers, stationers, dealers in music, pictures, musical instruments and curiosities	198	67	...	...	...	131
176	ORDER 40.—TRADE IN REFUSE MATTER (Group 134.) Dealers in rags, stable refuse, etc....	*9*	*3*	...	...	...	*6*
177	ORDER 41.—TRADE OF OTHER SORTS	*3,949*	*1,324*	*260*	*87*	*3*	*2,365*
178	135. Shop-keepers otherwise unspecified ..	2,687	828	185	53	3	1,674
179	136 Itinerant traders, pedlars, hawkers, etc. .	23	9	...	..	..	14

TABLE XV.

Occupation or Means of Livelihood.—Part—A. *(Continued).*

KOTTAYAM.						DEVIKULAM.						
Total No. of workers and dependants.	Actual Workers				Dependants.	Total No. of workers and dependants.	Actual Workers.				Dependants.	Number.
	Total.		Partially Agriculturists				Total.		Partially Agriculturists.			
	Males.	Females.	Males.	Females.			Males.	Females.	Males.	Females.		
26	27	28	29	30	31	32	33	34	35	36	37	
11,022	2,762	3,621	21	2	4,639	73	36	19	...	.	18	156
6,938	2,239	431	49	1	4,265	224	73	20	1	.	131	157
413	75	127	...	..	211	52	19	7	.		26	158
2,553	651	596	1	...	1,300	109	26	35			48	159
5,974	1,838	301	46	.	3,885	241	103	1		..	120	160
5,846	1,782	608	21	2	3,456	124	33	21		.	70	161
2,248	664	280	14	1	1,304	130	43	8	1		79	162
5	3	...	...	...	2		..	..	.	.	..	163
458	151	62	1	2	245	22	9	1		.	12	164
...	...	..	...	...	...	..	...	...	.	.	.	165
816	*203*	*103*	*5*	...	*540*	*18*	*7*	*3*	.	..	*8*	166
377	90	85	3	...	204	18	7	3		...	8	167
469	113	18	2	...	338	..	..	.	.	.	...	168
1,260	*411*	*123*	*8*	...	*726*	*78*	*25*	*6*	..	.	*17*	169
62	*[illegible]0*	...	..	...	*32*	*4*	*4*	.	..	..	...	170
218	*81*	*23*	...	.	*114*	.	.	.	..	..	..	171
173	*60*	.	..	..	*113*	...		.			.	172
53	21	...	..	.	32	.	..	.	.	.	.	173
10	5	..	.	.	5	.	.	..		.	.	174
110	31	.	.	.	76	.	..	..		.	.	175
5	*2*	...	.	..	*3*	.	.	.	..	.	..	176
3,733	*1,231*	*378*	*78*	*2*	*2,184*	*220*	*70*	*30*			*111*	177
2,468	767	225	48	1	1,476	156	57	26	..		73	178
8	2	.	.	.	6	...	.	..			.	179

TABLE XV.

Occupation or Means of Livelihood.—Part A. (General Table).

Number.	OCCUPATION	STATE. Total No. of Workers and Dependants	Actual Workers. Total. Males.	Actual Workers. Total. Females.	Partially Agriculturists. Males.	Partially Agriculturists. Females.	Dependants
	1	2	3	4	5	6	7
180	137. Conjurors, acrobats, fortune tellers, reciters, exhibitors of curiosities and wild animals	2,752	972	312	76	1	1,168
181	138. Other trades (including farmers of pounds, tolls and markets)	700	276		3	.	124
182	**CLASS C.—PUBLIC ADMINISTRATION AND LIBERAL ARTS**	**143,423**	**44,918**	**3,540**	**1,721**	**14**	**96,970**
183	**Sub-Class VI.—Public Force**	**9,239**	**3,480**		**430**	.	**5,309**
184	ORDER 42.—ARMY	*5,886*	*1,818*		*232*	.	*1,068*
185	139. Army (Imperial)	115	73				42
186	140. Army (Native States)	5,771	1,745	.	232		4,026
187	ORDER 43.—(Group 141) Navy						
188	ORDER 44.—POLICE	*3,103*	*1,662*		*198*		*1,711*
189	142. Police	3,103	1,662		198		1,711
190	143. Village watchmen				.		
191	**Sub-Class VII.—Public Administration**	**32,695**	**10,122**		**413**		**22,573**
192	ORDER 45.—PUBLIC ADMINISTRATION	*32,695*	*10,122*		*413*		*22,573*
193	144. H. H. the Maha Rajah and family	12	1				11
194	(a) Service of the State	26,155	8,066		171		18,089
195	145. Service of British India	187	59		2		128
196	(a) Service of other native and foreign State	81	5				76
197	146. Municipal and other local (not village) service	254	66		2		188
198	147. Village officials and servants other than watchmen.	6,003	1,925		235		4,078
199	**Sub-Class VIII.—Professions and liberal arts**	**97,729**	**29,645**	**3,256**	**833**	**11**	**64,823**
200	ORDER 46.—RELIGION	*33,714*	*10,993*	*2,064*	*379*	5	*20,658*
201	148. Priests, ministers, etc.	7,321	2,625	.	163	.	4,696
202	149. Religious mendicants, inmates of monasteries, etc.	495	119	130			246
203	150. Catechists, readers, church and mission service	4,033	969	190	7	1	2,874
204	151. Temple, burial or burning ground service, pilgrim conductors, circumcisers	21,865	7,279	1,744	209	4	12,842
205	ORDER 47.—LAW	*8,545*	*2,003*		*40*	.	*6,542*
206	152. Lawyers of all kinds, including Kazis, law agents and mukhtiars	5,758	1,247		19		4,505
207	153. Lawyers' clerks, petition writers, etc.	2,792	756		21		2,036
208	ORDER 48.—MEDICINE	*10,209*	*2,844*	*269*	*131*		*7,066*
209	154. Medical practitioners of all kinds, including dentists, oculists and veterinary surgeons	8,692	2,365	139	129		6,163
210	155. Midwives, vaccinators, compounders, nurses, masseurs, etc.	1,517	489	130	2		893

TABLE XV.

Occupation or Means of Livelihood.—Part A. *(Continued.)*

PADMANABHAPURAM.						TRIVANDRUM.						
Total No. of Workers and Dependants.	Actual Workers. Total.		Partially Agriculturists.		Dependants.	Total No. of Workers and Dependants.	Actual Workers. Total.		Partially Agriculturists.		Dependants.	Number.
	Males.	Females.	Males.	Females.			Males.	Females.	Males.	Females.		
8	9	10	11	12	13	14	15	16	17	18	19	
167	57	11	5	.	99	893	118	60	9		211	180
113	55	.	1	..	88	120	52	...	.	..	77	181
19,336	**5,541**	**652**	**247**	**2**	**13,193**	**41,045**	**11,880**	**813**	**469**	**2**	**18,352**	182
729	**331**		**57**	.	**398**	**6,061**	**1,862**	...	**198**	..	**4,199**	183
116	*80*	.	*26*		*66*	*5,180*	*1,468*	..	*148*	...	*3,712*	184
						115	73	.	.	..	42	185
116	80	.	26		66	5,065	1,395	.	148	..	3,670	186
		.	.	.	.	.	.	.	.	.	...	187
583	*251*		*31*	.	*333*	*881*	*394*		*50*	..	*487*	188
583	251		31	.	333	881	394		50		487	189
					.					.	.	190
3,943	**1,239**		**62**	.	**2,704**	**11,235**	**3,224**		**84**	.	**9,011**	191
3,943	*1,239*		*62*		*2,704*	*11,235*	*3,224*		*94*	.	*8,011*	192
			.		.	12	1	.		.	11	193
3,018	953		24		2,065	9,743	2,779	.	48	.	6,964	194
		.		.		164	53	.	2	..	115	195
			.		.	17	1	.		.	16	196
23	8			.	15	121	21	.	.	..	97	197
902	278		33	.	624	1,171	366	.	44	...	808	198
14,255	**3,828**	**646**	**123**	**2**	**9,781**	**21,258**	**6,122**	**721**	**135**	**1**	**4,415**	199
4,837	*1,315*	*457*	*25*	*1*	*3,035*	*6,144*	*2,068*	*411*	*72*		*3,965*	200
1,157	331	..	27	.	776	1,092	374		23	.	718	201
60	13	21			33	69	21	14	..	...	34	202
866	177	38	1	.	651	545	127	27	1	...	381	203
2,715	771	395	27	1	1,576	4,738	1,546	360	18	.	2,832	204
1,105	*333*		*11*		*1,073*	*1,980*	*113*	..	*11*	..	*1,368*	205
891	186		9	.	705	1,310	249	.	10	.	1,061	206
511	116		5		368	670	163	.	4	...	507	207
[illegible]	*303*	*11*	*16*		*931*	*2,801*	*706*	*15*	*27*	.	*2,020*	208
1,071	213	23	16	.	806	2,302	547	24	27	..	1,721	209
207	63	11		.	125	499	120	41	...	..	299	210

TABLE XV.

Occupation or Means of Livelihood.—Part A. (General Table.)

Number.	OCCUPATION.	QUILON. Total No. of workers and dependants.	Actual Workers. Total. Males.	Actual Workers. Total. Females.	Partially Agriculturists. Males.	Partially Agriculturists. Females.	Dependants.
	1	20	21	22	23	24	25
180	137. Conjurors, acrobats, fortune tellers, reciters, exhibitors of curiosities and wild animals	1,040	411	75	33	.	554
181	138. Other trades (including farmers of pounds, tolls and markets)	199	76	.	1	.	123
182	CLASS C.—PUBLIC ADMINISTRATION AND LIBERAL ARTS	**45,791**	**14,658**	**988**	**577**	**6**	**30,145**
183	**Sub-Class VI.—Public Force. .**	**1,322**	**675**	..	**94**	...	**647**
184	ORDER 42.—ARMY	*354*	*165*	..	*30*	.	*189*
185	139 Army (Imperial) ..			...		.	
186	140. Army (Native States) ..	354	165	...	30	.	189
187	ORDER 43.—(Group 141) Navy	...	..	..	...	..	...
188	ORDER 44.—POLICE	*968*	*510*	...	*64*	...	*458*
189	142. Police	968	510	...	64	..	458
190	143. Village watchmen	..	...	...	...	...	..
191	**Sub-Class VII.—Public Administration**	**9,443**	**3,024**	...	**138**	..	**6,419**
192	ORDER 45.—PUBLIC ADMINISTRATION ..	*9,443*	*3,024*	...	*138*	...	*6,419*
193	144. H. H. the Maha Rajah and family. ..	...	..	..	...	..	..
194	(a) Service of the State	7,348	2,362	..	56	.	4,981
195	145. Service of British India . . .	11	3	...	..	...	8
196	(a) Service of other native and foreign States	1	1	...	..	...	..
197	146. Municipal and other local (not village), service	65	20	...	1	.	45
198	147. Village officials and servants other than watchmen	2,023	638	...	81	.	1,385
199	**Sub-Class VIII.—Professions and liberal arts**	**33,333**	**10,413**	**891**	**329**	**4**	**22,079**
200	ORDER 46.—RELIGION	*11,004*	*3,662*	*448*	*137*	*2*	*6,894*
201	148. Priests, ministers etc. ..	2,713	984	..	64	.	1,729
202	149. Religious mendicants, inmates of monasteries, etc.	148	40	34	...	...	74
203	150. Catechists, readers, church and mission service .	1,522	368	68	3	1	1,086
204	151. Temple, burial or burning ground service, pilgrim conductors, circumcisers ..	6,621	2,270	346	70	1	4,005
205	ORDER 47.—LAW	*2,859*	*681*	..	*28*	...	*2,178*
206	152. Lawyers of all kinds, including Kazis, law agents and mukhtiars	2,022	153	..	21	..	1,869
207	153. Lawyers' clerks, petition writers, etc. .	837	228	...	7	..	609
208	ORDER 48.—MEDICINE .	*3,756*	*1,117*	*85*	*59*	...	*2,554*
209	154. Medical practitioners of all kinds, including dentists, oculists and veterinary surgeons .. .	3,324	971	42	58	...	2,311
210	155. Midwives, vaccinators, compounders, nurses, masseurs, etc.	432	146	43	1	..	243

TABLE XV.

Occupation or Means of Livelihood.—Part A. *(Continued).*

KOTTAYAM.						DEVIKULAM.						
Total No. of workers and dependants.	Actual Workers.				Dependants.	Total No. of workers and dependants.	Actual Workers.				Dependants.	Number.
	Total.		Partially Agriculturists.				Total.		Partially Agriculturists.			
	Males.	Females.	Males.	Females.			Males.	Females.	Males.	Females.		
26	27	28	29	30	31	32	33	34	35	36	37	
1,109	376	153	29	1	580	43	15	4	.	.	24	180
208	86	..	1	...	122	21	7	...	.	..	14	181
37,922	**12,242**	**1,077**	**408**	**4**	**24,603**	**1,284**	**597**	**10**	**20**	..	**677**	182
1,001	**502**	...	**73**	...	**499**	**176**	**110**	..	**8**	...	**66**	183
188	*96*	...	*27*	...	*92*	*18*	*9*	.	*1*	...	*9*	184
..	..	..	...	...	.	...	..	..	...	..	..	185
188	96	...	27	...	92	18	9	...	1	...	9	186
...	...	...	...	...	...	...	.	..	..	...	...	187
813	*406*	...	*46*	...	*407*	*158*	*101*	..	*7*	..	*57*	188
813	406	...	46	...	407	158	101	..	7	.	57	189
..	...	...	..	...	..	...	...	...		.	...	190
7,700	**2,455**	...	**111**	..	**5,245**	**374**	**180**	.	**8**	.	**194**	191
7,700	*2,455*	..	*111*	...	*5,245*	*374*	*180*	..	*8*	...	*194*	192
...	...	...	.	...	.	.	.	.	..	.	.	193
5,849	1,872	...	41	...	3,977	202	100	.	5	.	102	194
8	3	..	...	..	5	..	.	.		.	.	195
66	3	.	...	...	63	.	.		.	.	..	196
45	14	..	1	..	31	.	...	.	.		..	197
1,732	563	...	69	..	1,169	172	80	.	3	..	92	198
28,113	**8,980**	**988**	**213**	**4**	**18,145**	**720**	**302**	**10**	**4**	.	**408**	199
11,233	*3,842*	*746*	*113*	*2*	*6,645*	*196*	*75*	*2*	*2*	.	*119*	200
2,263	843	.	47	..	1,420	96	48		2	..	58	201
209	45	58	.	.	106	.	.	.			.	202
1,046	283	47	2	..	716	54	14	..	..	..	10	203
7,715	2,671	641	64	2	4,403	46	18	2	..		26	204
2,252	*359*	..	*14*		*1,698*	*49*	*19*	..	.	.	*30*	205
1,488	315		9	...	1,143	42	11	..	.	..	28	206
764	214	...	5	..	550	7	5		.	.	2	207
2,202	*674*	*60*	*27*	.	*1,468*	*172*	*71*	*8*	*2*	.	*93*	208
1,896	582	38	26	...	1,276	99	42	3	2	.	51	209
306	92	22	1	.	192	73	29	5	.	.	39	210

TABLE XV.

Occupation or Means of Livelihood.—Part A. (General Table).

Number.	OCCUPATION.	TOTAL NO. OF WORKERS AND DEPENDANTS.	STATE. ACTUAL WORKERS. Total. Males.	Females.	Partially Agriculturists. Males.	Females.	DEPENDANTS.
	1	2	3	4	5	6	7
211	ORDER 49.—INSTRUCTION (Group) 156. Professors and teachers of all kinds (except law, medicine, music, dancing and drawing) and clerks and servants connected with education.	*26,365*	*8,111*	*677*	*132*	*6*	*17,577*
212	ORDER 50.—LETTERS AND ARTS AND SCIENCES.	*18,896*	*5,665*	*246*	*121*	...	*12,985*
213	157. Public scribes, stenographers, etc.	...	...	..	..	...	...
214	158. Architects surveyors, engineers, and their employes.	4,274	1,152	...	6	...	3,122
215	159. Others (authors, photographers, artists, sculptors, astronomers, meteorologists, botanists, astrologers, etc)	7,459	2,352	90	58	...	5,017
216	160. Music composers and masters, players on all kinds of musical instruments (not military), singers, actors and dancers.	7,163	2,161	156	57	...	4,846
217	**Sub-Class IX.—Persons living on their income**	**5,715**	**1,671**	**284**	**45**	**3**	**3,760**
218	ORDER 51 —PERSONS LIVING PRINCIPALLY ON THEIR INCOME. (Group 161) Proprietors (other than of agricultural land), fund and scholarship holders and pensioners	*5,715*	*1,671*	*284*	*45*	*3*	*3,760*
219	CLASS D.—MISCELLANEOUS.	**447,663**	**113,297**	**121,341**	**593**	**69**	**213,025**
220	**Sub-class X.—Domestic service.**	**15,255**	**3,481**	**4,337**	**16**	**23**	**7,437**
221	ORDER 52.—DOMESTIC SERVICE	*15,255*	*3,481*	*4,337*	*16*	*23*	*7,437*
222	162. Cooks, water carriers, doorkeepers watchmen and other indoor servants	13,683	2,924	4,337	14	23	6,422
223	163. Private grooms, coachmen, dog boys, etc.	1,572	557	...	2	...	1,015
224	**Sub-Class XI.—Insufficiently described occupations.**	**424,789**	**106,593**	**114,635**	**577**	**46**	**203,558**
225	ORDER 53.—GENERAL TERMS WHICH DO NOT INDICATE DEFINITE OCCUPATION	*424,789*	*106,596*	*114,635*	*577*	*46*	*203,558*
226	164. Manufacturers, business men and contractors otherwise unspecified.	783	163	2	9	..	618
227	165. Cashiers, accountants, book-keepers, clerks and other employes in unspecified offices, warehouses and shops.	6,281	2,004	57	30	2	4,180
228	166. Mechanics otherwise unspecified.	..	..	..	..	...	..
229	167. Labourers and workmen otherwise unspecified.	417,725	104,339	114,576	538	44	198,810
230	**Sub-Class XII.—Unproductive**	**7,619**	**3,220**	**2,369**	..	...	**2,030**
231	ORDER 54.—INMATES OF JAILS, ASYLUMS AND HOSPITALS. (Group 168) Inmates of jails, asylums and hospitals	*1,740*	*1,164*	*95*	...	..	*481*
232	ORDER 55.—BEGGARS, VAGRANTS, PROCURERS, PROSTITUTES. (Group 169) Beggars, vagrants, procurers, prostitutes, receivers of stolen goods, cattle poisoners	*5,879*	*2,056*	*2,274*	..	...	*1,519*

TABLE XV.

Occupation or Means of Livelihood.—Part A. *(Continued).*

PADMANABHAPURAM.						TRIVANDRUM.						
Total No. of workers and dependants.	Actual Workers.				Dependants.	Total No. of workers and dependants.	Actual Workers.				Dependants.	Number.
	Total.		Partially Agriculturists.				Total.		Partially Agriculturists.			
	Males.	Females.	Males.	Females.			Males.	Females	Males.	Females.		
8	9	10	11	12	13	14	15	16	17	18	19	
4,410	*1,197*	*91*	*21*	*1*	*3,122*	*5,725*	*1,746*	*180*	*25*	*1*	*3,799*	211
2,325	*648*	*57*	*16*	..	*1,620*	*4,308*	*1,190*	*55*	*27*	.	*3,063*	212
...	...	..	..	..	...	...	.	...	...	..	...	213
795	197	...	1	.	598	1,755	416	..	2	...	1,339	214
537	164	24	6	...	349	1,370	410	45	11	...	915	215
993	287	33	9	...	673	1,183	364	10	14	..	809	216
459	**143**	**6**	**6**	...	**310**	**2,491**	**672**	**92**	**12**	**1**	**1,727**	217
459	*143*	*6*	*6*	.	*310*	*2,491*	*672*	*93*	*13*	*1*	*1,727*	218
24,801	**7,003**	**7,971**	**68**	**8**	**9,827**	**80,416**	**20,183**	**22,008**	**93**	**11**	**38,225**	219
1,656	**357**	**444**	**2**	**3**	**855**	**5,507**	**1,168**	**1,641**	**3**	**6**	**2,698**	220
1,656	*357*	*441*	*2*	*3*	*855*	*5,507*	*1,168*	*1,641*	*3*	*6*	*2,698*	221
1,564	323	444	2	3	797	4,663	866	1,641	2	6	2,156	222
92	34	...	...	.	58	844	302		1	.	542	223
22,106	**6,238**	**7,164**	**66**	**5**	**8,704**	**72,368**	**17,718**	**19,828**	**90**	**5**	**34,822**	224
22,106	*6,238*	*7,164*	*66*	*5*	*8,704*	*72,368*	*17,718*	*19,828*	*90*	*5*	*34,822*	225
225	50	...	3	..	175	152	35	2	1	.	115	226
926	293	10	4	.	623	1,200	359	11	5	.	830	227
...	..	..	.	..	..	.	.	.	.	...	.	228
20,955	5,805	7,154	59	5	7,906	71,016	17,324	19,815	84	5	33,877	229
1,039	**408**	**363**	..	.	**268**	**2,541**	**1,297**	**539**	.	.	**705**	230
119	*70*	*5*	.	.	*44*	*1,190*	*785*	*10*		.	*356*	231
920	*338*	*358*	...	..	*224*	*1,351*	*512*	*490*	.		*349*	232

TABLE XV.

Occupation or Means of Livelihood.—Part A. (General Table).

Number.	OCCUPATION.	QUILON. Total No. of workers and dependants.	Actual Workers. Total. Males.	Females.	Partially Agriculturists. Males.	Females.	Dependants.
	1	20	21	22	23	24	25
211	Order. 49.—Instruction (Group 156) Professors and teachers of all kinds (except law, medicine, music, dancing and drawing), and clerks and servants connected with education. ..	*9,276*	*3,012*	*278*	*63*	*2*	*5,986*
212	Order 50.—Letters and arts and sciences...	*6,488*	*1,941*	*80*	*42*	...	*4,467*
213	157. Public scribes, stenographers, etc. .	...	...	...	...	..	..
214	158. Architects, surveyors, engineers and their employés.	800	238	...	2	...	562
215	159. Others (authors, photographers, artists, sculptors, astronomers, meteorologists, botanists, astrologers, etc.) .	2,985	942	14	22	...	2,029
216	160 Music composers and masters, players on all kinds of musical instruments (not military), singers, actors and dancers ..	2,703	761	66	18	...	1,876
217	**Sub-Class IX.—Persons living on their income.**	**1,643**	**546**	**97**	**16**	**2**	**1,000**
218	Order 51.—Persons living principally on their income (Group 161). Proprietors (other than of agricultural land), fund and scholarship holders and pensioners..	*1,643*	*546*	*97*	*16*	*2*	*1,000*
219	CLASS D.—MISCELLANEOUS. .. .	**183,340**	**48,401**	**50,710**	**255**	**34**	**84,229**
220	**Sub-class X.— Domestic service.** ..	**4,172**	**1,090**	**1,047**	**7**	**7**	**2,035**
221	Order 52.—Domestic service. .. .	*4,172*	*1,090*	*1,047*	*7*	*7*	*2,035*
222	162. Cooks, water carriers, doorkeepers, watchmen and other indoor servants. ..	3,826	962	1,047	6	7	1,817
223	163. Private grooms, coachmen, dog boys, etc .	346	128	...	1	...	218
224	**Sub-Class XI.—Insufficiently described occupations**	**176,600**	**46,322**	**48,747**	**248**	**27**	**81,531**
225	Order 53.—General terms which do not indicate a definite occupation. ..	*176,600*	*46,322*	*48,747*	*248*	*27*	*81,531*
226	164. Manufacturers, business men and contractors otherwise unspecified. ..	375	71	...	5	...	304
227	165. Cashiers, accountants, book-keepers, clerks and other employés in unspecified offices, warehouses and shops . ..	2,276	715	18	12	1	1,543
228	166. Mechanics otherwise unspecified .	..	.	...	...	..	...
229	167. Labourers and workmen otherwise unspecified.	173,949	45,536	48,729	231	26	79,684
230	**Sub-Class XII.—Unproductive** .	**2,568**	**989**	**916**	..	..	**663**
231	Order 54.—Inmates of jails, asylums and hospitals. (Group 168) Inmates of jails, asylums and hospitals. . .	*334*	*240*	*28*	.	..	*66*
232	Order 55.—Beggars, vagrants, procurers, prostitutes. (Group 169) Beggars, vagrants, procurers, prostitutes, receivers of stolen goods, cattle poisoners. ..	*2,234*	*749*	*888*	...	..	*597*

TABLE XV.

Occupation or Means of Livelihood.—Part A. *(Continued).*

KOTTAYAM.						DEVIKULAM.						
Total No. of Workers and Dependants.	Actual Workers.				Dependants.	Total No. of Workers and Dependants.	Actual Workers.				Dependants.	Number.
	Total.		Partially Agriculturists.				Total.		Partially Agriculturists.			
	Males.	Females.	Males.	Females.			Males.	Females.	Males.	Females.		
26	27	28	29	30	31	32	33	34	35	36	37	
6,852	*2,115*	*128*	*23*	*2*	*4,609*	*102*	*41*	...	...	...	*61*	211
5,574	*1,790*	*54*	*36*	...	*3,730*	*201*	*96*	...	..	...	*105*	212
...	...	...	...	...	...	...	...	...	...	...	...	213
781	228	...	1	...	553	143	73	...	...	...	70	214
2,542	823	7	19	...	1,712	25	13	...	...	...	12	215
2,251	739	47	16	...	1,465	33	10	...	...	..	23	216
1,103	**305**	**89**	**11**	...	**714**	**14**	**5**	...	...	...	**9**	217
1,108	*305*	*89*	*11*	...	*714*	*14*	*5*	...	...	...	*9*	218
150,242	**35,351**	**37,850**	**155**	**14**	**77,041**	**6,864**	**2,359**	**2,602**	**22**	**2**	**3,703**	219
3,551	**733**	**1,141**	**3**	**7**	**1,677**	**369**	**133**	**64**	**1**	..	**172**	220
3,551	*733*	*1,141*	*3*	*7*	*1,677*	*369*	*133*	*64*	*1*	.	*172*	221
3,377	682	1,141	3	7	1,554	253	91	64	1	..	98	222
174	51	...	...	...	123	116	42	..	...		74	223
145,285	**34,123**	**36,177**	**152**	**7**	**74,985**	**8,430**	**2,195**	**2,719**	**21**	**2**	**3,516**	224
145,285	*34,123*	*36,177*	*152*	*7*	*74,985*	*8,430*	*2,195*	*2,719*	*21*	*2*	*3,516*	225
31	7	...	..	..	24	..	..	..	.	.	..	226
1,680	660	13	8	1	1,002	199	67	..	1	...	132	227
...	..	...	..	..	..	..	..	.	..	...	.	228
143,574	33,456	36,159	144	6	73,959	8,231	2,128	2,719	20	2	3,384	229
1,406	**495**	**532**	...	..	**379**	**65**	**31**	**19**	...	.	**15**	230
97	*69*	*13*	.	..	*15*	...	..	...	.	...	.	231
1,309	*426*	*519*	.	..	*364*	*65*	*31*	*19*	...	..	*15*	232

TABLE XV.

Occupation or Means of Livelihood.—Part A. (General Table.)

OCCUPATION.	WESTERN NATURAL DIVISION.						EASTERN NATURAL DIVISION.					
	Total workers and dependants.	Actual Workers.		Partially Agriculturists.		Dependants	Total workers and dependants.	Actual Workers.		Partially Agriculturists.		Dependants
		Males.	Females.	Males.	Females.			Males.	Females.	Males.	Females.	
1	2	3	4	5	6	7	8	9	10	11	12	13
Total Population ...	***1,976,154***	***560,405***	***289,844***	***4,556***	***220***	***1,125,905***	***1,452,821***	***404,697***	***166,700***	***2,111***	***118***	***881,424***
Class A.—Production of raw materials ..	**960,765**	**278,740**	**68,645**	**122**	**7**	**613,380**	**946,434**	**263,094**	**72,485**	**117**	**11**	**610,925**
Sub-Class I.—Exploitation of the surface of the earth .	*960,189*	*278,550*	*68,605*	*122*	*7*	*613,034*	*945,277*	*262,562*	*72,359*	*117*	*11*	*610,356*
1 Pasture and Agriculture .	896,418	253,926	66,098	107	7	576,394	943,005	261,644	72,293	116	11	609,068
(a) Ordinary cultivation .	784,887	218,755	59,777	6	..	506,355	831,015	222,559	59,856	8	..	548,600
(b) Growers of special products and market gardening . ..	102,258	31,898	4,828	39	4	65,532	104,598	36,266	11,498	45	7	56,904
(c) Forestry .	3,571	863	1,012	36	2	1,696	2,895	783	652	40	2	1,460
(d) Raising of farm stock .	5,699	2,407	481	26	1	2,811	4,497	2,036	357	23	2	2,104
(e) Raising of small animals .	3	3	.	.	..				..	..	.	
2. Fishing and hunting .	63,771	24,624	2,507	15	..	36,640	2,272	918	66	1	.	1,288
Sub-Class II.—Extraction of minerals ...	*576*	*190*	*40*	.	..	*346*	*1,157*	*462*	*126*	..	...	*569*
3 Mines	138	40	7	.	..	91	1,157	462	126	...	.	569
4. Quarries of hard rocks .	.	.	...	..	..	...		..		..	.	..
5. Salt, etc.	438	150	33	..	..	255		...	.	...	..	...
Class B.—Preparation and supply of material substances . ..	**677,414**	**190,268**	**152,577**	**2,938**	**163**	**334,569**	**251,271**	**74,855**	**37,956**	**1,176**	**74**	**138,460**
Sub-Class III.—Industry	*426,592*	*120,012*	*98,167*	*2,018*	*75*	*208,413*	*161,816*	*48,320*	*22,448*	*793*	*33*	*91,050*
6. Textiles	149,649	36,771	64,002	189	18	48,876	10,895	2,216	3,085	9	1	5,594
7. Hides, skins and hard materials from the animal kingdom	118	43	1	..	...	74	31	15	2	..	..	14

8. Wood	52,867	15,808	7,797	165	6	29,262	40,151	12,811	5,474	174	4	21,866
9. Metals . .	17,283	5,954	289	69	1	11,040	18,108	5,847	314	63	2	11,947
10. Ceramics .	8,134	2,410	1,160	26	2	4,564	6,100	2,190	1,457	22	4	2,453
11. Chemical products, properly so called, and analogous	17,165	6,082	2,396	115	11	8,737	2,838	875	312	18	2	1,651
12 Food industries .	121,862	33,629	11,911	1,098	12	76,322	46,545	12,984	6,023	319	7	27,538
13. Industries of dress and the toilet ..	36,154	11,043	9,624	217	24	15,487	24,734	7,290	5,495	132	11	12,039
14. Furniture industries	111	47	..	.	...	64	16	6		.	.	10
15. Building industries .	5,698	2,016	390	45	.	3,292	1,808	662	123	16	.	1,023
16. Construction of means of transport ..	387	283	.	4	...	154	.		.		.	
17. Production and transmission of physical forces (heat, light, electricity etc) ..	61	16	...	.	..	45		..		.	.	.
18. Industries of luxury and those pertaining to literature and the arts and sciences..	15,794	5,665	187	89	1	9,942	9,920	3,211	118	37	1	6,591
19. Industries concerned with refuse matter .	1,309	345	410	1	..	554	672	213	135	3	..	324
SUB-CLASS IV.—TRANSPORT . .	*37,385*	*15,888*	*3,759*	*61*	*1*	*17,738*	*17,557*	*6,836*	*2,162*	*39*	*1*	*8,559*
20. Transport by water .	20,796	9,056	1,512	18	..	10,228	3,099	1,150	261	1	..	1,688
21. Transport by road .. .	14,135	5,955	2,245	36	1	5,935	11,703	4,445	1,901	31	1	5,357
22. Transport by rail	141	58	.	.	..	83	788	509	...	2	..	279
23. Post Office, Telegraph and Telephone services	2,313	819	2	7	..	1,492	1,967	732	..	5	..	1,235
SUB-CLASS V.—TRADE . . .	*213,437*	*54,368*	*50,651*	*859*	*87*	*108,418*	*71,896*	*19,699*	*13,346*	*344*	*41*	*38,851*
24. Banks, establishments of credit, exchange and insurance ...	7,717	1,476	634	36	3	5,607	1,729	411	227	8	1	1,091
25 Brokerage, commission and export ..	747	231	26	4	..	490	80	28	.	1	.	52
26. Trade in textiles	41,749	11,439	9,479	129	10	20,831	8,472	997	478	14	1	1,997
27. Trade in skins, leather and furs .	261	91	3	.	..	167	247	93	.	1	..	154
28 Trade in wood	4,881	969	2,297	21	4	1,615	4,150	1,125	1,435	23	2	1,590
29. Trade in metals	42	16	.	...	..	26	36	14	.	..	...	22
30. Trade in pottery	1,220	320	374	7	..	526	1,069	300	261	5	...	508
31 Trade in chemical products . .	93	34	.	..	..	59	38	13		..	..	25
32 Hotels, cafes, restaurants, etc. ..	9,541	3,072	2,641	63	18	3,828	13,902	3,739	2,786	37	20	7,377
33. Other trade in food stuffs .	130,195	31,781	32,758	434	40	65,656	38,508	10,404	6,889	153	9	21,215
34. Trade in clothing and toilet articles ..	64	25	4	1		35	..	...	..	..	..	.
35. Trade in furniture . .	2,071	538	258	13	3	1,275	1,210	296	154	7	3	760
36. Trade in building materials .	3,421	880	619	15	3	1,922	1,583	483	243	6	1	857
37. Trade in means of transport .	633	215	4	1	..	414	304	116	4	..	...	184
38. Trade in fuel	2,644	665	984	1	1	995	1,438	360	464	1	..	614
39. Trade in articles of luxury and those pertaining to letters and the arts and sciences.	1,151	361	.	12	..	790	264	96	..	1	..	168
40. Trade in refuse matter .. .	31	11		.		20	7	2	...	..	..	5
41. Trade of other sorts	6,976	2,244	570	122	5	4,162	3,859	1,222	405	87	4	2,232
Class C.—Public administration and liberal arts. . ..	**97,507**	**29,356**	**2,234**	**1,102**	**9**	**65,917**	**47,921**	**15,562**	**1,306**	**619**	**5**	**31,053**
SUB-CLASS VI —PUBLIC FORCE . ..	*7,396*	*2,529*	..	*337*	...	*4,867*	*1,893*	*951*	...	*93*	..	*942*
42 Army	5,456	1,622	...	230	..	3,834	430	196	...	2	.	234
43. Navy			..		.			.	.	.	.	

TABLE XV.

Occupation or Means of Livelihood.—Part A. *(Concluded)*.

OCCUPATION.	WESTERN NATURAL DIVISION.						EASTERN NATURAL DIVISION.					
	Total Workers and Dependants.	Actual Workers.		Partially Agriculturists.		Dependants.	Total Workers and Dependants.	Actual Workers.		Partially Agriculturists.		Dependants.
		Males.	Females.	Males.	Females.			Males.	Females.	Males.	Females.	
1	2	3	4	5	6	7	8	9	10	11	12	13
44. Police	1,940	907	..	107	..	1,033	1,463	755	..	91	...	708
Sub-Class VII.—Public administration	*22,433*	*6,672*	...	*224*	..	*15,761*	*10,262*	*3,450*	...	*189*		*6,812*
45. Public Administration	22,433	6,672	...	224	...	15,761	10,262	3,450	.	189	.	6,812
Sub-Class VIII.—Professions and Liberal Arts ..	*63,414*	*18,917*	*2,054*	*507*	*7*	*42,443*	*34,315*	*10,728*	*1,202*	*326*	*4*	*22,385*
46. Religion	19,594	6,351	1,190	211	3	12,053	14,120	4,641	874	168	2	8,605
47. Law	6,008	1,338	..	44	..	4,670	2,537	665	..	26	..	1,872
48 Medicine	7,773	2,140	193	87	..	5,440	2,436	734	76	44	..	1,626
49. Instruction	18,368	5,727	514	86	4	12,127	7,997	2,384	163	46	2	5,450
50. Letters and arts and sciences	11,671	3,361	157	79	..	8,153	7,225	2,304	89	42	..	4,832
Sub-Class IX.—Persons living on their income .	*4,264*	*1,238*	*180*	*34*	*2*	*2,846*	*1,451*	*433*	*104*	*11*	*1*	*914*
51. Persons living principally on their income..	4,264	1,238	180	34	2	2,846	1,451	433	104	11	1	914
Class D.—Miscellaneous	**240,468**	**62,041**	**66,388**	**394**	**41**	**112,039**	**207,195**	**51,256**	**54,953**	**199**	**28**	**100,986**
Sub-Class X.—Domestic Service	*10,462*	*2,339*	*2,992*	*10*	*14*	*5,131*	*4,793*	*1,142*	*1,345*	*6*	*9*	*2,306*
52. Domestic Service	10,462	2,339	2,992	10	14	5,131	4,793	1,142	1,345	6	9	2,306
Sub-Class XI.—Insufficiently described occupations	*224,701*	*57,306*	*61,967*	*384*	*27*	*105,428*	*200,088*	*49,290*	*52,668*	*193*	*19*	*98,130*
53. General terms which do not indicate a definite occupation . ..	224,701	57,306	61,967	384	27	105,428	200,088	49,290	52,668	193	19	98,130
Sub-Class XII.—Unproductive	*5,305*	*2,396*	*1,429*	...	...	*1,480*	*2,314*	*824*	*940*	...	..	*550*
54. Inmates of jails, asylums and hospitals ..	1,620	1,083	80	...	...	457	120	81	15	..	..	24
55. Beggars, vagrants and prostitutes . .	3,685	1,313	1,349	...	...	1,023	2,194	743	925	..	...	526

TABLE XV.

Occupation or Means of Livelihood.

Part B.—Subsidiary Occupations of Agriculturists—Actual workers only.

TABLE XV.

Occupation or means of Livelihood. Part B.—Subsidiary Occupations of Agriculturists (actual workers only).

Subsidiary occupations returned by rent receivers	Males.	Females.
1	2	3
Total Rent receivers (actual workers)	***21,408***	***4,963***
(a) Agricultural	*847*	*314*
Rent payers	783	301
Agricultural labourers	64	13
(b) Non-agricultural	*1,737*	*71*
Government employes of all kinds	31	
Money-lenders and grain-dealers ..	408	18
Other traders of all kinds .	348	7
Priests	62	1
Clerks of all kinds (not Government)	143	.
School masters . . .	126	.
Lawyers	16	.
Estate agents and managers ..	18	.
Medical practitioners	33	
Artisans	138	2
Others	414	43

Subsidiary occupations returned by rent payers	Males.	Females.
1	2	3
Total Rent-payers (actual workers)	***345,150***	***55,260***
(a) Agricultural	*5,178*	*1,041*
Rent receivers	1,291	34
Agricultural labourers	3,887	1,007
(b) Non-agricultural	*20,351*	*994*
General labourers	2,311	219
Government employes of all kinds .	722	.
Money-lenders and grain-dealers	2,497	11
Other traders of all kinds	2,394	56
Fishermen and boatmen	654	.
Cattle-breeders and milk-men .	988	64
Village watchmen .		.
Weavers .	494	5
Barbers .	596	4
Oil-pressers .	23	.
Washermen .	51	4
Potters	326	51
Blacksmiths and carpenters	936	17
Others . .	8,534	563

Subsidiary occupations returned by agricultural labourers	Males.	Females.
1	2	3
Total Agricultural labourers (actual workers) . .	***74,171***	***59,405***
(a) Agricultural	*1,285*	*23*
Rent receivers .	188	1
Rent payers	1,097	22
(b) Non-agricultural	*3,994*	*373*
General labourers ..	987	63
Village watchmen	..	
Cattle breeders and milk-men ..	321	42
Mill hands	58	41
Fishermen and boat men .	30	..
Rice pounders ...	4	36
Traders of all kinds	59	5
Oil-pressers	44	..
Weavers	532	15
Potters . .	61	12
Leather workers	118	2
Blacksmiths and carpenters ...	29	...
Washermen	3	1
Others	1,158	156

TABLE XV.

Occupation or means of Livelihood.

Part C.—Showing for certain mixed Occupations the number of persons who returned each as (a) Principal and (b) Subsidiary Means of Livelihood.

TABLE XV.

Occupation or Means of Livelihood.

PART C.—SHOWING FOR CERTAIN MIXED OCCUPATIONS THE NUMBER OF PERSONS WHO RETURNED EACH AS (a) PRINCIPAL AND (b) SUBSIDIARY MEANS OF LIVELIHOOD.

DIVISION.	Grain-dealers and Money-lenders.							
	Total number of persons (actual workers) who returned 'grain-dealers' as their principal occupation.		Number of persons in the two preceding columns who returned 'money-lenders' as their subsidiary occupation.		Total number of persons (actual workers) who returned 'money-lenders' as their principal occupation.		Number of persons in the two preceding columns who returned 'grain-dealers' as their subsidiary occupation.	
	Males.	Females.	Males.	Females.	Males.	Females.	Males.	Females.
1	2	3	4	5	6	7	8	9
State	*7,447*	*4,490*	*255*	*81*	*1,887*	*861*	*51*	*12*
WESTERN NATURAL DIVISION	5,100	3,292	177	59	1,476	634	38	9
EASTERN NATURAL DIVISION	2,347	1,198	78	22	411	227	13	3

DIVISION.	Fibre industry and Toddy drawing.							
	Total number of persons (actual workers) who returned 'fibre industry' as their principal occupation.		Number of persons in the two preceding columns who returned 'toddy-drawers' as their subsidiary occupation.		Total number of persons (actual workers) who returned 'toddy-drawers' as their principal occupation.		Number of persons in the two preceding columns who returned 'fibre industry' as their subsidiary occupation.	
	Males.	Females.	Males	Females.	Males.	Females.	Males.	Females.
1	2	3	4	5	6	7	8	9
State	*25,583*	*65,268*	*145*	.	*45,251*		*58*	.
WESTERN NATURAL DIVISION	24,299	62,566	136	..	32,648		44	
EASTERN NATURAL DIVISION	1,234	2,702	9	.	12,603		14	.

DIVISION.	Fishermen and Boatmen.							
	Total number of persons (actual workers) who returned 'fishermen' as their principal occupation.		Number of persons in the two preceding columns who returned 'boatmen' as their subsidiary occupation.		Total number of persons (actual workers) who returned 'boatmen' as their principal occupation.		Number of persons in the two preceding columns who returned 'fishermen' as their subsidiary occupation.	
	Males	Females.	Males	Females.	Males.	Females.	Males.	Females
1	2	3	4	5	6	7	8	9
State	*25,519*	*2,571*	*4,095*		*7,098*	.	*85*	
WESTERN NATURAL DIVISION	24,630	2,508	3,942		6,439		78	.
EASTERN NATURAL DIVISION	839	63	153		659		7	.

TABLE XV.

Occupation or Means of Livelihood.
Part D.—Distribution by Religion.

TABLE XV.

Occupation or Means of Livelihood.

PART D.—DISTRIBUTION BY RELIGION.

OCCUPATION.	TOTAL WORKERS AND DEPENDANTS.	DISTRIBUTION BY RELIGION.			
		HINDU.	CHRISTIAN.	MUSALMAN.	ANIMIST.
1	2	3	4	5	6
Total ...	*3,428,975*	*2,282,617*	*903,868*	*226,617*	*15,773*
Class A.—Production of raw materials ..	**1,907,199**	**1,209,457**	**535,405**	**149,487**	**12,786**
SUB-CLASS I.—EXPLOITATION OF THE SURFACE OF THE EARTH	*1,905,466*	*1,208,375*	*534,933*	*149,354*	*12,740*
1. Pasture and Agriculture	1,839,423	1,184,811	503,685	138,134	12,729
2. Fishing and hunting . ..	66,043	23,564	31,248	11,220	11
SUB-CLASS II.—EXTRACTION OF MINERALS .	*1,733*	*1,082*	*472*	*133*	*46*
3. Mines	1,295	692	451	106	46
4 Quarries of hard rocks	...		.	..	..
5. Salt, etc.	438	390	21	27	...
Class B.—Preparation and supply of material substances	**926,685**	**655,672**	**224,976**	**47,857**	**144**
SUB-CLASS III.—INDUSTRY	*568,410*	*443 683*	*117,018*	*27,641*	*67*
6. Textiles . ..	160,544	99,595	43,275	17,674	..
7. Hides, skins and hard materials from the animal kingdom	149	115	23	11	.
8. Wood	98,018	61,810	27,312	8,829	67
9. Metals	35,391	28,871	4,719	801	
10 Ceramics	14,254	9 342	4,251	641	...
11 Chemical products, properly so called, and analogous	20,003	15,375	3,620	1,008	...
12. Food industries	168,407	151,393	15,275	1,739	.
13. Industries of dress and the toilet .	60,898	51,375	8,732	781	.
14. Furniture industries . .	127	99	26	2	..
15. Building industries .	7,506	4,072	1,991	543	..
16. Construction of means of transport	387	263	95	29	..
17. Production and transmission of physical forces (heat, light, electricity, etc)	61	17	41	3	..
18 Industries of luxury and those pertaining to literature and the arts and sciences..	25,714	18,436	6,841	437	
19 Industries concerned with refuse matter .	1,981	1,026	812	143	.
SUB-CLASS IV.—TRANSPORT . ..	*54,942*	*29,443*	*23,670*	*1,779*	*50*
20. Transport by water	23,895	7 933	15,016	946	
21 Transport by road . ..	25,838	17,627	7,414	765	32
22 Transport by rail . .	929	718	168	25	18
23 Post Office, Telegraph and Telephone services	4,230	3,165	1,072	43	.
SUB-CLASS V.—TRADE	*283,333*	*181,540*	*84,2[illegible]3*	*18,437*	*27*
24 Banks, establishments of credit, exchange and insurance . .	9,416	7,951	1,236	252	
25 Brokerage, commission and export ..	827	579	132	116	
26 Trade in textiles ..	45,[illegible]21	28,[illegible]95	13,172	3,231	.
27. Trade in skins, leather and furs	508	397	69	21	.

TABLE XV.

Occupation or Means of Livelihood.

PART D.—DISTRIBUTION BY RELIGION.

OCCUPATION.	TOTAL WORKERS AND DEPENDANTS.	DISTRIBUTION BY RELIGION.			
		HINDU.	CHRISTIAN.	MUSALMAN.	ANIMIST.
1	2	3	4	5	6
28. Trade in wood	9,031	6,574	2,146	306	5
29 Trade in metals	78	51	12	15	..
30. Trade in pottery	2,289	1,375	816	98	.
31. Trade in chemical products	131	86	39	6	.
32. Hotels, cafes, restaurants, etc.	23,443	16,779	6,368	296	..
33. Other trade in food stuffs	168,703	102,927	54,314	11,462	..
34. Trade in clothing and toilet articles	64	32	18	14	...
35. Trade in furniture	3,281	2,137	817	327	..
36. Trade in building materials	5,004	3,671	1,158	175	.
37. Trade in means of transport	937	628	243	63	..
38. Trade in fuel	4,082	2,585	974	510	13
39. Trade in articles of luxury and those pertaining to letters and the arts and sciences	1,415	970	314	131	..
40. Trade in refuse matter	38	21	13	4	..
41. Trade of other sorts	10,835	6,982	2,432	1,406	9
Class C.—Public administration and liberal arts.	**145,428**	**107,600**	**34,110**	**3,689**	**29**
SUB-CLASS VI.—PUBLIC FORCE	*9,289*	*8,958*	*92*	*239*	..
42 Army	5,886	5,739	56	91	..
43 Navy		..	..	,	...
44. Police	3,403	3,219	36	148	.
SUB-CLASS VII.—PUBLIC ADMINISTRATION	*32 695*	*23,746*	*8,618*	*331*	..
45. Public Administration	32,695	23,746	8,618	331	..
SUB-CLASS VIII.—PROFESSIONS AND LIBERAL ARTS	*97,729*	*70,718*	*23,924*	*3,058*	*29*
46. Religion	33,714	23,327	8,945	1,421	21
47. Law	8,545	6,312	2,205	28	
48. Medicine	10,209	7,856	2,264	89	
49 Instruction	26,365	20,792	5,128	445	
50. Letters and arts and sciences	18,896	12,431	5,382	1,075	8
SUB-CLASS IX.—PERSONS LIVING ON THEIR INCOME	*5,715*	*4,178*	*1,476*	*61*	..
51 Persons living principally on their income	5,715	4,178	1,476	61	.
Class D.—Miscellaneous	**447,633**	**309,838**	**109,377**	**25,584**	**2,314**
SUB-CLASS X.—DOMESTIC SERVICE	*15,255*	*11,063*	*3,432*	*745*	*10*
52 Domestic service	15,255	11,063	3,432	745	10
SUB-CLASS XI.—INSUFFICIENTLY DESCRIBED OCCUPATIONS	*424,789*	*294,526*	*103,521*	*23,953*	*2,789*
53. General terms which do not indicate a definite occupation	424,789	294,526	103,521	23,953	2,789
SUB-CLASS XII.—UNPRODUCTIVE	*7,619*	*4,294*	*2,424*	*886*	*15*
54 Inmates of jails, asylums and hospitals	1,740	1 048	529	148	15
55 Beggars, vagrants and prostitutes	5,879	3,243	1,895	738	

TABLE XV.

Occupation or Means of Livelihood
Part E.—Statistics of Industries.

TABLE XV.

Part E. Statistics of Industries. I.—State Summary.

DESCRIPTION OF FACTORY, MINE, ETC.	CLASSIFICATION OF FACTORY, ETC., ACCORDING TO NUMBER OF PERSONS EMPLOYED (INCLUDING MANAGEMENT).	NUMBER OF FACTORIES.	TOTAL NUMBER OF PERSONS EMPLOYED.		CLASSIFICATION OF PERSONS EMPLOYED.												REMARKS.
					DIRECTION, SUPERVISION AND CLERICAL WORK.				SKILLED WORKMEN.				UNSKILLED LABOURERS.				N. B.—The 'State of business' is indicated thus in figures.— (1)=Much brisker than usual. (2)=Brisker than usual. (3)=Somewhat brisker than usual. (4)=Normal. (5)=Somewhat slacker than usual. (6)=Slacker than usual. (7)=Much slacker than usual.
					EUROPEANS AND ANGLO-INDIANS.		INDIANS.		EUROPEANS AND ANGLO-INDIANS.		INDIANS.		AGE 14 AND OVER.		UNDER 14.		
			Males.	Females.	Males.	Females.	Males.	Females.	Males.	Females.	Males.	Females.	Males.	Females.	Males.	Females.	
1	2	3	4	5	6	7	8	9	10	11	12	13	14	15	16	17	18
STATE	...	*108*	*10,482*	*4,459*	*138*	*11*	*1,003*	*28*	*54*		*1,983*	*1,822*	*6,086*	*1,725*	*1,218*	*873*	*Power* — *State of business.*
Growing of special products.																	Steam 1 Electricity
1. Tea plantations.	**Total** ...	**12**	**647**	**347**	**4**	...	**37**	..	.	...	**71**	**14**	**454**	**266**	**81**	**67**	& water 1 — (1) 2
Plantations in which mechanical power is used.	*Total*	*9*	*368*	*213*	*3*	...	*32*	...	...	...	*62*	*14*	*225*	*153*	*46*	*46*	Water & steam 2 — (4) 6 Water 2 — (6) 1
	From 20 to 50	4	99	24	[illegible]	...	14	.	...	...	5	..	72	20	5	4	Oil 3 — 9
	„ 50 „ 100	4	166	113	...	..	13	...	..	.	52	14	82	76	19	23	9
	„ 100 „ 200	1	103	76	..	...	5	..	..	...	5	..	71	57	22	19	
Plantations in which mechanical power is not used.	*Total*	*3*	*279*	*134*	*1*	...	*5*	..	...	.	*9*	..	*229*	*113*	*35*	*21*	(1) 3
	From 50 to 100	2	76	56	..	.	2		...	.	4	..	60	49	10	7	*Steam 6 — (1) 1
	„ 200 „ 400.	1	203	78	1	..	3	..	..	...	5	..	109	64	25	14	Steam & oil 1 — (2) 8 Steam & water 1 — (3) 2 Electricity 4 — (4) 8
2. Tea factories*	**Total** ..	**25**	**1,047**	**421**	**23**	**1**	**89**	**3**	**8**	.	**129**	**9**	**615**	**318**	**183**	**90**	Electricity — (5) 2
Factories in which mechanical power is used.	From 20 to 50	21	568	109	20	1	65	3	7	..	111	9	337	94	28	2	& water 2 — (6) 2
	„ 50 „ 100	3	145	39	2	..	15	..	1		3	..	109	30	15	9	Water 4 — (7) 2
	„ 400 and over	1	334	273	1	..	9	..	..	..	15	...	169	194	110	79	Water & oil 1 — 25 Oil 4 Oil & gas. 1
3. Rubber plantations ...	**Total** ..	**10**	**1,505**	**586**	**21**	**2**	**49**	**4**	**1**	..	**142**	**40**	**1,080**	**398**	**212**	**142**	Gas 1 — (1) 1
Plantations in which mechanical power is not used	From 20 to 50	2	64	10	3	..	6	..	.	.	42	..	8	6	5	4	25 — (2) 1
	„ 50 „ 100	1	48	50	2	.	1	.		.	30	40	.	.	15	10	(1) 7
	„ 100 „ 200	2	207	27	.	..	10	.	.	..	7		164	16	26	11	(6) 1
	„ 200 „ 400	4	857	246	13	2	24	4	1	.	60		628	166	131	74	
	„ 400 and over	1	329	253	3		8	.	.	.	3	.	290	210	35	43	10

4. Rubber factories. ...	Total ..	**2**	**292**	**113**	**4**	.	**11**						**240**	**55**	**37**	**58**	Oil 2		(4)	2
Factories in which mechanical power is used	From 100 to 200	1	90	101	3	..	5	.	.		.	..	43	47	29	54				
	,, 200 ,, 400 ..	1	212	12	1	..	6	..	..	.	..		197	8	8	4				
Mines.																				
1. Plumbago mines. ..	Total ..	**3**	**803**	**225**	**10**	.	**32**	..	**5**	..	**279**	...	**444**	**189**	**33**	**36**	Steam Steam & oil	1 1 2	(4)	2
Mines in which mechanical power is used.	*Total* ..	*2*	*757*	*225*	*10*		*31*	.	*5*	..	*249*	..	*429*	*189*	*33*	*36*				
	From 100 to 200	1	101	63	2		10	.	..	.		..	88	61	1	2				
	,, 400 and over ..	1	656	162	8	.	21		5		249	.	341	128	32	34				
Mines in which mechanical power is not used.	*Total* .	*1*	*46*	.	..	...	*1*	.	.	.	*30*	.	*15*		..	.			(4)	1
	From 20 to 50 .	1	46	..			1	.	..	.	30	..	15	..	..	..				
Textile industries																				
1. Cotton spinning factories. ..	Total ...	**1**	**31**	**3**	**2**	.	**3**		**1**	..	**10**	..	**13**	**3**	**2**		Steam	1	(7)	1
Factories in which mechanical power is used.	From 20 to 50 .	1	31	3	2	.	3	.	1		10	...	13	3	2				(1)	1
2. Cotton weaving factories. ..	Total ..	**3**	**95**	..	..	.	**11**	...	.	..	**37**	.	**27**	...	**20**				(2)	2
Factories in which mechanical power is not used.	From 20 to 50 ..	3	95	..		.	11	.	.	.	37	..	27	..	29	.				3
3. Coir factories. ...	Total ..	**6**	**1,558**	**425**	**30**	..	**174**	**10**	**1**		**92**	**5**	**934**	**259**	**277**	**151**	Steam	2	(4)	2
Factories in which mechanical power is used	*Total* ..	*2*	*1,319*	*389*	*29*		*69*	..	.	.	*6*	...	*959*	*251*	*256*	*188*			(2)	3
	From 400 and over .	2	1,319	389	29		69			.	6	...	959	251	256	188			(4)	1
Factories in which mechanical power is not used.	*Total*	*4*	*239*	*36*	*1*	..	*105*	*10*	*1*		*86*	*5*	*25*	*8*	*21*	*13*				4
	From 20 to 50 ..	2	40	23	..	.	18	5	.		3		21	5	7	13				
	,, 50 ,, 100 ..	1	78	9			39	3	..	..	35	3	4	3		.				
	,, 100 ,, 200 .	1	112	4	1		43	2	1		48	2	..	.	14	.				
4. Fibre factories. ..	Total	**2**	**474**	**441**	**1**	..	**46**	**1**	.	.	**17**		**390**	**125**	**110**	**315**			(4)	1
Factories in which mechanical power is not used.	From 400 and over	2	474	441	1		46	1		..	17	..	390	125	110	315			(4)	1 2
Wood, etc., industries.																				
1. Carpentry works ...	Total .	**3**	**93**	..	..	.	**7**	.	.		**53**		**35**	.	**4**	..			(2)	2
Works in which mechanical power is not used	From 20 to 50 .	3	93	..	.	.	7	.	...	.	53	..	35	.	4	.			(1)	1 3
Metal industries.																				
1. Mints. ..	Total .	**1**	**23**		.	.	**4**	.	..	.	**7**	..	**15**	..	.	.				
Mints in which mechanical power is not used	From 20 to 50 .	1	23	..	...		4	...		..	7	..	15	..	.	...			(4)	1
2. Engineering workshops .	Total ..	**1**	**235**	..	**2**		**25**	.	**11**	.	**195**	.	**63**	..	**59**	...	Steam, oil & gas	1	(4)	1
Workshops in which mechanical power is used	From 200 to 400 ..	1	205		2		25	...	11	.	105	..	63		59	.				
3. Monazite sand factories .	Total ..	**1**	**17**	**11**	**1**	.	**1**	..	...	..	**15**	**11**	.	..	.	..			(6)	1
Factories in which mechanical power is not used	From 20 to 50	1	17	11	1		1	.			15	11			.					

TABLE XV.

Part E. Statistics of Industries. I.—State Summary.

Description of factory, mine, etc.	Classification of factory, etc., according to number of persons employed (including management).	Number of factories.	Total number of persons employed. Males	Total number of persons employed. Females	Direction, Supervision and Clerical work. Europeans and Anglo-Indians. Males	Direction, Supervision and Clerical work. Europeans and Anglo-Indians. Females	Direction, Supervision and Clerical work. Indians. Males	Direction, Supervision and Clerical work. Indians. Females	Skilled work men. Europeans and Anglo-Indians. Males	Skilled work men. Europeans and Anglo-Indians. Females	Skilled work men. Indians. Males	Skilled work men. Indians. Females	Unskilled labourers. Age 14 and over. Males	Unskilled labourers. Age 14 and over. Females	Unskilled labourers. Under 14. Males	Unskilled labourers. Under 14. Females	Remarks. N. B.—The 'State of business' is indicated thus in figures—(1)=Much brisker than usual. (2)=Brisker than usual. (3)=Somewhat brisker than usual. (4)=Normal. (5)=Somewhat slacker than usual. (6)=Slacker than usual (7)=Much slacker than usual
1	2	3	4	5	6	7	8	9	10	11	12	13	14	15	16	17	18
Glass and earthenware industries.																	Power. — State of business.
1. Brick and tile factories.	**Total** ..	**8**	**1,469**	**41**	**29**	...	**145**	...	**17**	...	**216**	**7**	**946**	**22**	**116**	**12**	
Factories in which mechanical power is used.	*Total*	*4*	*1,259*	*21*	*29*	..	*139*	.	*17*	.	*95*	..	*887*	*13*	*102*	*8*	Steam 2 — (2) 3
	From 100 to 200	2	280	12	..		18	.	...	.	75	.	160	4	27	8	Steam & oil 1 — (4) 1
	,, 200 ,, 400	1	361	6	16	.	28	.	.			..	305	6	12	.	Steam & gas 1
	,, 400 and over	1	618	3	13	.	83	...	17	.	20	..	422	3	63	..	4 — 4
Factories in which mechanical power is not used.	*Total*	*4*	*210*	*20*	...	.	*16*	..	...	...	*121*	*7*	*59*	*9*	*14*	*4*	(1) 1
	From 20 to 50	2	70	..	..		9	..	.	.	35	...	21	..	5	..	(4) 1
	,, 50 ,, 100	2	140	20	...	.	7	..	.		86	7	38	9	9	4	(5) 1 (6) 1 4
Industries connected with chemical products.																	
1. Salt factories.	**Total** ..	**3**	**699**	**49**	..		**11**	...	..	...	**170**	..	**479**	**47**	**39**	**2**	
Factories in which mechanical power is not used.	From 100 to 200	1	172	21	...	..	4	.	...	..	13		128	19	28	2	(1) 3
	,, 200 ,, 400	2	527	28	.		7	..	...	..	158		351	28	11	.	
2. Oil mills.	**Total** ..	**12**	**648**	**11**	**7**	..	**253**	**5**	**8**	...	**138**	.	**232**	**6**	**10**	.	Steam 11 — (2) 5
Mills in which mechanical power is used.	*Total*	*11*	*626*	*11*	*7*	.	*251*	*5*	*8*	..	*118*	..	*232*	*6*	*10*	..	(3) 1
	From 20 to 50	3	99	1	1	...	16	..	.	..	18	..	62	1	2		(4) 3
	,, 50 ,, 100	8	527	10	6	..	235	5	8	.	100	..	170	5	8		(5) 1 (7) 1 11
Mills in which mechanical power is not used.	*Total* ..	*1*	*22*	..			*2*	..	...	.	*20*	..	..	...	.	.	
	From 20 to 50..	1	22	...	...	.	2	...	...	...	20	.	...	..	..	...	(4) 1

3. Copra out-agencies ..	**Total** ...	**1**	**37**	..		...	**24**	..	.	...	...	...	...	...	**13**	..			
Those in which mechanical power is not used.	From 20 to 50 .	1	37	.	...	..	24	...	..	..	..	..	..	...	13	...		(2)	1
4. Paper mills .. .	**Total** ...	**1**	**92**	**8**	..	..	**8**	..	**2**	...	**6**	..	**64**	**8**	**12**	..			
Mills in which mechanical power is used.	From 100 to 200 .	1	92	8	..	..	8	...	2	..	6	..	64	8	12	..	Steam & water 1	(4)	1
5. Stamp manufactories ..	**Total** .	**1**	**35**	.	..	..	**10**	..	..	..	**22**	..	**3**	..	.	...			
Manufactories in which mechanical power is not used.	From 20 to 50 .	1	35	...	.	..	10	..	.	..	22	...	3	..	...	...		(4)	1
Food industries.																			
1. Rice mills. .	**Total** ..	**3**	**62**	**26**	..	.	**7**	..	.	..	**30**	..	**25**	**26**	..	..			
Mills in which mechanical power is used.	From 20 to 50 ...	3	62	26	..	.	7	...	..	.	30	.	25	26	.	...	Steam 3	(2) (4)	1 2 3
Industries of dress.																			
1. Lace making factories .	**Total** .	**1**	..	**1,749**	..	**8**	...	**5**	...	...	...	**1,736**	...	..	..	..			
Factories in which mechanical power is not used.	From 400 and over	1	...	1,749	.	8	...	5	..	..	..	1,736	..	..	..	...		(4)	1
Industries of luxury.																			
1. Printing presses . ..	**Total**	**7**	**521**	**2**	**4**	.	**51**	..	.	...	**416**	..	**38**	**2**	**10**	.			
Presses in which mechanical power is used.	*Total* .	*1*	*188*	.	*3*		*19*		..	.	*147*	..	*19*	.	..	..	Steam 1	(2)	1
	From 100 to 200	1	188	..	3	.	19	...	..	...	147	..	19	..	..	.			
Presses in which mechanical power is not used.	*Total*	*6*	*333*	*2*	*1*	..	*32*	...	...	..	*271*	..	*19*	*2*	*10*	.			
	From 20 to 50	3	103	.	..	.	6	...	..		91	..	8	.	3	.		(1)	3
	,, 50 to 100 ..	2	131	1	1	.	20	.	.	..	97	..	11	1	2	..		(2)	1
	,, 100 to 200 ..	1	99	1	..	.	6	.	.	...	88	.	5	1	5	.		(4)	2 6
2. School of arts . ..	**Total**	**1**	**60**	**1**	..	.	**5**	...	..	.	**26**	..	**29**	**1**	..	..			
School in which mechanical power is used.	From 50 to 100 .	1	60	1	.	.	5	...	.	.	26	..	29	1		..	Steam 1	(2)	1

TABLE XV.

Part E. Statistics of Industries. II.—Distribution by Divisions.

Description of Factory, Mine, etc.	Division.	Number of Factories.	Total number of persons employed: Males	Total number of persons employed: Females	Direction, supervision and clerical work — Europeans and Anglo-Indians: Males.	Direction … — Europeans and Anglo-Indians: Females	Direction … — Indians: Males.	Direction … — Indians: Females.	Skilled Workmen — Europeans and Anglo-Indians: Males.	Skilled Workmen — Europeans and Anglo-Indians: Females.	Skilled Workmen — Indians: Males.	Skilled Workmen — Indians: Females	Unskilled Labourers — Age 14 and over: Males.	Unskilled Labourers — Age 14 and over: Females.	Unskilled Labourers — Under 14: Males.	Unskilled Labourers — Under 14: Females.	Remarks.
1	2	3	4	5	6	7	8	9	10	11	12	13	14	15	16	17	18
	STATE .	*108*	*10,482*	*4,459*	*138*	*11*	*1,003*	*28*	*54*	.	*1,983*	*1,822*	*6,086*	*1,725*	*1,218*	*873*	
Growing of special products.	**Padmanabhapuram..**	**17**	**1,699**	**2,532**	**4**	**8**	**91**	**6**	.	.	**359**	**1,794**	**1,015**	**349**	**230**	**375**	
1. Tea plantations	do.	5	258	212		.	13	.		.	15		184	168	46	44	
2. Rubber plantations	do.	1	48	50	2	.	1				30	40	.	.	15	10	
Textile industries.																	
1. Cotton weaving factories .	do.	1	95		.	.	9		.		16	.	4		6		
2. Fibre factories	do	2	474	441	1		46	1			17		300	125	110	315	
Metal industries.																	
1. Monozite sand factories .	do.	1	17	11	1		1				15	11	.	..			
Glass and earthenware industries.																	
1. Brick and tile factories ..	do.	3	168	20	.	.	10		.	.	96	7	48	9	14	4	
Industries connected with chemical products..																	
1. Salt factories	do.	3	699	49	.	.	11	.			170	.	479	47	39	2	

Industries of dress.																
1. Lace making factories ..	do.	1	.	1,749	.	8	...	5	..		.	1,736	..	..		..
Growing of special products.	**Trivandrum.**	**15**	**1,615**	**231**	**21**	.	**133**	**3**	**16**		**700**	**4**	**643**	**218**	**100**	**36**
1. Tea factories	do.	4	106	32	5	.	23	3	2	..	17	4	55	25	4	.
Mines.																
1. Plumbago mines . .	do.	3	803	225	10	.	32	.	5		279	.	444	189	33	36
Metal industries.																
1. Mints	do.	1	26		.	..	4	.		..	7		15			.
2. Engineering workshops	do.	1	265	.	2	.	25	.	11	.	105	.	63	..	59	.
Industries connected with chemical products.																
1. Oil mills .	do.	1	48	2	..		6		..	.	30		10	2	2	
2. Stamp manufactories .	do.	1	35		.		10			..	22		3	..	.	.
Industries of luxury.																
1. Printing presses .	do.	3	272	1	4	.	28				214		24	1	2	.
2. School of arts .	do.	1	60	1	.		5	.		.	26	.	29	1	..	..
Growing of special products.	**Quilon.**	**33**	**4,790**	**1,098**	**81**		**615**	**15**	**30**	.	**458**	**5**	**2,883**	**716**	**723**	**362**
1. Tea plantations .	do.	3	264	109	2		6			.	13		211	87	32	22
2. Tea factories .	do,	1	334	273	1	.	9		.	.	15		169	194	140	79
3. Rubber plantations	do.	4	594	125	9		24		1	..	60		401	77	99	48
4. Rubber factories .	do.	1	80	101	3	.	5	..		.	.	.	43	47	29	54
Textile industries.																
1. Cotton spinning factories .	do	1	31	3	2		3	.	1		10		13	3	2	
2. Cotton weaving factories .	do.	1	38			.	1			.	9		17	...	11	..
3. Coir factories ..	do.	6	1,558	425	30	..	174	10	1		92	5	984	259	277	151
Glass and earthenware industries.																
1. Brick and tile factories .	do.	5	1,301	21	29	.	135		17	.	120	...	898	13	102	8
Industries connected with chemical products.																
1. Oil mills	do.	5	360	7	5	.	217	5	8	..	66	.	58	2	6	..
2. Copra out-agencies .	do.	1	37	..		.	24	..	.		..	.			13	.
3. Paper mills	do.	1	93	8			8		2	.	6	.	64	8	12	..
Food industries.																
1. Rice mills ..	do.	3	62	26	..	...	7			..	30	.	25	26	...	.

TABLE XV.

Part E. Statistics of Industries II.—Distribution by Divisions. *(Concluded).*

Description of Factory, Mine, etc.	Division.	Number of Factories.	Total number of persons employed.		Classification of persons employed.												Remarks.
					Direction, Supervision and Clerical work.				Skilled Workmen.				Unskilled Labourers.				
					Europeans and Anglo-Indians.		Indians.		Europeans and Anglo-Indians.		Indians.		Age 14 and over.		Under 14.		
			Males.	Females.	Males.	Females.	Males.	Females.	Males.	Females.	Males.	Females.	Males.	Females	Males.	Females.	
1	2	3	4	5	6	7	8	9	10	11	12	13	14	15	16	17	18
Industries of luxury.	**Quilon** *(Concld).*																
1. Printing presses ..	do.	1	39	..	.	..	2	..	..	..	37	..	.	..	.	..	
Growing of special products.	**Kottayam.**	**19**	**1,646**	**426**	**13**	**2**	**89**	**4**	..	..	**326**	.	**1,095**	**332**	**123**	**88**	
1. Rubber plantations .	do.	5	863	411	10	2	24	4	.	.	52	.	679	321	98	84	
2 Rubber factories . .	do.	1	212	12	1	..	6	...	..	.	..	...	197	8	8	4	
Textile industries.																	
1. Cotton weaving factories .	do.	1	22	..	..	..	1	..	.	.	12	..	6	...	3	..	
Wood, etc., industries.																	
1. Carpentry works ...	do.	3	99	..	..	.	7	.	..	.	53	...	35	..	4	..	
Industries connected with chemical products.																	
1. Oil mills .	do.	6	240	2	2		30	..	..	...	42	...	164	2	2	.	
Industries of luxury.																	
Printing presses . .	do.	3	210	1	...	..	21	..	...	..	167	.	14	1	8	.	
Growing of special products.	**Devikulam.**	**24**	**732**	**142**	**19**	**1**	**75**	.	**6**	.	**140**	**19**	**450**	**110**	**42**	**12**	
1. Tea plantations . ..	do.	4	125	26	2	..	18	..	.	..	43	14	59	11	3	1	
2. Tea factories	do.	20	607	116	17	1	57	..	6	...	97	5	391	99	39	11	

TABLE XV.

Part E. Statistics of Industries.
III.—Particulars as to ownership of factories, etc.

Description of factory, etc.	Number of factories.	Number owned by companies of which the Directors are: Europeans and Anglo-Indians.	Indians.	Of both races.	Number privately owned by: Europeans and Anglo-Indians.	Indians: Total.	Caste: Hindu: Brahman.	Chetti.	Izhava.	Konkani.	Nayar.	Reddi.	Vellala.	Christian.	Musalman.	Remarks
1	2	3	4	5	6	7	8	9	10	11	12	13	14	15	16	17
STATE	***108***	***50***	***15***	.	***11***	***27***	***5***	***1***	***2***	***2***	***2***	***1***	***3***	***7***	***4***	
Growing of special products.																
(1) Tea plantations	12	6	1	.	5	..	..	.		..	..	.	..	.	.	
(2) Tea factories	25	23	...	...	2	.	...	.	...	..	...	..	.	..	..	
(3) Rubber plantations	10	9	..	..	1	..	...	..	.	..	...	..	.	.		
(4) Rubber factories	2	2	..	..	..	.	...	.	..	...	...	.	.	.	..	
Mines.																
(1) Plumbago mines	3	3	..	.	..	...	..	.	.	..	...	..	.	..	..	
Textile industries.																
(1) Cotton spinning factories	1	.	.	.	...	**1**	..	.	..	..	1	..		.	.	
(2) Cotton weaving factories	3	.	.	..	..	**3**	.	.	1	...	1	..	...	1	.	
(3) Coir factories	6	1	.	.	1	**4**	.	.	1		.	..	..	.	3	
(4) Fibre factories	2	2	.		.	..	..	..	.	.	..	.	..	.	...	
Wood, etc. industries																
(1) Carpentry works	3	1	1		..	**1**	..		..		..	..		1		
Metal industries.																
(1) Mints *	1	.	.					.	.			.	.	.	.	
(2) Engineering workshops*	1	...	..	.	..	.		.	..	..	.	.	.	.	.	
(3) Monozite sand factories	1	1		..	..	.		.	.					.		
Glass and earthenware industries.																
(1) Brick and tile factories	8	1	3	.	2	**2**	..		.	.	.	.	.	2	.	
Industries connected with chemical products.																
(1) Salt factories	3		1	.	.	**2**	1	.	.	.			1			
(2) Oil mills	12		6	.	..	**6**	1	1	.	2	.		1	1	.	
(3) Copra out-agencies	1	.		.		**1**	.	.	.	.	.	.	..		1	
(4) Paper mills	1	.	.	.	..	**1**	..			.			1	.		
(5) Stamp manufactories *	1	..	.	.	.	.	..	.	.	.		.	.	.		
Food industries.																
(1) Rice mills	3		1	.	...	**2**	2	.	.	...	.		.			
Industries of dress.																
(1) Lace making factories	1	1	.	..	...	..	.		.	.	.	.		.		
Industries of luxury.																
(1) Printing presses †	7	.	2	.	.	**4**	1	.	.			1	.	2		
(2) School of arts *	1	..	.	.	..	..	.				.				.	

* Owned by Travancore Government.
† One owned by Travancore Government.

TABLE XV.

Part E. Statistics of Industries.

IV.—Particulars as to caste or race of the managers of factories, etc.

DESCRIPTION OF FACTORY, ETC.	Number of factories.	NUMBER MANAGED BY										
		Europeans and Anglo-Indians.	INDIANS.									
			Total.	CASTE.								
				HINDU.							Christian.	Musalman.
				Brahman.	Chetti.	Izhava.	Konkani.	Nayar.	Rodh.	Vellala.		
1	2	3	4	5	6	7	8	9	10	11	12	13
STATE ...	***108***	***61***	***42***	***5***	***1***	***2***	***2***	***2***	***1***	***3***	***18***	***8***
Growing of special products.												
(1) Tea plantations ...	12	11	**1**	...	...	...	...	...	...	...	1	...
(2) Tea factories	25	25	...	...	...	...	...	...	...	...	...	...
(3) Rubber plantations ...	10	10	...	...	...	...	...	...	...	...	...	...
(4) Rubber factories ...	2	2	...	...	...	...	...	...	...	...	...	...
Mines.												
(1) Plumbago mines ...	3	3	...	...	...	...	...	...	...	...	...	...
Textile industries.												
(1) Cotton spinning factories ...	1	...	**1**	...	...	...	...	1	...	...	...	...
(2) Cotton weaving factories ...	3	...	**3**	...	...	1	...	1	...	...	1	...
(3) Coir factories	6	2	**4**	...	...	1	...	...	...	...	...	3
(4) Fibre factories	2	2	...	...	...	...	...	...	...	...	...	...
Wood, etc. industries.												
(1) Carpentry works ...	3	1	**2**	...	...	...	...	...	...	...	2	...
Metal industries.												
(1) Mints*	1	...	...	...	...	...	...	...	...	...	...	...
(2) Engineering workshops* ...	1	...	...	...	...	...	...	...	...	...	...	...
(3) Monozite sand factories ...	1	1	...	...	...	...	...	...	...	...	...	...
Glass and earthenware industries.												
(1) Brick and tile factories ...	8	3	**5**	...	...	...	...	...	...	...	5	...
Industries connected with chemical products.												
(1) Salt factories ...	3	...	**3**	1	...	...	...	...	...	1	...	1
(2) Oil mills	12	...	**12**	1	1	...	2	...	...	1	5	2
(3) Copra out-agencies ...	1	...	**1**	...	...	...	...	...	...	...	...	1
(4) Paper mills	1	...	**1**	...	...	...	...	...	...	1	...	...
(5) Stamp manufactories* ...	1	...	...	...	...	...	...	...	...	...	...	...
Food industries.												
(1) Rice mills	3	...	**3**	2	...	...	...	...	...	...	...	1
Industries of dress.												
(1) Lace making factories ...	1	1	...	...	...	...	...	...	...	...	...	...
Industries of luxury.												
(1) Printing presses†	7	...	**6**	1	...	...	...	...	1	...	4	...
(2) School of arts*	1	...	...	...	...	...	...	...	...	...	...	...

* Owned by Travancore Government. † One owned by Travancore Government.

TABLE XVI.

Occupation by Selected Castes, Tribes or Races.

NOTE—For this Table, some castes shown separately in Table XIII (Castes, Tribes, Races or Nationalities) have been grouped together. The castes so grouped are those shown in the Note to Table IX.

TABLE XVI.

Occupation by Selected Castes, Tribes or Races.

CASTE.	TRADITIONAL OCCUPATION.	Population dealt with. Actual Workers. Males.	Actual Workers. Females.	Dependants. Males.	Dependants. Females.	Number of actual workers whose traditional occupation was returned as their Principal means of livelihood. Males.	Principal means of livelihood. Females.	Subsidiary means of livelihood. Males.	Subsidiary means of livelihood. Females.
1	2	3	4	5	6	7	8	9	10
HINDU.									
1. Ampalavāsi ..	Accessory service in temples ...	3,743	822	1 705	4,582	2,178	428	135	42
2. Ampattan ...	Barbers ..	8,012	1,808	2,984	9,022	7,680	880	31	..
3. Brahman (Malayāla and others)	Priests .	16,464	4,714	13.269	21,227	2,140	974	189	..
4 Chakkāla ...	Oil-pressers .	5,265	2,922	3,672	6,215	1,598	895	270	93
5. Chānnān ...	Toddy drawers ..	39,901	20,525	44,737	61,032	12,428	.	875	..
6. Chetti ...	Traders .	5,320	1,658	5,215	8,688	828	464	168	3
7. Izhavan ...	Toddy drawers ..	177,391	98,334	94,286	176,254	30,436	...	4,375	..
8. Kammalan ..	Artisans .	38,108	12,121	33,430	57,923	32,410	724	324	.
9. Kaniyān ..	Astrologers ...	3,269	1,235	2,886	4,597	1,565	43	12	...
10. Konkani .	Traders ..	2,579	1,296	2,777	3,567	1,220	125	128	49
11 Kuravan .	Labourers and fortune tellers ..	23,149	12,719	7,034	18,925	17,875	10,112	243	119
12. Marakkān .	Boatmen .	5,619	3,846	1,625	3,484	319		791	.
13. Marān ..	Pipers and drummers.	8,101	3,280	6,560	11,377	1,912	..	85	.
14. Nāyar .	Agriculturists ..	166,956	40,461	128,747	256,325	115,652	24,051	539	106
15. Parayan	Field labourers ..	22,425	22,163	12,706	13,260	18,358	9,090	643	418
16 Pulayan .	Field labourers ..	61,777	58,173	31,558	33,806	58,231	52,042	2,431	1,769
17. Sāliyan .	Weavers .	2,311	1,550	2,642	3,416	1,686	743	41	12
18. Vālan ..	Boatmen ..	6,050	4,490	2,538	3,670	4,146	.	120	.
19. Vāniyan .	Oil-pressers ..	5,932	2,074	2,788	6,046	4,161	1,426	68	38
20. Vēlan .	Sorcerers ..	5,041	2,895	1,309	3,712	805	93	11	4
21. Vellāla	Agriculturists .	12,267	3,736	11,507	20,969	6,878	1,214	216	49
22. Veluttēdan .	Washermen ..	3,023	2,104	2,695	3,534	2,611	1,964	91	36

NOTE.—The figures in column 13 onwards are exclusive of those in columns 7 and 8. Asterisks have been placed

TABLE XVI.

Occupation by Selected Castes, Tribes or Races.—*(Continued).*

Number of actual workers returning their traditional occupation as their principal means of livelihood who had some subsidiary occupation.		Recorded principal occupation of actual workers. I.—Exploitation of the surface of the soil. Income from rent of land.		Cultivators of all kinds.		Agents managers of landed estates planters etc.		Field labourers wood-cutters, etc.		Raisers of live stock, milkmen, etc.		Fishing and hunting.		Number.
Males.	Females.	Males.	Females.	Males.	Females.	Males.	Females.	Males.	Females.	Males.	Females.	Males.	Females.	
11	12	13	14	15	16	17	18	19	20	21	22	23	24	
71	25	91	24	1,072	149	...	...	50	..	...	...	..	...	1
18	5	27	3	183	126	...	..	25	95	...	...	5	..	2
293	...	695	84	3,260	729	26	...	..	...	...	...	...	...	3
154	81	139	26	1,890	426	...	...	75	...	34	23	...	.	4
639	...	1,571	319	10,831	2,579	7	...	2,358	1,746	170	26	...	..	5
103	41	926	45	2,479	416	...	...	161	...	18	...	..	..	6
1,639	..	3,549	697	40,619	4,420	25	...	30,476	15,278	393	48	145	...	7
118	..	113	46	2,410	1,931	..	..	220	126	95	..	..	.	8
61	.	13	3	428	341	...	...	247	89	19	..	...	..	9
82	16	46	8	611	93	..	..	84	...	48	11	...	..	10
94	38	71	9	2,411	917	...	..	982	819	63	.	259	..	11
48	..	5	.	502	60	..	...	68	37	.	.	3,580	84	12
67	.	49	11	5,130	925	3	...	43	71	42	..	.		13
2,479	1,165	*	*	*	*	59	..	8,905	3,115	755	226	116	..	14
96	69	..	.	1,754	3,125	...	..	*	*	63	10	336	398	15
816	753	14	.	716	213	..	.	*	*	176	101	291	15	16
69	75	16	5	116	29	...	...	65	...	..	.	.	.	17
45	...	5	...	170	90	.	...	119	26	..	..	816	263	18
53	19	29	8	497	94	.	.	106	19	26	..	..	..	19
32	8	..	.	1,933	914	.	.	618	443	.	...	.	..	20
619	35	*	*	*	*	24	...	539	60	170	47	...	..	21
24	13	19	6	259	96	...	.	40	.	.	.	.	.	22

against the figures in those columns which are affected by this arrangement.

TABLE XVI.

Occupation by Selected Castes, Tribes or Races.

CASTE.	TRADITIONAL OCCUPATION.	RECORDED PRINCIPAL OCCUPATION OF ACTUAL WORKERS.							
		II EXTRACTION OF MINERALS.				III INDUSTRIES.			
		Owners, managers, clerks, etc.		Artisans and other workmen, etc.		Owners, managers, clerks, etc.		Artisans and other workmen etc.	
		Males.	Females.	Males.	Females.	Males.	Females.	Males.	Females.
1	2	25	26	27	28	29	30	31	32
HINDU.									
1. Ampalavāsi ..	Accessory service in temples .	..	.	..	.	.	..	188	162
2. Ampa*tt*an ...	Barbers ..	.	.	..	..	.	..	* 26	* 625
3. Brahman (Malayā*la* and others) .	Priests ..	5	.	.	.	9	.	156	636
4. Chakkāla ...	Oil-pressers ..	..	..	..	.	* 3	*	* 98	* 872
5. Chānnān ...	Toddy drawers .	.	.	14	.	9	..	* 565	6,755
6. Che*tti* ..	Traders .	..	...	..	..	2	.	331	476
7. Izhavan ..	Toddy drawers	.	.	96	42	* 8	.	*27,416	31,624
8. Kammā*l*an	Artisans .	..	..	..	.	10	*	* 326	* 7,671
9. Ka*n*iyān .	Astrologers ..	.	..	..	..	..	.	832	626
10. Konka*n*i ..	Traders ..	.	..		..	2	..	411	990
11. Kuravan ...	Labourers and fortune tellers ...	..	..	20	5	..	..	1,285	1,205
12 Marakkan ..	Boatmen ...	..	...	26	1	.	.	898	8,218
13. Mārān .	Pipers and drummers ..	..	...	..	.	..	..	138	1,464
14. Nāyar .	Agriculturists ..	9	..	41	.	10	.	7,402	4,347
15 Pa*r*ayan ..	Field labourers ..		..	29	.	..	.	367	1,480
16 Pulayan .	Field labourers		..	75	29	.	..	524	476
17. *S*āliyan	Weavers	.	..	..	.			* 80	* 745
18. Vālan	Boatmen .		.	.		..	..	670	8,016
19. Vā*n*iyan ..	Oil-pressers .	.	.	.	.	*	*	* 66	* 264
20. Vēlan	Sorcerers .	..		..	.	..	.	819	702
21 Ve*ll*ā*l*a .	Agriculturists	.	.			4	..	1,220	689
22 Veluttē*d*an .	Washermen	..	..	.	.	*		* 40	* 23

TABLE XVI.

Occupation by selected Castes, Tribes or Races.—*(Continued).*

RECORDED PRINCIPAL OCCUPATION OF ACTUAL WORKERS.																
IV. Transport.				V. Trade.		VI. Public Force.		VII. Public Administration.		VIII. Arts and Professions.						
Owners, managers, ship officers, etc.		Labourers, boatmen, carters, etc.								Religions.		Lawyers, doctors and teachers.		Others.		
Males	Females.	Males	Females.	Males	Females.	Males.	Females.	Males.	Females	Males.	Females.	Males	Females	Males	Females.	Number.
33	34	35	36	37	38	39	40	41	42	43	44	45	46	47	48	
5	.	11	..	20	18	..	.	43	.	* 27	*	16	..		.	1
.		7	.	5	..	..	.	2	..	6	.	22	96		.	2
676	.	39	.	1,770	830	96	.	2,498	.	* 275	*	2,772	11	315		3
		78	69	125	91	2	.	86	.	.	.	19		2	.	4
18		1,178	296	6,431	4,583	.	.	6		.		35		4	.	5
26	.	216	.	*	*	29	.	35	.			24	.	3		6
42	.	3,093	675	18,939	16,216	18	.	102		149	.	92	13	27	14	7
8	.	13	.	1,235	76			6	.	45	.	11		9		8
2	..	5	.	15	7	.	.		.			8		*	*	9
15		24		*	*	.	.	7	.		...	13	.	.		10
2	.	98	43	69	87	.	.	...	.	18		26	9	19	25	11
* 14		* 76	40	146	375	.	.	..	.		.	.	..	.		12
9	..	13	.	35	521	..	...	24	..	426	65	39		*	..	13
920	5	3,912	146	5,984	3,771	2,763	.	3,827	.	672	164	5,479	374	434	53	14
.		58	93	65	47			...	..	59		..			.	15
.	.	348	199	263	113						..	.		13	.	16
5	.	71		218	16	..	.	12	.	.	.	11			.	17
* 2	.	* 25	9	49	13		.	.		..						18
9	.	96	13	167	91	4		6	.		.	5	.	5	..	19
	.	40	15	82	5	.	.	.	.	..		..				20
73		673		1,239	476	131		224	..	113	.	193	24	17		21
2	.	14	3	..	...			.	..	.	..	.			.	22

TABLE XVI.

Occupation by Selected Castes, Tribes or Races.—*(Concluded).*

RECORDED PRINCIPAL OCCUPATION OF ACTUAL WORKERS.

CASTE.	TRADITIONAL OCCUPATION	IX. PERSONS LIVING ON THEIR INCOME.		X. DOMESTIC SERVICE		XI. CONTRACTORS, CASHIERS AND CLERKS OTHERWISE UNSPECIFIED		XII. LABOURERS UNSPECIFIED		XIII. BEGGARS, PROSTITUTES AND CRIMINALS, INMATES OF JAILS.	
		Males.	Females.	Males.	Females.	Males.	Females.	Males.	Females.	Males.	Females.
1	2	49	50	51	52	53	54	55	56	57	58
HINDU.											
1. Ampalavāsi ..	Accessory service in temples ...	.	..	18	25	...	..	21	14	3	2
2. Ampattan ...	Barbers .	...	...	...	.	...	..	24	26	...	6
3. Brahman (Malayāla and others)	Priests ..	407	61	918	1,287	267	...	60	7	71	95
4. Chakkāla ..	Oil-pressers ...	4	...	29	16	5	..	1,065	494	13	10
5. Chānnān .	Toddy drawers ...	.	...	36	11	43	12	4,071	4,219	105	39
6. Chetti ..	Traders ..	6	..	...	...	8	..	215	244	16	13
7. Izhavan .	Toddy drawers ..	12	..	243	28	175	16	21,214	29,172	132	90
8. Kammālan .	Artisans ...	2	...	...	..	7	.	1,123	1,519	65	28
9. Kaniyān .	Astrologers ..	.	...	..	...	..	.	121	118	14	8
10. Konkani ..	Traders ..	.	.	..	.	19	..	81	64	3	5
11. Kuravan .	Labourers and fortune tellers ..		...	...	..	..	.	*	*	46	38
12. Marakkān .	Boatmen	.	..	.	.	9	...	43	25	13	11
13. Mārān	Pipers and drummers.	4	..	48	19	...		175	191	21	13
14. Nāyar ..	Agriculturists .	658	140	1,347	2,461	1,249	10	6,607	1,459	205	136
15. Parayan ..	Field labourers ..	..	.	..	..	.	..	1,321	7,916	11	4
16. Pulayan	Field labourers ..	.	..	86	47	...	.	1,019	4,926	26	12
17. Sāliyan	Weavers ...	.	.	..	...	..	..	31	12	..	.
18. Vālan ..	Boatmen .	.	.	..	..	.	..	39	1,066	9	2
19. Vāniyan .	Oil-pressers ..	..	.	.	..	14	.	128	153	13	6
20. Vēlan .	Sorcerers	..	.	90	11	...	..	674	712	.	.
21. Vellāla .	Agriculturists	89		40	..	86	8	1,489	1,201	65	17
22. Veluttēdan ..	Washermen .	..	..	10	3	...	.	24	9	4	

TABLE XVII.

Territorial Distribution of the Christian Population by Sect and Race.

NOTE.—There are in the State 1,121 Christians of the 'Yuyomayam' Sect and they are shown under the head 'Indefinite beliefs'.

TABLE XVII.

Territorial Distribution of the Christian Population by Sect and Race.

DENOMINATION.	TOTAL RETURNED.			DISTRIBUTION BY RACE.								
				EUROPEAN AND ALLIED RACES.			ANGLO-INDIAN.			INDIAN.		
	Persons.	Males.	Females.	Persons.	Males.	Females.	Persons.	Males.	Females.	Persons.	Males.	Females.
1	2	3	4	5	6	7	8	9	10	11	12	13
State.												
All Denominations	***903,868***	***461,165***	***442,703***	***399***	***250***	***149***	***1,750***	***911***	***839***	***901,719***	***460,004***	***441,715***
1. Anglican Communion	56,251	29,040	27,211	183	133	50	93	56	37	55,975	28,851	27,124
2. Baptist	3		3	..		..	...	..	...	3		3
3. Congregationalist	81,573	41,520	40,053	27	11	16	47	20	27	81,499	41,489	40,010
4. Greek	24	13	11	...	..	..	...	...	..	24	13	11
5. Lutheran	391	243	148	6	4	2	..	..	...	385	239	146
6. Methodist	1	1	.	1	1	..	..	...	..	..	..	...
7. Minor Protestant Denominations	1,537	747	790	17	11	6	34	14	20	1,486	722	764
8 Presbyterian	34	25	9	24	18	6	..	..	...	10	7	3
9 Protestants (unsectarian or sect not specified)	116	75	41	1	1	..	...	..	...	115	74	41
10. Roman Catholic	173,724	87,743	85,981	107	57	50	1,555	806	749	172,062	86,880	85,182
11. Salvationist	16,794	8,594	8,200	27	10	17	8	8	...	16,759	8,576	8,183
12. Syrian Chaldean	1,612	1,218	394	...	..	...	..	..	...	1,612	1,218	394
13. ,, Jacobite	202,059	102,601	99,458	..	.	..	..	..	...	202,059	102,601	99,458
14. ,, Reformed	74,866	39,301	35,565	...	...	..	..	..	...	74,866	39,301	35,565
15. ,, Romo	293,407	149,294	144,113	...	..	.	..	.	...	293,407	149,294	144,113
16. Sect not returned	355	190	165	6	4	2	13	7	6	336	179	157
17. Indefinite beliefs	1,121	560	561	..	..	...	...	...	..	1,121	560	561
Padmanabhapuram Divsion.												
All Denominations	***116,778***	***58,670***	***58,108***	***64***	***24***	***40***	***24***	***20***	***4***	***116,690***	***58,626***	***58,064***
1. Anglican Communion	6,778	3,311	3,462	1	1	..	..	...	..	6,772	3,310	3,462
2. Congregationalist	39,177	20,084	19,098	16	5	11	3	1	2	39,158	20,078	19,080
3. Greek	24	13	11	...	..	.	...	...	..	24	13	11
4. Lutheran	279	164	115	6	4	2	..	..	..	273	160	113

5. Presbyterian	1	1	...	1	1	..	..	...	..	...	..	...
6. Roman Catholic	62,138	30,778	31,360	18	5	13	..	..	..	62,099	30,754	31,345
7. Salvationist	8,310	4,252	4,058	23	8	14	21	19	2	8,288	4,244	4,044
8. Syrian Jacobite	24	16	8	...	..	..	..	.	..	24	16	8
9. ,, Reformed	13	13	..		..	..	.	.	.	13	13	..
10. ,, Romo	39	38	1		...	...	..	..	.	39	38	1

Trivandrum Division.

All Denominations	***77,305***	***39,371***	***37,934***	***91***	***50***	***41***	***817***	***378***	***439***	***76,397***	***38,943***	***37,454***
1. Anglican Communion	3,142	1,561	1,581	32	20	12	23	8	15	3,087	1,533	1,554
2. Congregationalist	37,443	19,121	18,322	6	2	4	34	9	25	37,403	19,110	18,293
3. Lutheran	1	1	.	..	..	..	.	..	...	1	1	..
4. Methodist	1	1	.	1	1	.	.	.	..	...	..	
5. Minor Protestant Denominations	670	331	339	17	11	6	34	14	20	619	306	313
6. Presbyterian	1	1	..	..	.	..	.	.	..	1	1	
7. Protestants (unsectarian or Sect not specified)	1	1	..	1	1	..	.	..	.	.	...	
8. Roman Catholic	29,077	14,769	14,308	23	9	14	711	338	373	28,343	14,422	13,921
9. Salvationist	6,273	3,176	3,097	5	2	3	2	2	..	6,266	3,172	3,094
10. Syrian Jacobite	203	152	51	...		...	..	.		203	152	51
11. ,, Reformed	64	51	13	..	..	..	.	.	..	64	51	13
12. ,, Romo	320	148	172	.	..	.		..		320	148	172
13. Sect not returned	109	58	51	6	4	2	13	7	6	90	47	43

Quilon Division.

All Denominations	***262,446***	***134,621***	***127,825***	***71***	***47***	***24***	***704***	***393***	***311***	***261,671***	***134,181***	***127,490***
1. Anglican Communion	20,591	10,723	9,868	21	20	1	46	33	13	20,524	10,670	9,854
2. Baptist	3	..	3	...	...	.	.	..	..	3	..	3
3. Congregationalist	4,846	2,243	2,603	3	3	..	9	9	.	4,834	2,231	2,603
4. Lutheran	71	51	20	...	..			...	...	71	51	20
5. Minor Protestant Denominations	533	226	307	...	...	..	...	..	.	533	226	307
6. Presbyterian	11	8	3	2	2	..	.	.	.	9	6	3
7. Protestants (unsectarian or Sect not specified)	106	68	38	..	.	..	.	..	..	106	68	38
8. Roman Catholic	35,775	18,161	17,614	45	22	23	643	345	298	35,087	17,794	17,293
9. Salvationist	1,512	791	721	..	..	...	6	6	.	1,506	785	721
10. Syrian Chaldean	21	16	5	..	...	.	..	.	.	21	16	5
11. ,, Jacobite	102,148	52,603	49,545	..	..	.	..	...	.	102,148	52,603	49,545
12. ,, Reformed	71,008	36,768	34,240	..	..	.	.	..	..	71,008	36,768	34,240
13. ,, Romo	24,622	12,355	12,267	...	..	..	.	..	..	24,622	12,355	12,267
14. Sect not returned	246	132	114	...	.	.	..	...	.	246	132	114
15. Indefinite beliefs	953	476	477	...	..	..	..	..	..	953	476	477

TABLE XVII.

Territorial Distribution of the Christian Population by Sect and Race.

DENOMINATION.	TOTAL RETURNED.			DISTRIBUTION BY RACE.								
				EUROPEAN AND ALLIED RACES.			ANGLO-INDIAN.			INDIAN.		
	Persons.	Males.	Females.	Persons.	Males.	Females.	Persons.	Males.	Females.	Persons.	Males.	Females.
1	2	3	4	5	6	7	8	9	10	11	12	13
Kottayam Division.												
All Denominations	**428,706**	**217,874**	**210,832**	**20**	**15**	**5**	**159**	**74**	**85**	**428,527**	**217,785**	**210,742**
1. Anglican Communion	21,031	10,668	10,363	8	4	4	21	12	9	21,002	10,652	10,350
2. Congregationalist	2	1	1	2	1	1	...	...	...	...	...	...
3. Lutheran	1	1	...	...	...	...	...	...	...	1	1	...
4. Minor Protestant Denominations	199	114	85	...	...	...	...	...	...	199	114	85
5. Protestants (unsectarian or Sect not specified)	9	6	3	...	...	...	...	...	...	9	6	3
6. Roman Catholic	44,050	22,311	21,739	10	10	...	138	62	76	43,902	22,239	21,663
7. Salvationist	699	375	324	...	...	...	...	...	...	699	375	324
8. Syrian Chaldean	1,591	1,202	389	...	...	...	...	...	...	1,591	1,202	389
9. ,, Jacobite	98,889	49,279	49,610	...	...	...	...	...	...	98,889	49,279	49,610
10. ,, Reformed	3,338	2,076	1,262	...	...	...	...	...	...	3,338	2,076	1,262
11 ,, Romo	258,729	131,757	126,972	...	...	...	...	...	...	258,729	131,757	126,972
12. Indefinite beliefs	168	84	84	...	...	...	...	...	...	168	84	84
Devikulam Division.												
All Denominations	**18,633**	**10,629**	**8,004**	**153**	**114**	**39**	**46**	**46**	...	**18,434**	**10,469**	**7,965**
1. Anglican Communion	4,714	2,777	1,937	121	88	33	3	3	...	4,590	2,686	1,904
2. Congregationalist	105	71	34	...	...	...	1	1	...	104	70	34
3. Lutheran	39	26	13	...	...	...	...	...	...	39	26	13
4. Minor Protestant Denominations	135	76	59	...	...	...	...	...	...	135	76	59
5. Presbyterian	21	15	6	21	15	6	...	...	...	...	...	...
6. Roman Catholic	2,684	1,724	960	11	11	...	42	42	...	2,631	1,671	960
7. Syrian Jacobite	795	551	244	...	...	...	...	...	...	795	551	244
8. ,, Reformed	443	393	50	...	...	...	...	...	...	443	393	50
9. ,, Romo	9,697	4,996	4,701	...	...	...	...	...	...	9,697	4,996	4,701

TABLE XVII.

Christian Population by Sect and Race.

Western Natural Division.

All Denominations	419,818	213,955	205,863	193	96	97	1,513	750	763	418,112	213,109	205,003
1. Anglican Communion	26,279	13,467	12,812	32	22	10	74	45	29	26,173	13,400	12,773
2. Baptist	3	...	3	...	...	...	...	...	.	3	...	3
3. Congregationalist	59,518	30,144	29,377	18	5	13	35	9	26	59,465	30,127	29,338
4. Greek	23	12	11	...	...	...	...	..	...	23	12	11
5. Lutheran	95	92	3	6	4	2	...	...	...	89	88	1
6. Minor Protestant Denominations	1,002	448	554	17	11	6	34	14	20	951	423	528
7. Presbyterian	10	7	3	2	2	...	...	..	..	8	5	3
8. Protestants (unsectarian or Sect not specified)	107	69	38	1	1	...	...	...	...	106	68	38
9. Roman Catholic	149,304	75,133	74,171	89	39	50	1,349	667	682	147,866	74,427	73,439
10. Salvationist	9,287	4,729	4,558	22	8	14	8	8	...	9,257	4,713	4,544
11. Syrian Chaldean	1,612	1,218	394	...	..	...	...	..	...	1,612	1,218	394
12. ,, Jacobite	60,599	31,398	29,201	...	...	...	...	...	..	60,599	31,398	29,201
13. ,, Reformed	47,719	24,526	23,193	...	...	..	...	..	..	47,719	24,526	23,193
14. ,, Romo	63,386	32,283	31,103	..	...	.	..	..	...	63,386	32,283	31,103
15. Sect not returned	321	173	148	6	4	2	13	7	6	302	162	140
16. Indefinite beliefs	553	259	294	...	...	..	.	..	..	553	259	294

Eastern Natural Division.

All Denominations	484,050	247,210	236,840	206	154	52	237	161	76	483,607	246,895	236,712
1. Anglican Communion	29,972	15,573	14,399	151	111	40	19	11	8	29,802	15,451	14,351
2. Congregationalist	22,055	11,379	10,676	9	6	3	12	11	1	22,034	11,362	10,672
3. Greek	1	1	...	..	...	..	...	...	...	1	1	.
4. Lutheran	296	151	145	...	..	...	...	...	..	296	151	145
5. Methodist	1	1	..	1	1	...	...	...	..	...	..	..
6. Minor Protestant Denominations	535	299	236	...	...	..	...	...	...	535	299	236
7. Presbyterian	24	18	6	22	16	6	...	...	..	2	2	..
8. Protestants (unsectarian or Sect not specified)	9	6	3	...	...	...	..	...	...	9	6	3
9. Roman Catholic	24,420	12,610	11,810	18	18	...	206	189	67	24,196	12 453	11,743
10. Salvationist..	7,507	3,865	3,642	5	2	3	...	...	...	7,502	3,863	3,639
11. Syrian Jacobite	141,460	71,203	70,257	...	...	..	...	...	...	141,460	71,203	70,257
12. ,, Reformed	27,147	14,775	12,372	...	...	...	..	..	...	27,147	14,775	12,372
13. ,, Romo	230,021	117,011	113,010	...	...	...	...	...	..	230,021	117,011	113,010
14. Sect not returned	-34	17	17	..	..	..	...	...	...	34	17	17
15. Indefinite beliefs	568	301	267	.	..	.	....	...	...	568	301	267

TABLE XVIII.

Europeans, Armenians and Anglo-Indians by Race and Age.

NOTE.—As there are no Armenians in the State, the heading 'Armenian' is omitted from the body of the Table.

TABLE XVIII.

Europeans, Armenians and Anglo-Indians by Race and Age.

DIVISION.	TOTAL.			BRITISH SUBJECTS.														
				ALL AGES.			0–12		12–15		15–30		30–50		50 and over.	
	Total.	Males.	Females.	Total.	Males.	Females.	Males.	Females.	Males.	Females.	Males.	Females.	Males.	Females.	Males.	Females.
1	2	3	4	5	6	7	8	9	10	11	12	13	14	15	16	17
STATE ..	*2,149*	*1,161*	*988*	*320*	*216*	*104*	*20*	*18*	*1*	*1*	*63*	*25*	*113*	*52*	*19*	*8*
PADMANABHAPURAM ..	88	44	44	30	12	18	1	2	1	...	1	2	6	11	3	3
TRIVANDRUM ...	908	428	480	68	42	26	5	6	...	1	6	5	28	13	3	1
QUILON	775	440	335	59	42	17	1	3	...	...	11	8	25	4	5	2
KOTTAYAM	179	89	90	11	7	4	...	...	...	...	...	1	7	3	...	..
DEVIKULAM ...	199	160	39	152	113	39	13	7	...	...	45	9	47	21	8	2
Western Natural Division ...	*1,706*	*846*	*860*	*121*	*68*	*53*	*7*	*11*	...	*1*	*15*	*15*	*39*	*22*	*7*	*4*
Eastern Natural Division ..	*443*	*315*	*128*	*199*	*148*	*51*	*13*	*7*	*1*	...	*48*	*10*	*74*	*30*	*12*	*4*

DIVISION.	OTHERS.													ANGLO-INDIANS.												
	ALL AGES.			0-12		12-15		15-30		30-50		50 and over.		ALL AGES.			0-12		12-15		15-30		30-50		50 and over.	
	Total.	Males.	Females.	Males.	Females.	Males.	Females.	Males.	Females.	Males.	Females.	Males.	Females.	Total.	Males.	Females.	Males.	Females.	Males.	Females.	Males.	Females.	Males.	Females.	Males.	Females.
1	18	19	20	21	22	23	24	25	26	27	28	29	30	31	32	33	34	35	36	37	38	39	40	41	42	43
STATE ..	*79*	*34*	*45*	*1*	...	..	...	*10*	*20*	*19*	*24*	*4*	*1*	*1,750*	*911*	*839*	*256*	*255*	*115*	*81*	*256*	*238*	*182*	*181*	*102*	*84*
PADMANABHAPURAM ..	34	12	22	1	..	..	.	2	13	8	9	1	..	24	20	4	2	...	5	...	3	2	3	2	7	..
TRIVANDRUM ..	23	8	15	..	..	...	..	3	5	4	9	1	1	817	378	439	115	111	45	37	104	132	71	108	43	56
QUILON	12	5	7	.	.	...	..	2	2	3	5	...	..	704	393	311	106	117	58	37	113	77	77	61	39	19
KOTTAYAM	9	8	1	...	.	...	...	3	..	4	1	1	..	159	74	85	21	27	6	7	21	27	16	15	10	9
DEVIKULAM ..	1	1	...	.	...	...	...	..	..	...	.	1	...	46	46	...	12	...	1	..	15	...	15	...	3	..
Western Natural Division ..	*72*	*28*	*44*	*1*	...	..	..	*8*	*20*	*17*	*23*	*2*	*1*	*1,513*	*750*	*763*	*217*	*233*	*107*	*76*	*206*	*212*	*136*	*167*	*84*	*75*
Eastern Natural Division .	*7*	*6*	*1*	...	...	...	...	*2*	...	*2*	*1*	*2*	...	*237*	*161*	*76*	*39*	*22*	*8*	*5*	*50*	*26*	*46*	*14*	*18*	*9*

PROVINCIAL TABLE I.

Area and Population of Taluks and Towns.

NOTE.—The areas given in this Table represent (1) the final result of the survey of the State which was only in progress at the last Census and (2) the adjustments made for inter-taluk transfers of areas since 1901.

PROVINCIAL TABLE I.

Area and Population of Taluks and Towns.

TALUK OR TOWN.	AREA IN SQUARE MILES.	NUMBER OF		NUMBER OF OCCUPIED HOUSES.	POPULATION.				Percentage of variation.		Number of persons per square mile in 1911.
					1911.			1901 Both sexes.	1901 to 1911.	1891 to 1901.	
		TOWNS.	VILLAGES.		Persons.	Males.	Females.				
1.	2	3	4	5	6	7	8	9	10	11	12
STATE ...	*7,593·76*	*11*	*3,965*	*663,153*	*3,428,975*	*1,731,363*	*1,697,612*	*2,952,157*	*+ 16·2*	*+ 15·4*	*452*
1. Tovala ...	115·00	...	150	7,774	34,503	16,991	17,512	32,410	+ 6·5	+ 8·9	300
2. Agastisvaram ...	94.00	1	311	22,567	104,910	51,282	53,628	93,513	+ 12·2	+ 7·2	1,116
4. Eraniel ...	98·00	...	340	25,019	123,783	62,638	61,145	110,161	+ 42·4	+ 4·8	1,263
5. Kalkulam ...	169·00	...	169	15,864	76,211	38,266	37,945	70,247	+ 8·5	+ 18·1	451
5. Vilavankod ...	137·00	...	121	15,977	90,680	46,136	44,544	78,244	+ 15·9	+ 16·1	662
6. Neyyattinkara	233·35	...	226	31,933	178,703	91,797	86,906	141,292	+ 26·5	+ 26·3	765
7. Trivandrum ...	97.26	1	73	27,367	155,138	78,155	76,983	134,196	+ 15·6	+ 19·9	1,595
8. Nedumangad ...	365·97	...	70	17,522	88,147	44,685	43,462	67,771	+ 30·1	+ 22·1	241
9. Chirayinkil ...	146·57	...	90	25,221	135,877	66,588	69,289	112,823	+ 20·4	+ 15·1	927
10. Kottarakara ...	202·03	...	154	17,290	90,309	45,176	45,133	77,065	+ 17·2	+ 7·8	447
11. Pattanapuram	425·67	...	88	11,154	56,769	28,503	28,266	49,575	+ 11·5	+ 25·7	133
12. Shencottah ..	129·14	1	43	8,916	38,303	18,734	19,568	38,970	— 1·7	+ 21·4	297
13. Quilon ..	147·41	1	147	29,263	163,798	81,716	82,082	129,658	+ 26·3	+ 6·3	1,111
14. Kunnattur ...	171·49	...	128	17,828	91,390	46,226	45,164	81,725	+ 11·8	+ 11·5	533
15. Karunagapalli...	88·99	1	121	27,666	137,420	67,914	69,506	124,312	+ 10·5	+ 14·2	1,544
16. Kartikapalli ...	74·26	...	89	20,781	111,570	55,103	56,467	96,755	+ 15·3	+ 5·2	1,502
17. Mavelikara ...	111·43	...	121	25,833	130,738	66,154	64,574	116,830	+ 11·9	+ 12·5	1,173
18. Chengannur ...	925·97	...	152	24,557	126,439	64,843	61,596	108,540	+ 16·5	+ 15·5	137
19. Tiruvalla ..	172·18	1	169	32,131	173,768	89,384	84,384	140,926	+ 23·3	+ 15·4	1,009
20. Ambalapuzha..	115·74	1	71	20,981	112,867	57,020	55,847	105,927	+ 6·6	+ 11·8	975
21. Shertallay ...	118·03	...	45	35,531	156,580	78,563	78,017	140,888	+ 11·1	+ 20·1	1,327
22. Vaikam ...	139·55	...	75	24,756	119,824	60,894	58,930	109,095	+ 9·8	+ 17·5	859
23. Ettumanur ...	105·89	...	60	16,821	90,591	46,471	44,120	81,911	+ 10·6	+ 17·5	856
24. Kottayam ...	172·84	1	86	21,535	112,139	57,317	54,792	92,911	+ 20·7	+ 22·4	649
25. Changanachery	134·29	1	51	17,914	96,241	49,019	47,222	78,959	+ 21·9	+ 26·2	717
26. Minachil ..	139·69	...	68	15,149	78,871	40,276	38,595	66,033	+ 19·4	+ 17·9	565
27. Muvattupuzha	472·34	...	165	27,321	138,392	69,611	68,781	127,721	+ 8·4	+ 24·0	293
28. Todupuzha ...	561·01	...	87	7,635	38,426	19,904	18,522	32,571	+ 18·0	+ 29·2	68
29. Kunnatnad ...	293·88	...	146	22,311	118,693	58,419	60,274	101,730	+ 16·7	+ 15·6	404
30. Alangad ..	127·34	1	112	20,431	103,836	51,574	54,262	97,144	+ 12·0	+ 6·0	855
31. Parur ...	53·89	1	64	14,566	80,508	40,982	39,526	70,644	+ 14·0	+ 9·3	1,494
32. Devikulam ...	625·32	...	80	4,761	23,458	13,038	10,420	11,520	+ 103·6	+ 46·8	38
33. Peermade ...	629·23		52	8,746	45,104	24,954	20,150	30,090	+ 49·9	+ 30·9	72
TOWN ...	...	...	...	*38,317*	*212,090*	*107,668*	*104,423*	*183,835*	*+ 15·3*	*+ 70·7*	...
1. Nagercoil ...	3·29	...	...	6,213	29,883	14,553	15,330	25,782	+ 15·9	+ 130·5	9,083
2. Trivandrum ...	9·89	...	...	10,485	63,561	32,292	31,269	57,882	+ 9·8	+ 107·6	6,427
3. Shencottah ...	3·20	...	...	2,473	10,309	4,905	5,404	9,039	+ 14·0	+ 3·6	3,221
4. Quilon ...	4·24	...	...	3,123	18,839	9,649	9,190	15,691	+ 20·0	+ 2·1	4,443
5. Kayankulam ...	...	...	...	1,079	5,830	2,772	3,058	5,745	+ 1·5	...	...
6. Tiruvalla ...	...	...	...	1,211	7,969	4,268	3,701	...	...	...	...
7. Alleppey ...	3·54	...	...	5,152	25,665	13,370	12,295	24,918	+ 3·0	+ 9·4	7,250
8. Kottayam ...	...	...	...	2,655	15,141	7,863	7,278	17,552	− 13·7	+ 147·6	...
9. Changanachery	...	...	...	2,865	17,242	8,826	8,416	14,264	+ 20·8	...	...
10. Alwaye ...	...	...	...	578	3,859	2,103	1,766	...	...	...	...
11. Parur ...	...	...	...	2,483	13,782	7,067	6,715	12,962	+ 6·3	...	...

PROVINCIAL TABLE II.

Population of Taluks and Towns by Religion and Education.

PROVINCIAL TABLE II.

Population of Taluks and Towns by Religion and Education.

TALUK OR TOWN.	DISTRIBUTION BY RELIGION.					
	HINDU.		MUSALMAN.		CHRISTIAN.	
	Males.	Females.	Males.	Females.	Males.	Females.
1	2	3	4	5	6	7
STATE. ...	*1,145,511*	*1,137,106*	*116,488*	*110,129*	*461,165*	*442,703*
1. Tovala ...	13,374	13,876	752	819	2,827	2,785
2. Agastisvaram ...	36,826	38,526	1,606	1,954	12,650	13,148
3. Eraniel ...	40,240	39,202	2,151	1,947	20,247	19,996
4. Kalkulam ...	25,297	25,458	1,351	1,378	11,050	10,623
5. Vilavankod ...	32,397	31,224	1,359	1,334	11,896	11,556
6. Neyyattinkara ...	63,240	60,028	3,825	3,689	23,886	22,460
7. Trivandrum ...	61,081	60,011	7,802	7,440	9,261	9,495
8. Nedumangad ...	34,311	31,674	4,063	3,904	4,884	4,522
9. Chirayinkil ...	54,633	56,845	10,043	10,131	1,340	1,457
10. Kottarakara ...	33,018	33,346	3,630	3,481	7,435	7,249
11. Pattanapuram ...	20,421	20,483	3,511	3,440	3,999	3,816
12. Shencottah ...	16,790	17,632	1,300	1,310	637	620
13. Quilon ...	58,897	59,611	9,494	9,042	13,322	13,399
14. Kunnattur ...	36,215	35,789	2,270	1,981	7,703	7,847
15. Karunagapalli ...	51,918	51,211	9,623	8,951	6,314	6,341
16. Kartikapalli ...	41,730	46,641	4,540	4,289	5,833	5,537
17. Mavelikara ...	50,935	50,403	3,229	2,856	11,996	11,315
18. Chengannur ...	40,698	39,293	2,080	1,900	21,978	20,320
19. Tiruvalla ...	48,275	46,133	1,701	1,568	39,370	36,650
20. Ambalapuzha ...	36,180	35,896	4,820	4,717	16,010	15,231
21. Shertallay ...	56,567	57,450	2,888	2,816	19,104	17,751
22. Vaikam ...	47,767	46,735	2,890	2,554	10,237	9,611
23. Ettumanur ...	21,893	20,927	372	197	24,206	22,996
24. Kottayam ...	30,316	28,981	937	773	26,020	24,974
25. Changanachery ...	23,962	23,405	1,694	1,414	23,824	22,363
26. Minachil ...	15,711	14,626	789	600	23,777	23,323
27. Muvattupuzha ...	31,911	32,102	5,143	4,924	34,397	31,571
28. Todupuzha ...	9,317	8,659	2,186	1,913	7,572	7,199
29. Kunnatnad ...	31,416	32,781	5,014	4,779	21,953	22,678
30. Alangad ...	27,486	28,297	10,267	9,515	16,819	16,450
31. Parur ...	25,681	21,983	2,805	2,641	12,465	11,886
32. Devikulam ...	9,842	8,251	179	44	2,209	1,328
33. Peermade ...	14,056	11,551	2,018	1,522	8,420	6,676
TOWN. ...	*72,466*	*70,591*	*12,186*	*11,732*	*22,963*	*22,078*
1. Nagercoil ...	10,996	11,483	1,391	1,531	2,166	2,313
2. Trivandrum ...	26,180	25,166	2,475	2,173	3,626	3,926
3. Shencottah ...	4,447	4,930	423	449	85	25
4. Quilon ...	5,149	4,733	1,736	1,622	2,761	2,832
5. Kayankulam ...	1,609	1,812	608	598	555	618
6. Tiruvalla ...	2,797	2,463	8	8	1,463	1,224
7. Alleppey ...	6,676	5,956	3,299	3,370	3,987	2,966
8. Kottayam ...	3,935	3,612	323	254	3,605	3,412
9. Changanachery ...	4,509	4,527	1,002	853	3,315	3,036
10. Alwaye ...	692	601	424	370	985	795
11. Parur ...	5,476	5,269	497	501	1,065	931

PROVINCIAL TABLE II.

Population of Taluks and Towns by Religion and Education.

DISTRIBUTION BY RELIGION.—(Concluded).				NUMBER OF LITERATE PERSONS.						
Animists.		Others.		0—15		15—20		20 and over.		
Males.	Females.	Males.	Females.	Males.	Females.	Males.	Females.	Males.	Females.	Number.
8	9	10	11	12	13	14	15	16	17	
8,123	*7,650*	*76*	*24*	*47,002*	*19,317*	*50,805*	*16,271*	*331,142*	*48,512*	
38	32	...	...	565	117	362	103	3,722	276	1
...	...	...	...	1,854	813	1,655	549	10,155	1,547	2
...	...	...	...	1,483	1,307	1,329	826	11,852	2,215	3
568	486	...	...	897	473	843	824	6,297	1,014	4
484	430	...	...	966	804	1,048	243	6,329	695	5
845	729	1	...	2,065	764	1,982	610	14,060	1,723	6
...	...	11	4	3,333	1,793	3,598	1,314	22,995	4,195	7
1,427	1,362	...	...	584	172	748	194	5,832	679	8
622	553	...	...	1,221	327	1,323	858	9,473	966	9
1,054	1,054	...	...	737	257	964	195	6,793	565	10
572	527	...	...	505	99	609	121	4,725	855	11
7	6	...	...	451	86	406	66	3,110	147	12
...	...	8	...	2,448	767	2,087	632	13,419	1,853	13
38	47	...	...	576	158	956	205	7,051	557	14
...	...	...	...	1,718	618	1,696	505	10,391	1,548	15
...	...	...	...	1,664	599	1,918	518	11,401	1,632	16
...	...	...	...	1,760	847	1,960	629	12,040	1,642	17
87	88	...	...	2,202	822	2,238	639	14,484	1,797	18
85	83	...	...	4,028	1,844	4,094	1,558	22,472	3,945	19
...	...	10	3	1,798	694	2,184	817	14,299	2,641	20
...	...	4	...	1,647	508	1,965	516	15,298	2,047	21
...	...	...	...	1,889	843	2,089	465	13,245	1,616	22
...	...	...	...	1,151	387	1,757	416	10,206	1,871	23
74	64	...	...	2,163	956	2,785	908	15,155	2,756	24
39	40	...	...	1,761	863	2,009	911	11,445	2,788	25
49	46	...	...	1,764	599	1,650	779	11,482	1,597	26
160	184	...	...	1,514	360	1,616	427	10,221	1,491	27
829	741	...	...	546	186	683	151	4,111	398	28
36	86	...	...	699	129	1,088	223	7,246	580	29
...	...	2	...	872	346	1,106	803	7,472	1,286	30
...	...	91	16	1,487	991	1,243	493	7,960	1,627	31
794	796	14	1	141	47	236	36	1,849	208	32
465	401	...	...	518	241	684	237	4,652	755	33
...	...	*63*	*21*	*6,502*	*3,146*	*6,300*	*2,324*	*34,245*	*7,594*	
...	...	...	...	709	413	778	261	3,368	707	1
...	...	11	4	2,386	1,367	2,267	923	14,606	2,949	2
...	...	...	...	194	18	155	17	975	28	3
...	...	3	...	329	212	400	158	2,184	513	4
...	...	...	...	220	146	153	94	681	295	5
...	...	...	...	872	143	308	137	1,505	338	6
...	...	8	8	750	250	699	135	3,314	821	7
...	...	...	...	776	313	712	303	3,186	928	8
...	...	...	...	312	171	489	166	2,668	611	9
...	...	...	...	117	24	123	21	493	82	10
...	...	29	14	337	89	316	100	1,315	322	11